GOSPEL BEARERS,
GENDER BARRIERS

Previously Published in
The American Society of Missiology Series

American Society of Missiology Series, No. 32

GOSPEL BEARERS, GENDER BARRIERS

Missionary Women in the Twentieth Century

Edited by
Dana L. Robert

ORBIS BOOKS

Maryknoll, New York 10545

Founded in 1970, Orbis Books endeavors to publish works that enlighten the mind, nourish the spirit, and challenge the conscience. The publishing arm of the Maryknoll Fathers and Brothers, Orbis seeks to explore the global dimensions of the Christian faith and mission, to invite dialogue with diverse cultures and religious traditions, and to serve the cause of reconciliation and peace. The books published reflect the opinions of their authors and are not meant to represent the official position of the Maryknoll Society. To obtain more information about Maryknoll and Orbis Books, please visit our website at www.maryknoll.org.

Manufactured in the United States of America.
Manuscript editing and typesetting by Joan Weber Laflamme.

Library of Congress Cataloging-in-Publication Data

Gospel bearers, gender barriers : missionary women in the twentieth century / edited by Dana L. Robert.
    p. cm.
Includes bibliographical references and index.
  ISBN 1-57075-425-X (pbk.)
  1. Women missionaries—History—20th century. I. Robert, Dana Lee.
BV2610 .G59 2002
266'.0082—dc21
                    2001008114

Contents

PART TWO
EVANGELIZATION, LIBERATION, AND GLOBALIZATION, 1945-2000

EVANGELIZATION AND WOMEN'S RIGHTS
IN LATE-TWENTIETH-CENTURY PROTESTANT MISSION

LIBERATIONIST PERSPECTIVES AND COLLABORATIVE STRUCTURES
AMONG ROMAN CATHOLIC WOMEN MISSIONERS

THE GLOBALIZATION OF WOMEN IN MISSION

Preface to the ASM Series

The purpose of the ASM (American Society of Missiology) Series is to publish—without regard for disciplinary, national, or denominational boundaries—scholarly works of high quality and wide interest on missiological themes from the entire spectrum of scholarly pursuits relevant to Christian mission, which is always the focus of books in the Series.

By *mission* is meant the effort to effect passage over the boundary between faith in Jesus Christ and its absence. In this understanding of mission, the basic functions of Christian proclamation, dialogue, witness, service, worship, liberation, and nurture are of special concern. And in that context questions arise, including, How does the transition from one cultural context to another influence the shape and interaction between these dynamic functions, especially in regard to the cultural and religious plurality that comprises the global context of Christian mission?

The promotion of scholarly dialogue among missiologists, and among missiologists and scholars in other fields of inquiry, may involve the publication of views that some missiologists cannot accept, and with which members of the Editorial Committee do not agree. Manuscripts published in the Series reflect the opinions of their authors and are not understood to represent the position of the American Society of Missiology or of the Editorial Committee. Selection is guided by such criteria as intrinsic worth, readability, and accessibility to a range of interested persons and not merely to experts or specialists.

The ASM Series, in collaboration with Orbis Books, seeks to publish scholarly works of high merit and wide interest on numerous aspects of missiology—the study of mission. Able presentations on new and creative approaches to the practice and understanding of mission will receive close attention.

The ASM Series Editorial Committee
Jonathan J. Bonk
Angelyn Dries, O.S.F.
Scott W. Sunquist

Preface

The experiences of women missionaries in the twentieth century illustrate the tensions captured in the title of this book: *Gospel Bearers, Gender Barriers*. The essays herein explore both the remarkable accomplishments and the ambiguities of gender in the work of twentieth-century missionary women. While missionary women have found personal liberation and spiritual inspiration from sharing the gospel across cultures, they have often found themselves struggling against gender limitations—imposed either by the mission societies that send them, the indigenous churches that they serve, or both. They also find themselves caught between secular scholarship that characterizes mission work as unwarranted proselytism and cultural imperialism, and doctrinal conservatives who condemn aspects of their work as illegitimate simply because it is being done by women. Within individual denominations or faith missions, the ministries of missionary women have been the casualties of doctrinal struggles between modernists and fundamentalists in the early twentieth century, or between liberals and conservatives in the late twentieth century. Believing in both the freedom of women through Christ and the evangelistic mandates of the Bible, missionary women have often found their work negated by destructive church squabbles.

Probably the most significant ambiguity in the work of twentieth-century missionary women has been their lack of recognition. Outnumbering men by two to one on the mission field during much of the century, women's own distinctive contributions to mission practice and theory have been ignored by scholars until fairly recently. In the scholarly literature from mainline churches there has been virtually no dialogue between feminist or womanist theology and missiology—despite the fact that women missionaries have represented the cutting edge of much of western Christian involvement in non-western cultures. In conservative circles, because of supposed fear of "feminism," gender has been ignored by church-growth theorists as a separate category by which to analyze cultural realities in the expansion of Christianity. Lessons learned from the "woman's missionary movement" of the early twentieth century seem to have been completely lost or ignored by scholars of church growth and expansion. Yet with estimates that at least two-thirds of the new Christians in the global church are women, it is a scandal in mission studies to ignore the socio-political and cultural realities particular to the female gender.

When I first joined the American Society of Missiology in 1984, the number of women professors of mission in North America could be counted on one hand despite the historic numerical domination of women in actual mission practice. The paucity of women missiologists has undoubtedly contributed to the general lack of research on mission and women's issues. With the typical modesty and activism of women missionaries, "insider" scholarly reflection on their own history has been scarce.

The genesis of this project lay in the limitations of my book *American Women in Mission: A Social History of Their Thought and Practice* (Mercer Press, 1997). While the book identified major themes in mission thought and practice that characterized the work of Catholic and Protestant missionary women from the United States, the narratives of mainline Protestant, Roman Catholic, and evangelical segments of women's missions ended at different points in the twentieth century. The lack of scholarly research into twentieth-century missions simply did not provide enough building blocks with which to construct even a tentative narrative of missionary women through the century. With a grant from the Currents in World Christianity Project, based at Cambridge University in England and funded by The Pew Charitable Trusts, in 1999-2000 I held a seminar series at the Boston University School of Theology titled "Women and Mission in the Twentieth Century." The seminar series facilitated recent scholarship on the subject, as historians and practitioners came to the university to present their research and meet with graduate students in missions and church history. Some of the papers in this volume were first presented at the Boston University seminars.

In the meantime, the American Society of Missiology saw a sudden and welcome increase in the number of women professors of mission in the late 1990s, as something of a renaissance in mission studies began occurring in Protestant theological seminaries. In particular, the decision of the Presbyterian Church, U.S.A., to push for a mission professorship in each of its theological seminaries led to the hiring of several female professors of mission. The ongoing leadership of Catholic women religious in the area of mission studies provided another source of papers from women connected with the American Society of Missiology. Although not all the authors of papers are connected with the American Society of Missiology, the majority are active members. It is appropriate, therefore, that this volume is published by Orbis Books as part of the ASM Series.

The purpose of the volume is to promote scholarship on the history and practice of missionary women in the twentieth century. While North American women are the organizing center of the book, the relationships between western missionary women and non-western women have been at the heart of the mission enterprise. Some of the papers, therefore, represent the opening wedge of much-needed scholarship on the missionary activities and reflections of non-western or ethnic-minority women. With authors from diverse theological traditions and scholarly training—notably history, anthropology, or missiology—there was no preset agreement among them on precise definitions of mission, except to assume that it involves the communication of the gospel beyond the boundaries of church and across cultures. Each writer assumed the definition of mission appropriate to his or her ecclesial background or subject matter. But whatever the topic, the creative tension between missionary roles and gender identity runs like a thread through all the papers.

The papers are organized roughly in chronological order, beginning with historical articles on women's missionary activity in the early twentieth century and ending with the reflections of active missiologists on selected aspects of their work. I have provided a chronological framework in which to place the various papers—an attempt that is by definition tentative and subject to revision by future historical research. It can do little more than highlight major trends and historical moments, indicate how the papers break new ground, and sketch out areas in need of further research. As I am solely responsible for the historical framework in which I place their papers, the authors of individual essays are not responsible for how I have situated their work and may not entirely agree with or endorse my interpretations. I thank them, however, for being willing to participate in the first cooperative project ever undertaken by North American women missiologists.

I wish to thank all the people who have supported this project, including the women scholars who participated in the Boston University seminars on women and mission in the twentieth century but who do not have papers in the volume—Ann Braude, Virginia Brereton, Juanita Leonard, Ruth Tucker, Alice Mathews, and others. Thanks go to The Pew Charitable Trusts for funding the seminars through the Currents in World Christianity Project of Cambridge University, and its director Dr. Brian Stanley. I appreciate the ongoing support of my colleagues and students at the Boston University School of Theology, especially Dr. Carter Lindberg. I also wish to thank the DeFreitas Foundation for supporting my sabbatical, which has made it possible to produce this volume.

I would like to thank Alan Neely, Rena Yocom, Bonnie Sue Lewis, and Inus Daneel for reading the introductory essay and providing valuable feedback. I very much appreciate the hard work of the Reverend Kendal Mobley, who has assisted in the seminars, in copyediting the volume, and in preparing the bibliography.

Finally, I thank my family—Marthinus, Samuel, and John. I dedicate this book to my deceased mother-in-law, Tina Muller Daneel, who spent many decades as a Dutch Reformed missionary in Rhodesia (Zimbabwe). A linguist, evangelist, musician, and educator, she taught both the European missionaries and the Shona pastors. Her spirit of creativity and dedication exemplified the work of women missionaries and has lived on in her children.

1

Introduction

Historical Themes and Current Issues

Dana L. Robert

In 1975, with Saigon falling and the last of the Americans leaving Vietnam, missionary Penelope Hall was evacuated from Vietnam for the fourth and final time. She was a Christian and Missionary Alliance missionary serving with the Hoi Thanh Tin Lanh, the only Protestant church officially recognized by the South Vietnamese government. Hall had been working in Vietnam since 1966, first near Saigon, and then as a Bible translator among the Jarai, a tribal people of Malayo-Polynesian extraction who centuries before had been pushed into the interior by the coastal invasion of the Vietnamese from the north. As Bible translator whose facility for languages was such that she mastered over two dozen, Hall was assigned to translate the Old Testament into Jarai. She also checked earlier translations of the New Testament against the original Greek, standardized the orthography, and translated the Book of Hebrews herself. Two weeks before the final evacuation, the church held a dedication service for the newly published New Testament and Psalms. Upon her escape from Vietnam, all she could carry with her were some of the precious translations. She left the Jarai people a manuscript of the Old Testament that was 80 percent complete.

When speaking of her years in Vietnam—a period in which several groups of Christian and Missionary Alliance missionaries were captured, tortured, or killed by the Viet Cong; in which Hall repeatedly fell under fire; and in which she suffered tropical diseases and several miscarriages—Penelope Hall recalls that it was a "fabulous time" to be a missionary there. For during the war the church was preparing and strengthening itself for what was to come—years of persecution and suffering under communist rule. In addition to her translation work, she prepared Jarai pastors for ministry by teaching them homiletics, theology, and the arts of ministry—including how to give communion, baptize, and conduct funerals.

The women's Bible study she led grew into a church. While the small group of women were praying on behalf of a woman whose husband severely and repeatedly abused her, the man dropped dead in a field nearby. The apparently immediate answer to the women's prayers, along with the conversion of a leading female traditional religious practitioner, sparked the transformation of the women's Bible study into a full-blown church. Within six months there were 153 baptized members and a building.

Covert messages from the Jarai have continued to reach Hall and the other missionaries who were torn from Vietnam over twenty-five years ago. Despite persecution by the Vietnamese, who consider them a primitive minority, and hostility from communists, who oppose their Christianity, the Jarai church continues to grow. The New Testament that was finalized by the translation team on which Hall served is still being used by the Jarai and other tribal groups who share cognate languages.

Penelope Hall experienced her work in Vietnam as a form of liberation, just as the gospel she carried liberated the Jarai from their fears of evil spirits who punished them for violating various cultural taboos. One incident stands out in her mind as emblematic of the freedom in Christ brought through her work. To the Jarai, the human body is sacred, and discussion of its private parts is forbidden except in special initiation ceremonies. Yet in her role as Bible translator, Hall needed to write the words relating to circumcision, knowing that such forbidden language would be read aloud in the church. She recalled,

One day while reviewing some New Testament manuscripts, I came across the expression that they were using for circumcision, *sí klí*, which simply meant "cut skin" to me. Although we had not yet needed to find a word or words to express this concept in the stories we were working on in the Old Testament, I knew that sooner or later we would need an expression to cover this concept. I also knew that no form of circumcision was practised among the Jarai and I was curious as to what they understood from *sí klí*.

When Ama Bol, one of my informants and trainee translators, arrived the next day, I asked him very carefully what he understood by the term, all the while aware of the Jarai taboo against verbalizing the specific parts of the body. He calmly replied that it meant *sí klí*.

"But, do you know where?" I asked.

"Oh, just anywhere," he replied while gesturing to his finger and then his arm.

"No, not just anywhere," I countered, suddenly wondering how I was going to get myself out of this impossible situation of confronting a taboo head-on.

"Well then, where?" he countered.

Not wanting to offend him, I explained that I was aware of certain taboos with regard to spoken language, so I would prefer to write the answer for him. He read the description that I wrote for him, and after registering considerable shock that I even knew the right words to use to describe the action, he said, "You're not a woman; you're not a man; you're not even a Jarai; you're just a translator, so we can talk about this." And talk we did. He explained the situation to Ama H'Lak, my other informant/trainee translator, and all three of us talked about the practice of circumcision. We then began a discussion, which lasted for months, about the problem of expressing the concept in Jarai, searching for a way to convey the proper meaning that would not be offensive when the words were read aloud.

Although they understood clearly the description of circumcision which I had written down for them, they agreed that such a description could never be used in the translation because it could never be read aloud. In the end we had to stay with *sí klí* for the time-being; nevertheless, we did make a decision that if the Old Testament were ever to be published, we would add a glossary of terms for reference purposes which would never need to be read aloud.

As a result of our continuing discussion, my translation helpers came to the understanding that the importance of the sign of circumcision from a Biblical perspective is that it was the sign that marked the Israelites as a distinctive people, set apart for God. They understood it within the context of tribal markings like the distinctive patterns they wove into their loin clothes, into the borders of their skirts, and into the baskets they used in the fields to identify themselves as Jarai.

Yet the most important lesson that came out of this discussion was the experience of a transforming freedom in Christ. As members of the Body of Christ, they could be free from their taboos, free to appreciate and express their delight in the world and the body that the Creator had provided for them. . . . The transforming power of the gospel message brings a freedom to all areas of the human experience—language, culture, relationships. As members of the body of Christ our relationships can be transformed, moving us into a realm where the usual male-female differences, hindrances and rivalries are no longer obstacles to our effectiveness. This power brings a liberating dynamic that elevates us into a knowledge of what it means to be children of God—not just men and women, but joint heirs of the riches of our heavenly Father. (Hall 2000, 3-6)

Missionary Penelope Hall experienced the liberating power of Jesus Christ in her work as "gospel bearer" among the Jarai. Not only did the gospel break the power of taboos over the Jarai, but it freed Hall from some of the restraints of gender discrimination. While the negation of her gender might seem odd from a twenty-first century western perspective, in the Jarai context, gender neutrality allowed her to work with male Jarai in the traditionally male missionary role of translating the Bible. It allowed her to claim as her own heritage that of the New Testament, "For in Christ Jesus you are all children of God through faith. . . .

There is no longer Jew or Greek, there is no longer slave or free, there is no longer male and female; for all of you are one in Christ Jesus" (Gal 3:26, 28, *NRSV*). Her freedom in Christ sustained Hall through the years in Vietnam and in the 1980s when she and her husband lived in the Ecuadorian Amazon, overseeing work among the Waorani. Penelope Hall's freedom in Christ sustained her during the 1990s, when for health reasons the Halls could not return to a ministry in the tropics. This seeming setback, however, allowed her to pursue doctoral studies. Her freedom in Christ has sustained her since 1998, when she began using her linguistic skills to work for the International Council of the Theological Library Association, directing a project to index catalogues from over three thousand theological libraries in Europe that can be accessed from a website in thirty-six languages.

Yet Penelope Hall—despite her remarkable skills and gifts for ministry, despite the broken health of her family and their suffering in violent situations both in Vietnam and Ecuador, despite translating the scriptures from Greek and Hebrew and teaching men the arts of ministry, despite founding a church—is not eligible to be an elder under the United States branch of the Christian and Missionary Alliance. As a Canadian, she originally went to Vietnam under a mission jointly administered by the American and Canadian branches of the denomination. Originally founded as a faith mission by Presbyterian A. B. Simpson in 1887, the Christian and Missionary Alliance was noteworthy in its early years for its pioneer women missionaries and the support of its founder for the rights of women to preach. Yet in June 2000 the General Council of the Alliance in the United States ruled that women can no longer be elders in the church and that all women in church-related positions must submit themselves to the rule of a male elder. The changed constitution reads:

> The elders shall be male members of this church and shall be elected as specified in the church bylaws. With authority from Christ the Chief Shepherd and confirmed by the church membership, the pastor and the other elders are the highest level of servant leadership in the local church. As undershepherds, elders shall serve with the senior pastor to oversee the local church and its ministries to accomplish Christ's mission.

Because of increasingly conservative notions of male authority, in one stroke the Alliance severed its own noble history of empowering women. In the year 2000 the U.S. branch of the Alliance also ruled not to accept the credentials of any Canadian workers, thereby making it difficult for female leaders like Penelope Hall to serve under it.

The tensions faced in her work by Penelope Hall were not unique to her experience. Women led the churches in mission in the twentieth century, while simultaneously facing obstacles and limitations because they were women. What follows is an attempt to place research on the work of women missionaries into a historical framework so that patterns of both their contributions and difficulties become visible.

EXPANDING THE MOVEMENT:
OPTIMISM AND GROWTH TO 1920

For North American missionary women, the twentieth century was born amid hope and tangible signs of women's progress in the churches and in the world. After hard-fought struggles for acceptance, women's mission organizations existed in nearly every Protestant denomination. Local auxiliaries of church women were devoted to the cause. Missions occupied the central spot in women's hearts because they provided opportunities for leadership in the church. With their focus on reaching women and children, women's missionary societies had carved out a vital niche and power base from which women could participate in lay ministry. In addition to denominational women's societies, newly founded non-denominational "faith missions" were attracting women devoted to evangelizing parts of the world unreached by the denominational societies. The twentieth century thus began auspiciously for Protestant missionary women.

While the Europeans fought each other, resources for their missionaries shrank. America's share of the total Protestant missionary force was approximately one-third at the beginning of the twentieth century. In the early years of World War I the North American percentage of the global Protestant missionary force climbed to 44 percent. Growing numbers of American women in the overall missionary force were a major factor in the expanding American presence in foreign missions. In the year 1900 approximately 57 percent of the nearly six thousand American Protestant foreign missionaries were women. By 1916 the percentage of women in the North American mission force of twenty-four thousand had grown to 62 percent. The presence of unmarried women along with missionary wives meant that missionary women outnumbered missionary men by nearly two to one in the major mission fields.

The dramatic growth in the number and percentage of North American women missionaries in the early decades of the twentieth century was partly due to political and social developments beyond women's control. Since the late 1880s a vibrant student mission movement had been recruiting college women and men across the country. Students saw missions as part of a progressive social movement to spread the gospel—and the best ideals of western democracy—around the world. After winning the Spanish-American War of 1898, the United States entered its experiment in colonialism by sending shiploads of school teachers to found a public-education system in its new colony, the Philippines. Protestant missionary women received appointments as teachers, physicians, social workers, and evangelists to newly opened missions in Southeast Asia, Africa, and Latin America. They also pushed their schools and clinics to higher levels in the older missions of India and East Asia.

The unity of Protestant women also undoubtedly contributed to the strength of their commitment to missions in the early twentieth century. In the 1890s, leaders of denominational women's societies had begun meeting regularly in the World's Missionary Committee of Christian Women as they crafted an ecumenical movement of joint cooperation that burst upon the scene in the new century. The women's ecumenical joint study program for missions published its first book in 1900, selling over fifty thousand copies of a mission history textbook despite the predictions of male nay-sayers. As women in local churches studied the volumes published annually, they learned about Christianity in different parts of the world, as well as about the needs of women and children in other cultures. Although one-third of the world was Christian at the beginning of the century, the vast majority were of European stock. The ecumenical mission study materials opened the eyes of ordinary church women to realities beyond their own communities, and they responded with an outpouring of support for women missionaries to reach women beyond the confines of European ethnicity.

Public awareness of women's missionary work flowered at the Ecumenical Conference of 1900, the most popular missionary conference in history. Held in New York City from April 21 to May 1, 1900, the Ecumenical Conference consisted of missionary meetings held in churches around town, a missionary exhibit of cultural artifacts from around the world, and up to 200,000 people in attendance at over sixty formal sessions. Mission boards sent twenty-five hundred official delegates to a conference attended by the U.S. president William McKinley, former president Benjamin Harrison, and future president Theodore Roosevelt. Women mission leaders had carefully planned a series of meetings to showcase their accomplishments as part of the conference. In midweek over four hundred female missionaries mounted the stage at Carnegie Hall, while thousands waved handkerchiefs. Later that evening "young Christian women from China, Japan, Armenia, India, and Turkey were introduced in indigenous dress" (Askew 2000, 148). The sight of educated, articulate Christian women from "heathen" nations was the capstone of the women's meeting. After hearing Professor Lilavati Singh, head of the Methodist women's college in India, speak on the need for higher education for non-western women, former President Harrison uttered his much-quoted statement, "If I had given a million dollars to foreign missions, I should count it wisely invested if it led only to the conversion of that one woman" (quoted in ibid.).

In 1910 the Protestant women's mission boards celebrated the fifty-year anniversary of the gender-separate "woman's missionary movement" with celebrations in forty-eight major cities and numerous smaller locations. Increased ecumenical cooperation followed the jubilee celebration, as women began organizing nondenominational women's groups in its wake. After the leaders of the woman's missionary movement determined that women around the world were clamoring for higher education, they raised three million dollars to fund seven ecumenical colleges for women in India, China, and Japan in the belief that education was the key to the emancipation of women everywhere. During the 1910s American women in local mission societies across a wide denominational spectrum engaged in mission studies with a common curriculum, raised money for the ecumenical causes of women's higher education and Christian literature for women and children around the world, supported a World Day of Prayer for both foreign and home missions, and held ecumenical summer schools of missions that attracted thousands of women and girls every summer. Their annual study books, issued by an ecumenical committee of women from a rotating list of denominations, sold two million copies by 1921.

During the early 1900s the increasing momentum of American Protestant foreign missions spilled over into American Catholicism (see Dries 1998). With the United States itself an official mission field of the Propaganda Fide until 1908, nineteenth-century American Catholics expended most of their energy building institutions and expanding the church across the vast North American continent. With few exceptions those American Catholic women drawn to cross-cultural missions, other than among Native Americans, went under the umbrella of European-based religious congregations. There were no American-based congregations of Catholic religious devoted to overseas missions. But in 1903 a Smith College junior, Mollie Rogers, a devout Roman Catholic, was deeply moved by the sight of a crowd of Smith College girls singing "Onward Christian Soldiers" as five of their classmates prepared to sail to China as missionaries. After meeting Father James A. Walsh, Boston director of the Society for the Propagation of the Faith, Mollie Rogers devoted herself to spreading mission information to American Roman Catholics. After Walsh and Father Thomas Price founded in 1911 the first American men's missionary order, the Catholic Foreign Mission Society of America, Mollie Rogers and a group of like-minded women became Catholic sisters and founded the Foreign Mission Sisters of St. Dominic (Maryknoll Sisters). With its canonical approval in 1920, the Maryknoll Sisters became the first American women's Catholic congregation devoted to foreign missions, thus setting the stage for major overseas commitments by American Catholic women after the First World War.

The cultural and theological attitude of the woman's missionary movement at the beginning of the twentieth century was characterized by its motto: "Woman's work for woman" (see Robert 1997, chap. 4; Flemming 1989; Hunter 1984; and Montgomery 1910). With mid nineteenth-century assumptions that males and females occupied different roles in society, "woman's work for woman" emphasized that it took women to reach other women and their children with the gospel. Notions of gender separatism had originally created a small space for women's ministry—a space that missionary women enlarged by founding missionary schools, hospitals, orphanages, and ultimately evangelistic ministries. "Woman's work for woman" was the first significant gender-linked mission theory. Behind it lay middle-class western assumptions that western women needed to help liberate their sisters around the world by reaching them in their homes, teaching them to read, and providing medical care for their bodies. Conversion to Christianity would not only provide eternal salvation for women everywhere, but it would help raise their self-worth and improve their social positions in oppressive, patriarchal societies. While maternalistic, "woman's work for woman" nevertheless revealed its origins in democratic society by assuming that all women around the world were equal, even if their circumstances differed. "Woman's work for woman" was uncritical about its origins in western modernity, but its holistic unity of spiritual and material progress and its operation along gender-separate lines were effective mission strategies in traditional Asian societies. As a mission philosophy, it "worked"—both for the North American women seeking to expand their own vocational and career choices and for women in the gender-separate societies of India, China, Japan, Korea, and the Near East.

THE INTEGRATION AND FRAGMENTATION
OF WOMEN'S MISSIONS, 1920-1945

The Protestant "Woman's Missionary Movement"

In 1918 World War I ended; in 1920, American women received the right to vote and with their newfound power promptly voted Prohibition into effect. The apparent victory of "the war to end all wars," combined with achieving the fondest hopes of many Christian women for civil rights and the end of the liquor industry, seemed at first to mark the dawn of a glorious new era for American women. But sober realities soon set in for the woman's missionary movement. The changing of the generations marked by the end of the war ushered in the "roaring twenties." The gay young women in flapper dresses, who could now vote and claim equality with men, had less use for the gender-separate social causes of the prewar progressive era—including those of the woman's missionary movement. While more young women than ever before sought to be foreign missionaries in the early 1920s, a fundamental shift in American society toward gender equality made separate women's causes start to seem old-fashioned.

Along with a decline in the traditional rationale for gender-separate organizations, revulsion against the horrors of the First World War made many educated Americans begin rethinking their notions of western cultural superiority. After all, the war had been fought among ostensibly Christian nations. Spokespersons for women's missions during the 1920s led a movement in the mainline denominations to embrace "internationalism"—emphasizing the rights of self-determination for peoples—and pacifism. Women's study texts emphasized missions as a moral alternative to war and the separability of Christianity from western culture. The woman's missionary movement began rejecting the unconscious westernized focus of "woman's work for woman." Rather, a missiology of world friendship, with emphasis on partnership with non-western women, suffused women's missions in the mainline churches (see Robert 1997, chap. 6). Along with the YWCA and international Christian student movements, women's missionary societies gave renewed attention to helping create female Christian leaders in the non-western world. Thus the women's societies supported higher education, including medical schools, for women in the mission fields. Advances in sociology and home economics encouraged women missionaries to initiate baby-care clinics and kindergartens, home-economics demonstration schools, and training in child-welfare methods in the missions.

In terms of public recognition, probably the high point of the woman's missionary movement after the war occurred when Helen Barrett Montgomery became the first woman to head a major denomination. In 1920 she was elected president of the Northern Baptist Convention. Widely acknowledged as the leading theoretician and organizer for women's missions, she wrote numerous best-selling study books for the woman's missionary movement. In them she argued for the emancipation of women through conversion to Christianity. Her classic history of women in mission, *Western Women in Eastern Lands* (1910), sold over 100,000 copies. Along with mission leaders Lucy Waterbury Peabody (Baptist) and Clementina Butler (Methodist), Montgomery organized ecumenical support for women's higher education in Asia, the World Day of Prayer, and Christian literature for women and children.

But while Helen Barrett Montgomery was presiding over the Northern Baptist Convention in 1921, fundamentalists introduced a resolution to require doctrinal conformity among Baptists. As the fundamentalist-modernist controversy exploded in the 1920s, it threatened to splinter the Northern Baptist and Presbyterian denominations, two of the strongest bases of support for women's leadership in foreign missions. Although scholars have studied the impact of the fundamentalist-modernist movement on women, little has been written about the pernicious effect of doctrinal in-fighting on women's missionary work (see Bendroth 1993; DeBerg 1990).[1] As fundamentalist movements swept through denominations and faith missions, biblical literalists began emphasizing the subordination of women to men. Separate women's mission organizations were undermined from both sides when the "modern" younger generation challenged evangelistic, gender-separate movements as old-fashioned, and fundamentalists claimed that the Bible restricted the ministry of women. The traditional holism of women's mission work made it vulnerable. Decades of combining evangelism with higher education and social work characterized women's missions: for lay women missionaries, teaching had long been the female counterpart to male preaching. Yet fighting between fundamentalists and liberals resulted in a polarization in the churches between direct evangelism and advanced education, and between biblical literalism and the social gospel. The loss of common ground between conservatives and liberals eroded the holistic middle, thereby undercutting women's leadership in missions.

In the name of efficiency and centralization, but with strong sub-texts of theological division and male domination, the very denominations whose recent missionary expansions had been carried by the women began dismantling their women's missionary societies and dividing the remains under various male-dominated church agencies. Part of the motive was to gain control of the money, since women continued faithfully raising their own funds even when the overall church collections lagged. Since women typically had no rights to speak or to vote in denominational church councils, they were powerless to stop the dissolution of women's missionary organizations. The process started with the Southern Methodists in 1910, when the all-male general conference, without considering

---

[1] On the impact of the fundamentalist-modernist controversy on male-led missions, see Longfield 1991.

input from women, forcibly merged the women's foreign and home mission societies into one women's mission council. In 1923, without even consulting the women, the Presbyterian Church U.S.A. eliminated its national female mission organization. One women's society followed another, so that by the time the Second World War broke out, the woman's missionary movement had been reduced to a shadow of its former self. Only a few autonomous women's organizations remained. The unforeseen result of the dissolution of many women's societies was to put into motion decades-long struggles for lay and clergy rights by women in the churches. Ironically, a movement that had sought empowerment for Christian women around the world found itself disempowered by patriarchal forces within the western churches themselves.

In retrospect, it is hard to pinpoint the specific causes for the decline of the separate woman's missionary movement. Broader attitudinal changes toward gender in American society, the destructive effects of the Great Depression on mission funding in the 1930s, theological changes that questioned the nature of women's missionary work, denominational cults of efficiency, church politics that sought to centralize power, male patriarchy in the church, and even doubts about the evangelistic mandates of the Bible—all played a part in the decline of women's missionary organizations during the 1920s and 1930s. The integration of women's missionary societies into the larger structures of the churches led to a broadening of women's interests in the mainline churches, but the focus on cross-cultural missions lost its central importance for many.

While a number of studies exist on the collapse of the women's mission societies at the home base (Beaver 1980; Robert 1997; Hill 1985; Verdesi 1976; Boyd and Brackenridge 1983; MacDonell 1987), there has been little research on the impact of decline in the mission field. Did the loss of women's power in the churches have implications for women's mission work? What happened to women's ministries when support and resources declined from women at home, or when men took over their work? In chapter 2, in her article on the training of Nez Perce as pastors by three unmarried Presbyterian women from 1874 to 1932, Bonnie Sue Lewis tells the remarkable story of how unordained women missionaries without theological education succeeded in training eighteen Native American men for ordination in the Presbyterian Church and stimulating the planting of six churches. Supported by Presbyterian women at home, the McBeth Mission represented a partnership of mutual dependence between women missionaries and Native American males, who needed each other to gain recognition from the church. After white, male-dominated mission structures replaced the women of the mission, only half a dozen Nez Perce were ordained in the following decades.

Lewis's research illustrates the interplay among race, gender, and power in the relationships of missionary women with their students. But she also shows how the relative lack of formal power by the women, that is, ordination, created a space in which the Native American men's leadership was able to flourish. Later, when ordained white males took over supervision of the work, in the name of efficiency and raising standards, they exerted authority over the Indian pastors that undermined their independence.

By the late 1920s, many denominations were experiencing declining donations on behalf of missions. Doctrinal in-fighting and schisms, economic factors foreshadowing the Depression, over-expansion of missions after the war, and donor fatigue connected with massive ecumenical fund-raising schemes combined to affect receipts. Always operating on tight budgets, Protestant missions began to retrench. The elimination of separate women's mission organizations affected funding for women's projects in many denominations, either by depressing receipts or by deliberate diversion of women's money to other causes by denominational executives.

A missiology of "world friendship," combined with active nationalist movements in China, India, and other parts of Asia, also emphasized that the older missions should be turned over to the indigenous Christians. "Devolution," the process by which foreign missions turned over decision-making authority and control of funds to the "younger churches" they had founded, became an active priority in the late 1920s and 1930s. In 1927 the Nationalist government of China required that all foreign mission institutions be turned over to the Chinese, with Chinese put in charge of mission schools and hospitals. The nationalization of mission institutions followed a period of anti-Christian riots in China. Missionary women, who only a few years before had collected three million dollars for ecumenical women's colleges in Asia, found themselves caught between declining funds from home and demands for autonomy from nationalist Christians, including their own restless students. An added impetus to devolution came when economic hardships caused substantial shortfalls in giving to mission causes, and self-support became an urgent necessity in many mission fields.

In 1927 women connected with the International Missionary Council (IMC) issued the first report ever made on the condition of women in the world church. Entitled *The Place of Women in the Church on the Mission Field*, the report was compiled from surveys submitted by women in different mission fields. One of the themes noted by the report was the movement both in the United States and the United Kingdom to merge women's mission societies into the general foreign mission boards for the sake of efficiency and centralization. The report affirmed the superiority of the Christian religion for women, because "women find in it a religion that compliments them by ignoring them as women. Christ laid down no rules for women as separate from men" (IMC 1927, 37). Reports from around the world affirmed that western missions had provided valuable education and leadership training for women. Highly capable, educated Christian women now stood organized in churches throughout Asia. As nationalist movements and modernization were breaking down traditional societies throughout the world, women stood in situations of rapid social change that could be navigated only with great difficulty. Overall, women throughout the world seemed to be moving toward greater economic independence and equality with men in home, church, and larger society.

The generally rosy picture painted of the rising movement for women's equality around the world indicated that as mission work was being turned over to national churches, non-western women were sometimes assuming positions of leadership beside men because of the women's high level of education. But the report warned of discouraging factors in the devolution process: "Over and over again we find that women do not begin to avail themselves of the privileges that are theirs. . . . They are shy and unresponsive, fearful still of expressing their own ideas in groups where the predominating voice is that of man" (ibid., 56). Leadership training was slow, and women hesitated to lead. They were, in the words of Quaker missionaries from Africa, "present, but silent." An undercurrent of worry marked the report's discussion—unless women's education is maintained and women's issues promoted, the turning over of women's mission work to national churches might result in a movement backward in terms of women's progress.

Melissa Heim's ground-breaking study traces the impact of devolution on women's work in the American Madura Mission, one of the oldest missions of American Congregationalists in India. In 1934 the mission transferred its authority to the *Sangam,* an association of Tamil-speaking churches. With a long tradition of missionary women, the American Madura Mission had educated many Indian women leaders, who sat with men on the *Sangam*. By examining the work of three women, one Indian and two American, during the time of devolution, Heim uncovers the ambiguities of gender, race, and power relations between Indians and Americans, and between women and men, in the Indian churches. In effect, the collapse of support from the defunct women's missionary society in America, combined with the male-dominated devolution process, resulted in a loss of power for both missionary and Indian women. Women's education, the work of "Bible women" (native female evangelists), and other ministries promoted by missionary women were the first to suffer when missions cut back their funds in the devolution process and male Indian supervision took over. Heim's case study confirms the concerns broached in the 1927 IMC report on women.

By the 1930s the decline of the gender-separate woman's missionary movement was being felt both at home and on the mission field. From one perspective, women's missions had been successfully integrated into larger denominational concerns. Though a minority, women sat on mission boards and ecumenical Christian councils around the world. The voices of educated non-western women were increasingly featured in women's denominational periodicals. With a huge push from missionary women, the 1938 meeting of the IMC had the largest representation of non-western Christian women in the history of ecumenical Protestantism, as seventy women from around the world took their places as delegates to the IMC meeting in Madras. The appearance of the "Christian Home" on the meeting agenda proved that women's concerns were being integrated into the highest levels of the Protestant ecumenical movement (Robert 1998). Yet integration of women into denominational structures came at the price of subsuming women's missionary interests under many denominational concerns.

Struggles over ordination and women's rights in the churches demanded increased attention. The split between liberals and conservatives eroded the connections between women's ministry and evangelism, forcing many women to take sides.

Evangelical Women in the Mission Field

One of the least researched areas in the history of twentieth-century women's missions is their evangelistic work (see Tucker 1988). In their own devotion to evangelism, women's mission organizations in the early twentieth century supported three times as many indigenous women as evangelists as they did foreign missionaries, even though salary levels were lower than for westerners. Typically, women missionaries assigned to evangelism worked in teams with Bible women. Evangelistic missionaries engaged in a variety of activities, including itinerating through villages, house-to-house visitation, and the running of Bible-training schools for women. Energized by their own deep piety, evangelistic missionaries cultivated the spiritual aspects of missions as well as the often intimate relationships that occurred in leading other women to faith in Christ.

By the 1890s the number of women desiring to be evangelistic missionaries was overwhelming the ability of the denominational organizations to support them. Inspired by new premillennial mission theories of preparing for the Second Coming of Jesus Christ, as well as by piety drawn from the holiness movement, women began joining newly founded nondenominational faith missions. Faith missions such as the China Inland Mission, the Christian and Missionary Alliance, the Africa Inland Mission, the Central American Mission, and others began moving into hitherto unevangelized areas, often the interiors of continents unreached by older denominational missions. Because faith missions prioritized evangelism over establishing institutions like schools and hospitals, women of low education and economic status could join them as long as they raised their own financial support. As a result, an even higher percentage of women joined faith missions than denominational ones. The relatively untold history of faith missions should be written as a woman's story (see Fiedler 1994; Tucker 1988; Robert 1997, chap. 5).

As Christina Accornero demonstrates in chapter 4 below, discussing Susan Beamish Strachan, faith missions opened new opportunities for missionary service for North American and British women at the beginning of the century. Sent by the Regions Beyond Missionary Union to Argentina, Strachan began working in one of the most difficult mission fields for Protestants early in the century, namely Latin America, where the Roman Catholic Church exercised both popular and political power. Strachan's story illustrates both the creative potential and the limitations of working for a faith mission. Because she and other missionary women felt restricted from ministry because of their gender, in 1917 she organized women from different missions into the League of Evangelical Women in Argentina. Launching an evangelistic movement with her husband in Costa Rica, the Strachans founded their own faith mission, the Latin

America Mission. While Harry traveled and raised funds in the United States, Susan edited the publications of the movement and founded a girls' school in their home with the financial support of American women. By 1941 her school had grown into the Seminario Biblico Latinamericano, the leading Protestant theological seminary in Central America, training primarily men. Throughout her ministry Susan Strachan insisted on a holistic approach to evangelism that included education and ministries of compassion, an approach typical of women missionaries whether in denominational or nondenominational missions (Robert 1997, 411-15; see also Israel 1998; Robert 2000b; Leonard 1998; Wood 1983; Parker 1988).

Besides joining faith missions, a sizeable number of pietistic women launched out on their own as independent holiness missionaries in the early twentieth century. Independent holiness missionaries believed in a process of spiritual development by which they could live on an elevated plane of Christian spiritual life, following the direct leading of God through the power of the Holy Spirit. Coming originally from Methodism, holiness thought pervaded denominational missions as well as emboldened women to set out on their own. In the early twentieth century freelance Wesleyan holiness missionaries linked up to found the mission forces of the Church of the Nazarene, the Church of God (Anderson, Indiana), and other new holiness denominations (see Hassey 1986). Holiness women played major roles in their missions. For example, women dominated the Church of God missions in Kenya at mid-century (see Leonard 1998). They were numerically dominant in the Church of the Nazarene mission in Mozambique, and during World War II the Nazarene presence there was entirely female (see Restrick 2001).

After pentecostalism swept through many holiness circles in the 1910s, tongues-speaking holiness women missionaries also became the founding missionaries of such pentecostal denominations as the Assemblies of God (see McGee 1986, 1998). Besides the Methodist version of holiness, which stressed distinct stages of spiritual progress along with the theoretical possibility of living without sin, a more Reformed version called Keswick theology spread through missionary communities at Bible conferences and summer retreats. In Keswick thought, spiritual progress was gradual and believers remained tainted by sin, yet the Holy Spirit empowered them to live "higher Christian lives" devoted to Christian service. The higher Christian life movement was encouraged among missionaries and indigenous converts by Keswick speakers, who conducted conferences on spiritual deepening in the older mission fields of India and China.

The spirituality of holiness, both in Wesleyan and Keswick forms, pervaded women's missionary spirituality well into the twentieth century, especially through the continued popularity of such writers as Andrew Murray, Jessie Penn-Lewis, F. B. Meyer, and E. Stanley Jones. Yet the pervasive impact of holiness spirituality scarcely has been researched in mission history and practice. The rise of a doctrinally rigid fundamentalism in the 1920s, with an emphasis on the subordination of women, obscured the history of holiness women in both denominational and nondenominational missions. In the history of missions, by the 1930s conservatism had become equated with fundamentalist negativity toward the leadership of women. But two articles in this volume demonstrate the importance of recovering the rich, if unfamiliar, stories of women inspired by the power of the Holy Spirit to leadership in evangelistic mission. In chapter 5 Kevin Xiyi Yao writes of two American women, Grace Woods and Ruth Paxson, whose holiness spirituality underpinned revivals among missionaries and Chinese Christians in the turbulent 1920s. The significance of their stories includes how holiness thought empowered missionary women, but also how the fundamentalist-modernist controversies of the era pushed holiness women ultimately to give their support to the fundamentalist cause, even at the risk of losing a more irenic, less doctrinal, experiential form of evangelicalism.

The greatest significance of Yao's article, however, lies in the impact that holiness women had on forming evangelical Chinese leadership in the early twentieth century. Women mentored the first generation of Chinese evangelists—men who like Watchman Nee, Witness Lee, Leland Wang, and others, who went on to found indigenous Chinese churches, as well as revivalists like John Sung, still considered by many to have been the greatest Chinese revivalist of the twentieth century. Dan Bays estimates that one-fourth of all Chinese Christians were members of indigenous churches by the time of the Communist takeover (see Bays 1996, 310).

Silas Wu in chapter 6 takes the story of holiness women in China further with his essay on Dora Yu, the leading Chinese woman evangelist of the early twentieth century. Dora Yu's life story illustrates the trajectory from "woman's work for woman," to ministry as Bible woman, to independent holiness evangelist, to influence upon the formation of indigenous Chinese Christianity. The general trend of moving from denominational "woman's work" to freelance evangelism was followed by a number of prominent holiness women, both missionaries and their converts, in the early twentieth century. Both Yao and Wu's articles raise the issue of the major contribution made by evangelical women missionaries to the rise of non-western evangelical Christianity, as well as the decline of women's leadership by the 1930s under the fundamentalist onslaught. Challenges to women's missionary activity were not confined to denominational hierarchies but also occurred through processes of routinization and doctrinal rigidification on the mission field, as well as through assertion of patriarchal customs by indigenous male Christian leaders. In the history of Christianity the charismatic leadership of women has often been supplanted by more formalized male leadership; cross-cultural church planting provides numerous examples of this general trend.

Case studies of Protestant missionary women in the first half of the twentieth century, both mainline and independent evangelical, reveal the familiar story of women gaining power only to lose it to male-led bureaucracies or doctrinal watchdogs. Yet while nineteenth-century "woman's work for woman" confined women missionaries to work with women and girls, a fascinating development—explored in the articles by Lewis, Accornero, Yao, and Wu—was the influence of mature women teachers and mentors on early generations of male church leaders around the world, a tradition continued by female Bible translators such as Penelope Hall. The same gender limitations that officially relegated women to secondary, lay teaching positions in missions paradoxically at times made their instruction more acceptable to native men than that of ordained western male competitors, especially in the formative years before the development of strong male hierarchies in mission or church. Further research is needed into the power dynamics at the intersection of gender, ethnicity, and clerical status between missionary women and indigenous church leaders. Another fruitful topic needing research is the interaction among gender, spirituality, and doctrines affecting women's leadership in twentieth-century missions.

Spreading Storm Clouds

By 1938 the clouds of war were spreading rapidly. Women's significant international presence at the IMC's decennial meeting in Madras, India, masked the fragility of the now venerable western woman's missionary movement. Many gender-separate women's mission societies had disappeared through integration with denominational mission boards, the middle ground of women's missionary holism was weakened by a fundamentalist-modernist split, and economic depression and devolution undercut the support for independent women's ministries in the mission field. In the United States the women's ecumenical mission study series and conference of women's mission boards merged into what became the National Council of Churches. The generation of strong-minded missionary women whose careers had been formed by strong gender-separate models of leadership before World War I were retiring and dying, in many cases with no successors.

When World War II began in 1939, the missionary movement entered a survival mode. Many missions were cut off from their funding sources or found themselves in enemy territory and were forced to withdraw. After bombing Pearl Harbor on December 7, 1941, the Japanese militarists quickly interned missionaries in concentration camps in Southeast Asia and the South Pacific. Despite the best efforts of the International Missionary Council, the Vatican and religious orders, and devoted Christians of many nationalities, mission work suffered all over the world. After the war ended, mission work had to be rebuilt completely, but this time without the benefit of a separate women's missionary movement in most of the Protestant denominations. Concern for relief work, nation building, and founding the long-delayed World Council of Churches took top priority in mainline mission circles after the war.

EVANGELIZATION, LIBERATION,
AND GLOBALIZATION, 1945-2000

After World War II ended, missions faced a vastly different world. One of the side effects of global conflagration was the inevitable decline of European colonialism. As nationalist independence movements flourished after the war, postwar mission leaders began strategizing about the new context for mission facing western missionaries (see Yates 1994). In the more established mission fields, nationalism, devolution, and partnership became the reigning motifs of postwar mission. The new World Council of Churches, founded in 1948, created an international forum for the negotiation of changing global realities that affected the churches. A massive geographical shift was also under way, as the old mission fields of China and India were increasingly closed off by communism and anti-western nationalist movements, resulting in the redeployment of missionaries from those areas. New evangelistic mission enterprises turned their attention to tribal areas of Latin America, Africa, and Papua New Guinea, with their thousands of languages and small ethnic groups, each in need of its own scriptures.

Further scholarly research is desperately needed into the relatively uncharted history of missionary women in mission after World War II. Three major themes that emerged in the late twentieth century included a tension between mission and women's rights in the church, the emergence of theologies of liberation and collaborative structures of governance within Catholic women's mission congregations, and the globalization of mission issues and personnel. Other issues for late-twentieth-century women in mission will certainly emerge as scholarly reflection deepens on the subject.

Evangelization and Women's Rights in Late-Twentieth-Century Protestant Mission

In the postwar context of nation building, mainline Protestant missionary women encouraged ecumenical causes like literacy crusades, public-health campaigns, the church center for the United Nations, and continuing support for established missionary institutions like schools and hospitals. Racial justice and the self-determination of all peoples also remained major issues for mainline missionary women. Although women missionaries continued in great numbers during the 1950s and early 1960s, home base leaders of the stature of Helen Barrett Montgomery were relegated to the memories of a bygone age. Each denomination had its own female mission leaders, but the woman's missionary movement had lost its distinctive visibility within the ecumenical movement. In 1956 both the Methodist and Presbyterian churches voted to ordain women. It is not surprising that the first women ordained in both denominations had served as missionaries or evangelists, the major arena for women's church service earlier in the century.

Although support for missions remained strong in mainline churches during the postwar period, the emphasis on international justice issues and theologies of partnership meant that the percentage of missionaries in denominations affiliated with the Division of Overseas Ministries of the National Council of Churches began dropping relative to increasing numbers of missionaries sent by conservative evangelical and independent missions. Repudiation of proselytism also characterized the ecumenical mission movement, and in some quarters any form of evangelism was seen as destructive to Christian unity. In the postwar period, conservative evangelicalism reached a new stage of maturity, with well-established educational institutions, including a continued culture of support for cross-cultural, evangelistic missions. By 1968 the numbers of missionaries from theologically conservative churches and faith missions such as the Southern Baptists, Christian and Missionary Alliance, Wycliffe Bible Translators, and so forth surpassed those of the mainline Methodists, Presbyterians, Disciples of Christ, and others. This major trend in the postwar period meant that the mainline denominational issue of women's rights in the church, including ordination, became separated from support for women missionaries except in the smaller denominations with traditions of women's ordination. By the late 1960s the public image of the Protestant woman missionary had become an increasingly conservative one, both theologically and culturally.

One way to examine the complex dynamic between women's rights issues in the churches and traditional missionary commitment in late-twentieth-century Protestantism is to compare the history of women's organization for mission in Methodism with that of Southern Baptists from the 1950s through the 1980s. Unlike the Presbyterians, Congregationalists, Episcopalians, and others, both Methodists and Southern Baptists maintained women's organizations devoted to missions into the 1960s. During the first half of the twentieth century, Methodists had the strongest women's mission organization and sent the most missionaries of any denomination. While education and evangelism progressed in tandem in Methodist missions, Methodist missionary women at mid-century had a strong progressive image and facilitated denominational concern over issues of social justice, including women's rights. But with the creation of the United Methodist Church in 1968, women's control over their holistic mission program was gutted in the name of bureaucratic efficiency, even though the new Women's Division retained a separate existence and therefore more autonomy than in most denominations (see Hoover 1983; Magalis 1973; Campbell 1983). The number of Methodist missionaries began dropping at the same time as the new denomination was created, although it is unclear whether there was a relationship between the two developments. While the new United Methodist Women maintained some of the old missionary energy, denominational restructurings stripped women of their control over such time-honored areas as mission curricula for children and the deployment of women missionaries. Despite excelling in social-justice work for women and children, and global ecumenical issues, United Methodist Women did not retain traditional cross-cultural, evangelistic missions as their major focus in the late twentieth century. Rather, their mission commitments became centered on challenging systemic injustices both in the West and the rest of the world.

By the late 1990s there were signs of hope that traditional women's mission issues—concern for women and children—were gaining stature in the church at large. With over forty years of ordained women in the denomination, including many women bishops, the church rallied to a Bishops' Initiative on making the issue of children and poverty a denominational priority. Yet one doubts that traditional, cross-cultural missions will ever again monopolize United Methodist girls the way they did earlier in the century before women could be ordained. Mission outreach was essentially a lay women's cause earlier in the century, and remains so in the present. New models for mission commitment needed to be explored once women's leadership was integrated into the central structures of the church. The Methodist situation raises the interesting question of what happens to women's support for missions when ordained women lead the church and gender equality is the official policy. How do the traditional mission interests of Methodist lay women carry over into the feminist theology of its seminary-trained elites? Can commitment to evangelism meaningfully intersect with feminism, as in the holistic model of previous generations of Methodist women? What is the effect on the mission of the church when women begin wielding formal power in church hierarchies, or when gender-separate and mixed-gender institutions coexist in the same denomination? These delicate issues need to be addressed in mainline churches that both ordain women and have strong missionary traditions.

Among Southern Baptists, the Woman's Missionary Union (WMU), Auxiliary to the Southern Baptist Convention (SBC), remained a consistent voice for cross-cultural missions since its founding in 1888. Never as independent as the Methodist women, who sent their own missionaries, the WMU pursued the single-minded goal of assisting missions by providing mission curricula and by raising nearly half of the mission budget of the Convention through the annual Lottie Moon Christmas Offering,[2] named for a Southern Baptist missionary woman in China who died of malnutrition in 1912. The strong women's organization with its single-minded focus on missions propelled the Southern Baptist Convention into being the leading mission-sending church in the United States in the late twentieth century. In 1967 not only did the Southern Baptists pass the United Methodists as the largest denomination in the United States, but the number of Southern Baptist missionaries mushroomed until the denomination was sending the most missionaries of any Protestant church in North America.

Even as Methodists in the 1960s were emphasizing church union and ecumenical and social-justice causes, Southern Baptist churches made a conscious decision to focus on starting Sunday schools and churches, and on foreign missions. In chapter 7 on Southern Baptist girls' education for mission, Lydia Huffman Hoyle analyzes the culture and writings of the Girls' Auxiliary, the central organization for inculcating missionary commitment into Southern Baptist girls during the 1950s and 1960s. Even as other denominations lost their focus on missionary service, the WMU of the SBC conducted a study program and rite of passage for missions commitment that was the major means by which girls expressed leadership in the church. In the absence of broad support for women's ordination or pastoral roles, the highest, socially approved church leadership role

---

[2] The Lottie Moon Christmas Offering goal for 2001 is $120 million, or 47 percent of the International Mission Board budget of $254.1 million.

for Baptist women was aspiring to be a missionary. Many adult Southern Baptist women who grew up to be professionals, but not necessarily missionaries, cherished their early formation for leadership by the Girls' Auxiliary.

But in 1970 the WMU was asked to restructure its children's mission organizations to coordinate them with other denominational entities. The end of the Girls' Auxiliary accompanied other subtle changes in Southern Baptist life that reflected the separatist youth culture of the decade, including social uproar over the Vietnam War and the Civil Rights movement. Between 1964 and 1986, approximately 230 women were ordained by Southern Baptist churches.

While neither supporting nor opposing the ordination of women, the WMU was nevertheless the chief power base for women in the church, as it promoted women's calls to church vocations. In the 1980s a growing fundamentalist movement in the SBC, partly responding to trends in modern society including feminism, moved to diminish the power of women in the SBC by attacking the WMU. In 1984 it also passed a prohibition on women's ordination. In chapter 8 Catherine Allen, who served as executive vice-president of the WMU at that time, traces the outlines of the fundamentalist assault on the WMU during the 1980s and 1990s. Once again, as in the 1920s, doctrinal and political in-fighting threatened to derail a woman's missionary movement, this time in the SBC. While Allen's article focuses on the internal conflict, it does not recount the practical impact of the fundamentalist movement on Baptist ministries worldwide. But a longer version of her paper, and anecdotal evidence shared among female missionaries in the 1990s reveal that the attack on the WMU is only part of a larger pattern of fundamentalist leadership shutting down holistic educational and other women's mission projects around the world.

In October 2000 the Southern Baptists of Texas voted to reduce drastically the amount of money sent to Southern Baptist seminaries under the control of fundamentalists. Texas Baptists raised objections both to the restrictive position of the SBC against women and to a narrowing of the definition of evangelism that excluded the historic holistic, social work-oriented missions of Southern Baptists. A leading characteristic of women's mission theory has been its holism—its tendency to oppose a dichotomy between evangelization and education or social work. Even in conservative evangelical denominations like the Southern Baptists, and in the work of faith missionaries like Susan Strachan of the Latin American Mission, women have often tended to use a broader definition of evangelism than is comfortable for doctrinal purists. For if evangelistic mission is reduced to proclamation only, then in conservative denominations that do not allow women to preach, women's mission work becomes relegated to secondary status. Paradoxically, in the history of theologically moderate and conservative mission organizations, women's devotion sustained the missionary enterprise.

Comparing the trajectories of Methodist and Baptist women's support for missions in the late 1900s is a bit like comparing former first ladies Rosalynn Carter, a devout Southern Baptist, with Hillary Clinton, a devout United Methodist. While both first ladies were vastly influential, they exercised their power and chose their outreach in different ways. As her husband's partner, Mrs. Carter worked beside him in Habitat for Humanity Projects, hammering and sawing and erecting houses for the poor all over the world. As her husband's partner, Mrs. Clinton used her training and influence to launch policy initiatives of her own. Her book *It Takes a Village*, on how it requires a whole community to raise a child, reflects the historic commitments of the United Methodist Women and their woman- and child-centered approach to mission. Both deeply religious women, the lives of Mrs. Carter and Mrs. Clinton reflect different, yet powerful gendered denominational traditions on the mission of the church.

Unraveling the intricate relationship between theologies of evangelism and women's roles in the church is an urgent agenda for scholarly reflection in the twenty-first century. Why have women's missionary societies been threatened when doctrinal disputes and structural reorganizations, largely engineered by men, occur? Tentative analysis indicates that women's mission approaches have often reflected a "messy" alliance between evangelism and "this-worldly" concerns, including the health and leadership of women in home and family, church, and society. By definition, therefore, women's missionary movements have prepared a context for the formal empowerment of women, even if, like the WMU, they have studiously avoided becoming involved in "women's rights." Yet unless women are allowed freedom to promote missions according to their own priorities, history shows that women's commitment to missions begins to decline. Moreover, without women, the mission of the church shrinks. As historians of women's movements in the church, Hoyle, Allen, and others are concerned that the neutralizing of the WMU foreshadows the decline of missions in the SBC in the twenty-first century.

Liberationist Perspectives and Collaborative Structures among Roman Catholic Women Missioners

During the last half of the twentieth century issues of gospel and gender took a different point of departure for Catholics than for Protestants because of the tradition that vowed religious life was the normal mode for Catholic women in mission. Unlike in Protestantism, where married women opened the way for unmarried women as missionaries, in Catholicism it was the reverse. Yet Catholic and Protestant women missionaries shared similar challenges in that both had to prove themselves missionaries in their own right. While Protestant wives were labeled "assistant missionaries" to their husbands in the nineteenth century, Catholic sisters were similarly considered "auxiliaries" to the missionary priests. Both Catholic and Protestant missionary women worked as educators, especially of women and girls, and in ministries of compassion such as nursing and care of orphans. In both traditions the ideology of "woman's work for woman" was the key rationale that justified women's involvement in foreign missions independent from that of men.

While scholars have explored the parameters of "woman's work for woman" among Protestant women in both sending and receiving cultures, "woman's

work for woman" has been little researched as a gender-based mission theory
that functioned among American Roman Catholic women through the 1960s.
With the later beginnings of American Catholic foreign missions, the Catholic
emphasis on home and family as women's central priority, and the continued
emphasis on religious vocations as a gender-separate phenomenon, the ideology of "woman's work for woman" thrived in twentieth-century Catholicism.
Undergirded by a philosophy that men and women have different, complementary natures, Catholic mission thought retained a gender-separate rationale even
after such views were becoming less popular in mainline Protestant circles.

Angelyn Dries, O.S.F., gives a preliminary overview of "woman's work for
woman" as a guiding motif for Catholic missionary women in the twentieth
century. She explores how the ideology legitimated mission involvements for
American Catholic women ranging from fund-raising and the establishment of
mission circles in local parishes, to medical missions, lay women as missionaries, and the "direct apostolate," that is, direct evangelism of non-Christians by
women religious. Catholic women religious faced challenges not common to
Protestants, such as the prohibition against performing medical work until canon
law was changed in 1936. The communal support of Catholic sisterhoods, however, gave Catholic women advantages over more isolated Protestant women.
Yet in a pattern remarkably similar to that of Protestant women, Catholic
women's mission work tended toward holism, concerned both with body and
soul. Both Catholic and Protestant women pushed the boundaries of the church
beyond four walls. Dries also shows ways in which Catholic women's mission
thought foreshadowed changes made in Catholic theology by the Second Vatican
Council from 1962 to 1965.

During the 1960s, amid broad social change, the religious identity of sisters
was transformed. They discarded traditions like wearing habits, taking religious
names, and living in large convents according to strict rules. Empowered by
theologies of the church as the people of God rather than a hierarchical institution, they began moving out of institutional ministries like parochial schools
and hospitals into positions of more direct contact with the poor. The de-institu-
tionalization of Catholic sisters accompanied their own research into their distinctive charisms, the spiritual gifts exemplified by their founders. As sisters
began studying their own traditions, they began rediscovering that many of their
congregations began in mission, with strong priorities toward outreach that had
been suppressed by male hierarchies or institutionalized over the years (see
Neal 1984; Dries 1998; Robert 1997, chaps. 7-8).

The context for many congregations' self-discovery was Latin America, which
after World War II became a major destination for foreigners ejected from China
by the communists. The Maryknoll Sisters, America's first congregation devoted to foreign missions, established a strong Latin American presence in the
1950s. When, in 1961, Pope John XXIII called for religious to send 10 percent
of their members as a "tithe" to Latin America, communities who had not thought
of themselves as "missionary" found themselves grappling with cross-cultural
issues. With Maryknollers as guides, non-missionary congregations found a

portion of their sisters radicalized by their experiences of plunging into Latin American realities of extreme poverty and wealth, oligarchy, and military rule (see Costello 1979). Experiencing the United States as an oppressor, sisters in Latin America adopted liberation theologies that made mission a matter of "accompanying the poor" and "animating" poor people to control their own destinies. As the missionary sisters returned to the United States for policy-setting chapter meetings in the early 1970s, they spread liberation theology to other segments of their communities, including to mission fields in Asia and Africa. Catholic sisters became the leading edge of a theology of mission as liberation.

Mary Jo Maher, I.H.M., explores in chapter 10 the mission history of the Servants of the Immaculate Heart of Mary, a congregation principally of teachers that began sending sisters abroad as missionaries after World War II, primarily to Africa and Latin America. In 1973 their Latin American Assembly voted to take a "fundamental option for the poor," de-emphasizing their previous institutional commitments in favor of direct involvement with the very poor. This priority involved pastoral ministries, conducting Bible studies, leading women's groups, forming Base Christian Communities, and assisting the poor toward self-sufficiency. Such work came into direct conflict with the military rulers of Brazil and other dictatorships, as the I.H.M. Sisters found themselves opposing the rich and powerful over such issues as land rights and economic justice. In Africa, I.H.M. Sisters did some of their most difficult yet inspirational work as teachers under terrible conditions of deprivation, apartheid, and violence.

With two hundred sisters in mission from 1948 to the end of the century, the I.H.M. Sisters exemplify the experience of non-missionary congregations who responded to the call of the pope for overseas personnel. Their collaborative model of decision-making and centrality of a reign-of-God missiology typify the liberationist perspective of many late-twentieth-century missionary congregations. With the kingdom of God as their central priority, religious sisters have been involved in social justice ministries around the world. The communities of Catholic missionary sisters have supported them in taking risks not many missionary women with families would be willing to take. A key gender issue raised by the I.H.M. case study is whether collaborative, non-hierarchical, holistic mission theologies are strategies typical of the female experience. In a church known for rigid, hierarchical structures, the mission practice of female religious since the 1960s stands out as an alternative model of constructing mission theology from the ground up rather than the top down. Catholic women religious are very conscious of the ambiguity between church dogma that limits formal power to men in sacramental ministry and the range of grassroots ministries they practice on the mission field.

Besides the switch from a "church-centric" to a "kingdom-centric" theology among Catholic women religious after the 1960s, another issue for Catholic women in mission was the decline of vocations. In the late 1960s vocations began steadily dropping both for Catholic priests and for religious sisters. By the 1980s, years went by without a North American novice joining established congregations. In the United States parochial schools were nearly emptied of

women religious, who simultaneously began taking on greater pastoral responsibilities because of a growing shortage of priests. For congregations with overseas missions, a new challenge presented itself as non-western women began
joining them. The process of mission, in other words, had opened possibilities
for cross-cultural spiritual formation and vocational choices that stood to change
the ethnic identities of North American congregations. Margaret Guider, O.S.F.,
examines how North American Franciscan Sisters in Brazil began incorporat-
ing Brazilians into their membership. Unlike explicitly missionary institutes
like the Franciscan Missionaries of Mary or the Maryknoll Sisters, most North
American Franciscans did not go through cross-cultural formation. When they
sent sisters to Latin America in response to the pope's request in the 1960s,
therefore, they faced identity problems in knowing how to relate their North
American traditions to South American women who wished to join them. The
process of cross-cultural mission led to tremendous challenge and growth not
only for the receiving population but for the mission force as well.

As more non-western sisters join, and as North American vocations decline,
a very real possibility exists that what were formerly North American congregations will become entirely "foreign" in the twenty-first century. How do these
evolving congregations retain their Franciscan, Dominican, or other roots while
also adapting to changing realities? Will North American congregations in mission become extinct? With vowed lifestyles losing favor in the United States
and Europe, what will become of the missionary tradition of North American
Catholic religious? In a missiology of the kingdom, where North American
missionary women have become one with the poor, succeeding in the difficult
task of missionary identification, they are like seeds who are dying to give birth
to something new—a world church with its center of gravity in the southern
hemisphere. Paradoxically, as gender-separate communities lose their attrac-
tion in the more egalitarian West, they are finding new life in non-western cultures, especially Africa, where women and men retain traditional separate-gen-
der roles (Burke 1993). Non-western sisters have discovered their own apostolic
vocations as they push the margins of the church into new contexts, as did their
European and North American sisters before them.

The Globalization of Women in Mission

The changing ethnic identity of North American Franciscans points to the
most important trend in the evolving world of late-twentieth-century women in
mission, namely, the globalization of the world church and its mission force.
The end of European colonialism after World War II marked the beginning of
massive growth in the Christian populations of Asia, Africa, and Latin America.
With the simultaneous decline of Christianity in the North and West, the numerical balance of the Christian population shifted to the southern hemisphere.
While approximately one-third of the world was Christian both in the year 1900
and in 2000, the church's ethnic composition changed radically from the largely
European church of the year 1900 (Barrett and Johnson 2001; see also Robert

2000a; Hutchinson and Kalu 1998; Dempster, Klaus, and Petersen 1991). In some respects, this shift represents the successful conclusion of the western missionary era (Bosch 1991; Shenk 1996).

Preliminary gender breakdowns indicate that the growing world church is predominantly composed of women. The female majorities in the new Christian communities were not always a sure thing. The 1927 report *The Place of Women in the Church on the Mission Field*, for example, indicated that the Chinese church at that time was largely a male phenomenon. Yet the postwar expansion of the church appears to be driven predominantly by female membership. Catholic sisterhoods are growing rapidly in sub-Saharan Africa; women's organizations flourish in Protestant churches; Chinese house churches and Korean cell groups are led mostly by women. Recent studies of Christian growth in Latin America indicate that Protestant women join churches to promote better family life, and Catholic women are active in Base Christian Communities to improve social conditions for their families (Martin 1990; Brusco 1995; Drogus 1997). Christian family life remains an important concern for women in traditional societies. In Africa, women in both African Initiated Churches and historic denominations are at the cutting edge of their missionary expansion during a period of explosive growth in African Christianity. Gender is clearly an important factor that needs to be analyzed in understanding various church growth movements in the late twentieth century, and many more studies are needed.

What are the implications of the global church for women in mission? The final papers in this volume represent the reflections of several practicing women missiologists on gender issues in the world church of today. Each assumes that mission is a multidirectional enterprise in a global context, rather than the monopoly of a European church going into a non-western area. Each also implicitly assumes that interaction with indigenous world views, including cultures and non-Christian religions, are a given in current missiological reflection. Perhaps the most interesting aspect of the following papers is that they represent a new generation of missiologists—ethnically diverse, educated, and female, with theological views ranging from evangelical to pluralistic. In themselves they represent the globalized and diverse future of world mission.

In her article on gender issues among Indonesian church women, Frances Adeney explores what happens when a western missionary woman carries her assumptions of gender equality into a society dominated by traditional, patriarchal values. In many respects Adeney's journey parallels the experiences of earlier generations of mainline Protestant missionary women who sought to promote women's leadership in societies in which forces of tradition and modernization battled each other. Adeney points out that despite government policies on gender equality, being centered in the home is still the normative cultural assumption for Indonesian women. Women often experience their calls to ministry as a conflict with their domestic responsibilities, and they are prevented from exercising pastoral leadership by lack of community support. Her observations imply the continued relevance of gender-separate mission theories such as "woman's work for woman" despite their decline in North America in the late twentieth century. While emphasizing the importance of missionary women listening to and identifying with women in traditional societies, Adeney affirms her belief that gender equality is a universal value cherished by women all over the world. With assumptions of mission as a partnership among women of different cultures, Adeney urges that women in mission develop a deeper and broader understanding of egalitarianism that is sensitive to diverse cultural realities. Her paper implicitly raises the knotty issue of the interaction between universal gospel values and the gendered contexts in which the values must be lived out.

One of the most rapidly growing churches in the late twentieth century was that of South Korea, which may become the first Confucian country to become predominantly Christian. With a Protestant missionary history that began with American missionaries, and the subsequent events of the twentieth century, including the Korean War (1950-53), the relationship between Christians in South Korea and the United States has been close. Korean immigrants to the United States, like many groups of immigrants before them, established a strong immigrant church.

Korean-American missiologist Young Lee Hertig tackles one of the problems of missionary globalization in examining how a gendered institution developed in one context was carried to another and then stagnated. Her paper raises the thorny question of the transference of gender roles from one setting to another in the context of a globalized church. The idea of Bible women developed in the missionary era and then was imported into the United States with Korean immigrants. What began as an innovative missionary role for Korean women a century ago, centered in a view of the church as "household," became a Confucianized patriarchal structure in which women leaders remained nameless and faceless. The evangelistic role of the Bible woman has today become a dead end for Korean-American women in denominations that do not ordain women. Analyzing case studies of two Korean-American Bible *jeondosa,* or Bible women, Hertig uncovers a disturbing pattern of patriarchal abuse of female ministry. She argues for a "Yinist" paradigm of mutuality and interdependence, drawn from Taoism, to replace the Confucian one in which the Bible woman is currently situated. Hertig's paper underscores the necessity for gender analysis in cross-cultural mission, as the roles of women become frozen in time in the church history of particular cultures. By her Yinist methodology, she also shows how the categories derived from non-Christian religions are brought into new church practice, whether the churches are aware of it or not.

In an age of globalization, in which all parts of the world are in contact with other parts, the issue of how to relate to non-Christians is a huge question consuming western theologians. Given the decline of Christianity in large segments of the "post-Christian" West, missiological engagement with one's non-Christian neighbors has become a live issue for ordinary Christians as well. Marsha Snulligan Haney's paper brings missiology into dialogue with reflections on a non-Christian religion, and with gender analysis—in this case with womanist thought. Haney reflects on the startling growth of Islam among African-Americans and the need for the Black church to recognize that African-Americans are now a religiously plural community. She advocates using a womanist paradigm through which to engage in the "dialogue of life" with African-American Muslim women. With womanist assumptions that the unity of the African-American community is more important than its differences, Haney urges the acceptance of religious pluralism and the development of a womanist hermeneutic common to both Muslim and Christian women. Ultimately, the womanist missiologist must ask what the Christian message means to a religiously diverse community, rather than focus on the divisive question of salvation.

The final paper in this volume, by evangelical mission anthropologist Miriam Adeney, concerns itself with missions and gender in Africa—the place of the most dramatic Christian growth in the late twentieth century. Mission statisticians David Barrett and Todd Johnson estimate the existence of over 600 million Christians in Africa by the year 2025, thereby making Africa the second largest Christian continent in terms of population (Barrett and Johnson 2001, 25). While statistics are not completely certain, it appears that up to 80 percent of church membership in some parts of Africa is female. Raising questions about the relationship between gender and Christian identity in Africa is thus a cutting-edge issue for missiology in the twenty-first century.

Adeney explores the fierce debate as to whether Christian missions have raised or lowered the status of women in Africa. Anthropologists have typically argued that colonialism, domesticated missionary perceptions of women's roles, and the bureaucratization of church structures have marginalized women in Africa. Yet from a Christian perspective the equality of men and women before God is intrinsic to the good news. Missions have taught that women are persons of eternal value. Conversion to Christianity gives new freedom in Christ that endures despite the church's sins of not upholding women's leadership and of putting into place bureaucratic structures that deny women's freedom in Christ. Adeney's paper illustrates the need for social-scientific and theological approaches to mission to relate to each other, as the two approaches provide different evidence regarding the impact of Christianity on the women of Africa. Once again, the freedom of the gospel bearer collides with gender barriers—in the culture of both the missionary and of the new Christians.

CONCLUSION

Discussion of the relationship between women's freedom in Christ and gender restrictions in African missions returns us full circle to the experiences of the late-twentieth-century missionary woman Penelope Hall, with whom we opened this chapter. By the second half of the twentieth century, not only did women make up the majority of the mission force, both Catholic and Protestant, but they also constituted the majority of the global church. Missionary women in the twentieth century were "gospel bearers" who rejoiced in the liberation they found, and shared with others, in Jesus Christ. As the third millennium of

Christianity dawns, women of diverse cultures, ecclesial traditions, and theological perspectives stand on the threshold of even greater contributions to God's mission in the world.

Yet the history of twentieth-century women in mission reveals numerous tensions, difficulties, and reversals because of "gender barriers." The paradox of Christian mission is that while missionary women affirm the good news that saves, frees, and liberates, the patriarchal contexts in which it is practiced continue to overshadow the message. Even as women have mentored men of other cultures for ministry, they have been denied elderships themselves. At the height of successful women's denominational mission movements, they were undercut in the name of bureaucratic efficiency and centralization. At the point of inculturation and identification with the poor, the numbers of North American missionary sisters have declined. Accusations of "false consciousness" continue to underscore the lack of dialogue between women who believe in evangelism and feminist theologians. Mission history and anthropology remain dominated by one-dimensional portrayals of women as the leading edge of cultural imperialism. In missiological analysis, gender studies lag far behind approaches based on class and ethnicity.

Difficulties notwithstanding, as women challenge boundaries to bear the good news and live in faithful hope of God's reign, they embody the *missio Dei*—the mission of God. The study of women in mission is important because it represents not only the past but the future of the church.

PART ONE

THE INTEGRATION AND FRAGMENTATION OF WOMEN'S MISSIONS, 1920-1945

2

Women Missionaries and the Formation of Native Presbyterian Pastors in the Pacific Northwest

Bonnie Sue Lewis

Early in the twentieth century Presbyterian Nez Perce minister James Hayes penned a note to missionary Kate McBeth. He was awaiting the stage in Bruneau, a small town in southern Idaho, to take him to preach in Owyhee, Nevada, at the Duck Valley Reservation of the Shoshone-Paiutes. In his note to let her know about the difficulties in reaching his destination, he reflected upon his morning scripture reading:

> This morning I read I Cor. 3 from 1st to the last. [D]ear Miss [Sue] McBeth you [know] what Paul says, I have planted, Apollos watered but God gave the increase. I have never forget what my teacher told me before I leave my home for Umatilla Indians since from at that time I remember her and her works among Nez Perce Indians. Althought [sic] she has been go[ne] to Heaven long time ago.[1]

Hayes's tribute to his teacher, Sue McBeth, in this letter to Kate McBeth, was a testimony to the nature of the strong ties that bound the women teachers and many of their Nez Perce ministerial students of the McBeth Mission.

Between 1879 and 1927 sixteen Nez Perces, one Spokane, and one Makah received pastoral training by women missionaries in the Pacific Northwest and ordination into a Presbyterian church that did not ordain women. This unusually

---

[1] Unless otherwise noted, quotations come from documents preserved in the following collections: Allen and Eleanor Morrill Papers, University of Idaho Library; Kate C. McBeth Papers, San Francisco Theological Seminary; and McBeth/Crawford Collection, Idaho State Historical Society.

large number of native pastors is a credit to the effectiveness of the relationship between the Native American students and their women teachers. It was a relationship embedded in ambiguous space where native authority and women's authority often collided, frequently coalesced, and eventually collapsed under the more dominant authority of white churchmen. For a time, however, the women of the McBeth Mission and their native students were able to make use of their ambiguous space, their fluid social and cultural roles, and the virtual absence of white male authority at the mission to establish mutual positions of respect and leadership in the church. In doing so, these women and men contributed to each other's status in the church.

The McBeth Mission, dubbed a "one-woman Presbyterian theological school," was unusual for both its accomplishments and its composition. It began in 1874 when Sue McBeth took over the education of a small group of native helpers of Henry Spalding upon his death. When Sue McBeth laid down the mantle at her death in 1893, her sister, Kate McBeth, took it up. Upon her death in 1915, her niece, Mary Crawford, continued the work until the school was closed in 1932. Their friend, Helen Clark, served alone among the Makahs for the first twenty years of the twentieth century and contributed to the work of the school. These four women, neither seminary trained nor ordained, raised up nearly single-handedly a generation of native ministers in the Pacific Northwest. Perhaps their greatest legacy to these pastors was an independent spirit that at times proved a mixed blessing in their relationships with their students.

Like many of the single women missionaries at the height of the missionary movement, the McBeth sisters, Mary Crawford, and Helen Clark imbued all the ideals of true womanhood but wrapped them around a steely determination to serve the Lord they loved.[2] These strong women insisted on preparing "preachers," not "helpers," thus setting the Nez Perce mission school apart from most other schools and paving the way for a strong native church leadership.[3]

The state of the national church and the nature of the missionary enterprise by the 1890s was responsible for much of what transpired at the McBeth Mission. Fueled by the proliferation of women's missionary societies, women missionaries made up more than 60 percent of the entire American Protestant missionary force (Hill 1985, 14, 54; Hunter 1984, xiii). Despite their proven abilities of administration and leadership, women's roles within the church remained circumscribed by their gender. Women could teach but not preach; they could raise money and send out missionaries but they could not do so without male oversight. Only children and Native Americans had less power in the church.

---

[2] A growing body of literature on women in mission has produced significant general works including Beaver (1980), Hill (1985), Robert (1997), and Tucker (1988). Works of a more specialized nature include Carpenter and Shenk (1990), Hunter (1984), and Zwiep (1991).

[3] There were a few other such women, most notably Charlotte (Lottie) Moon, Southern Baptist missionary to China, and Isabella Nassau, a Presbyterian missionary in West Africa (see Allen 1980; Penfield 1977).

For women who taught native men, it often seemed that the marginalized were leading the marginalized. At times there was competition for limited power, and both native pastors and missionaries turned to constructs of race, class, or gender in order to support claims to contested and restricted power. Ultimately, however, the women and the native men served to bolster each other's position in the church. Physical isolation from the church hierarchy allowed a certain amount of autonomy in the work of both the native pastors and the missionary women. Friendships between these independent-minded women and men often strengthened their marginal positions, but even together they could not prevail against white male dominance.

The women's missionary movement was reined in by the men's reorganization of the mission boards in the 1920s, signaling the end of an era for the women as well as the Native American pastors. The closing of the McBeth School in the 1930s ended an opportunity for both the women and their students to broaden the base of their power in the church organization. While six Nez Perce congregations came of the McBeth years, only half a dozen Nez Perces have been ordained to serve those churches since the 1930s.

I

From the beginning, the McBeth Mission was led by strong-minded women. Susan Law McBeth, the first of the missionary women, set a high standard. She arrived in 1873 during the Church Women's Decade as a government teacher for the children. Within a year of her arrival, Henry Spalding, a veteran of the original Oregon Mission of the American Board of Commissioners for Foreign Missions (ABCFM), died after a fall from his horse. McBeth took it upon herself, with the board's initial approval, to carry on the work Spalding had begun in training a select group of native helpers for the church. She preferred the work of teaching adults to that of teaching children (*AIC:* 31[N]/1).

The Civil War years were instrumental in forming this new breed of independent, single, women missionaries. McBeth's missionary career began among the Choctaws in 1860 but was interrupted within a year by the war. Wanting to continue in service, she worked among the wounded in the role of a chaplain with the U.S. Christian Commission. It was such expansion of women's roles during the war that allowed women to gain "administrative and technical knowledge, confidence in their stamina and abilities, security in working outside the home, and respect for one another" (Boyd and Brackenridge 1983, 14). By the time of her appointment to Idaho in 1873, McBeth felt well equipped to perform the task before her, and society was better prepared to accept her contributions. The Civil War had served to escalate a national trend toward a "'masculinization' of the ideology of benevolence," which valued patriotism, efficiency, and professionalism over the more feminine virtues of "charity and compassion" (Ginzberg 1990, 172, 173). Assuring the board that she was not "what is called a Women's Rights Woman," nor even "Strong Minded," she had the tenacity to stand up to board members, Indian agents, and even Indians who disagreed with her. She also learned that the marginalized had to take every advantage to gain entrance and acceptance into the dominant culture. Ordination for Indian pastors gave them that advantage, while it enhanced her own status and influence.

McBeth's role in the classroom expanded even as her presence in the church diminished. Restricted by lack of ministerial credentials and a physical disability that impaired her mobility and often confined her to her cabin, McBeth used her teaching and counsel in the schoolroom to give her a formidable influence over the church.[4] When the board criticized her for overstepping her boundaries as a woman, she was quick to point out that her "preaching, of course, is done only through the lips of her pupils" (*AIC:* 31[N]/1).

McBeth's students, though a select group who showed interest in ministry, included church elders and Sunday School teachers as well as potential pastors. She taught them not only "for the sake of their church duties and influence . . . that they may be good and intelligent" leaders, but so they could have an impact on the tribe (*AIC:* 21[D]/327; Crawford 1936, 40). Her own influence upon the church, therefore, was widespread. But it was not without its limits. When her students felt she was too heavy-handed, they protested by staying away from school.[5] That she seldom darkened the door of the church allowed the natives to retain control over their congregations and kept them from appearing subordinate to a woman.

Perhaps due to illness that made her look older than her forty-five years, Sue McBeth's students called her Pika, or Mother, and afforded her the respect given elder members of the tribe (Hoyle 1999, 478). Most of the Nez Perce she trained looked to Sue McBeth as guide, counselor, and friend, reporting to her regularly and conferring with her frequently even after being ordained. According to her letter to Lowrie, dated February 2, 1878, McBeth's pragmatic teaching, which covered studies of the church's doctrinal confessions and catechism and focused on scripture, concentrated on preparing the ministers for preaching on Sundays (*AIC:* 22[E]/18). The students translated biblical passages into Nez Perce and practiced sermons the class had worked out together. The strength of the McBeth Mission was the continued emphasis on practical ministry in the churches and the ability of the students to retain positions of respect among their own people. As the article entitled "Foreign Missions" in the May 1893 edition of *The Church at Home and Abroad* indicates, the board came to regard the school, no doubt reluctantly, as a "sort of Theological Seminary." Indeed, it provided the means for Native American Christian leaders to gain enough biblical knowledge and understanding of church history and polity to pass ordination exams given by the local presbytery.

---

[4] McBeth had apparently suffered a stroke during the war years that left her partially paralyzed. Kate McBeth noted that "Miss McBeth seldom appeared among the people" (McBeth 1993, 221); see also Crawford 1936, 40, 91. For General O. O. Howard's description of her classroom, see McBeth Papers, 1897, 18; McBeth 1993, 91.

[5] Kate McBeth noted in her diary in 1881 that Sue's attempts to place the church leadership in a position to govern the tribe were opposed even by her students. Kate McBeth wrote, "There is not the eagerness to attend S[chool] that there was last year."

McBeth, the Little Mother, however, was unremitting in viewing the Nez Perces as "her boys." This contributed to a tendency to infantilize her male students. As endearing as those references may have been, such an attitude at times failed to prepare McBeth, and the women who followed her, to meet with native men as adults and peers. Believing their students tractable as children, the women never seemed quite at ease when challenged by Nez Perce men who disagreed with them.

Archie Lawyer, for example, nearly became Sue McBeth's undoing. Lawyer was the son of the former Chief Lawyer, an early convert, who was appointed by American government personnel as head chief in 1848. He was the brother of James (Jimmy) Lawyer, Chief Lawyer's oldest son, who served for two years before the federal government disposed of the office of chief altogether in 1881. An aura of nobility clung to the Lawyer line, and Chief Lawyer's sons, both James and Archie, continued to use their former status to influence the tribe.

James and Archie Lawyer both attended Sue McBeth's school when she took it over in 1874 following the death of Spalding. Robert and Mark Williams, two sons of one of the first converts, also attended, along with James Hines, an older convert and cousin of the Lawyers (McBeth 1993, 88; *AIC:* 21[D]/320). As late as 1878 McBeth claimed in a letter to Lowrie that her students were "from the 'pick' of the tribe," and Archie Lawyer along with Robert Williams became the "principal preachers—and good preachers" (*AIC:* 22[E]/18). From the beginning she envisioned a native ministry establishing native churches throughout the western tribes. While not antagonistic to her vision, the Lawyer brothers challenged her. Already respected for their ancestry, they were also quick-witted, fun loving, and not reluctant to torment their humorless teacher. They also had their own ideas about where and how ministry should evolve. They let her know that they were not accustomed to taking orders from a woman (Morrill and Morrill 1978, 34).

Faced with the graver challenge of having to convince the mission board that she was capable of teaching theology to students, McBeth chose to downplay her trouble with the Lawyers for several years (ibid., 33-37). Sent by the government in 1879 to minister to Chief Joseph's people exiled in the Oklahoma Territory, Archie returned to a popular following among both those in Kamiah and the exiles who were eventually returned to the reservation. McBeth believed that the time in Oklahoma only strengthened his taste to rule. She recommended he be kept from assuming his own pulpit in Idaho. She wished to discredit him by virtue of his behavior and his upbringing; the former could be changed, the latter could not.

Lawyer challenged his teacher by showing an independence of spirit that kept him beyond her control. The more McBeth tried to circumscribe his activities, the more he defied her. She refused to endorse him for ordination, claiming he was trying to set up his own church, over which he would rule as "an absolute Monarch" and also that his mother was a "tewat" (medicine woman) and his upbringing ill-fitted him to Christian leadership (*AIC:* 21[D]/236 and 21[D]/ 309, 320; see also *AIC:* 2-2/17). Her sister, Kate McBeth, remarked in her diary on Christmas 1879: "These Lawyers, how they do trouble people. . . . So much intriguing & plotting for power"; yet she still believed her sister was responsible for the rift between the two (McBeth Papers, 1891, 6). Acknowl-edging that there was some justification for her assessment of the Lawyers, Kate attributed the difficulties to Sue's "jealousies & maneuvering to enthrone & establish Robert [Williams, the first ordained Nez Perce] even at the expense of Archie" (ibid., 26).

Lawyer turned to "Brother" George Deffenbaugh, the mission superinten-dent from 1878 to 1888, to speak on his behalf. Deffenbaugh blamed McBeth for causing the rivalry because of "her prejudice [against the Lawyers] more than anything else" (*AIC:* 1-1/263). Although he feared Lawyer would "never prove a successful pastor" due to "slight pulpit preparations," an "*innate* taste for display," and an inclination "to be domineering," Deffenbaugh regarded Lawyer as morally upright and "standing fairly and squarely in the faith as it is revealed in God's Word" (ibid.). He defended Lawyer's Christian commitment and his 1881 ordination, which made Lawyer a member of the fraternity of Presbyterian pastors to which McBeth could never belong.

The Presbytery, concerned over the evidence of strong factions within the Nez Perce community, endorsed Deffenbaugh's idea of splitting the Kamiah congregation to allow Lawyer to establish the Second Presbyterian Church of Kamiah across the river from the first. In "Facts regarding the two Spokane Churches Wellpinit and Spokane River," Kate McBeth described how, before Deffenbaugh could formally separate the congregation, Lawyer had taken half of the 280 members of the First Kamiah Church, built a new church on land donated by one of the group, and "organized" a new congregation (McBeth/Crawford Collection, 4).

As a respected leader among his own people, and an ordained minister, Law-yer had the upper hand over McBeth. Nevertheless, her letters to Kate McBeth show how she tried to discredit the new church in the eyes of the board. By pointing to its rather unorthodox beginnings, she tried to loosen Lawyer's hold on it, but to no avail. The split between Lawyer and McBeth, and ultimately between the First and Second churches, might have been avoided had McBeth been ordained. In a letter to J. C. Lowrie, McBeth begged the board to consider her the Rev. S. L. McBeth, if only "for an hour" (Morrill and Morrill 1978, 36). The distrust and recriminations may have sprung from legitimate concerns on both sides, but the inability to come to an amicable decision was exacerbated by the struggle for authority. In the end, Lawyer's ministerial status left him in a better bargaining position than McBeth. In the ambiguous space where they negotiated their relationship, her gender kept McBeth from participating in the fray with Lawyer as an ecclesiastical equal. His gender helped enable Lawyer to retain his independence and to achieve his end: a native Presbyterian church more tolerant of native ways. While it was, perhaps, to the Nez Perces' advan-tage that the Little Mother was kept from sharing the pulpit with them, Sue McBeth did prove a true friend to the Nez Perce Christians, including Lawyer. By the time of her death, McBeth had trained ten native pastors.

II

Ordination did not always give native pastors the advantage over women missionaries in struggles that pitted native authority against women's authority. The balance of power was fairly even, so that in the ambiguity of contested space, authority had to be negotiated. At times church governing bodies, personalities, and circumstances helped to swing the balance more in favor of one party than another. Despite the lack of ordination, missionary women's authority in the church was formidable and could be used to prevail over native pastors. Kate McBeth and Helen Clark used their authority in different ways but achieved the same ends. Kate McBeth arrived on the Nez Perce Reservation in 1879 to teach the women. Fearful of losing her hold on the men's school and being replaced by a male teacher, Sue McBeth begged the Board to send a teacher for the women so that she would not be pressed into service in that capacity. Her sister, the popular and more outgoing of the two, was not her choice. Jealousy and petty disagreements marred the relationship from the first and Miss Kate (the appellation the Nez Perces used to distinguish her from the older Miss McBeth) was left entirely on her own to make her way into the culture, lives, and hearts of the Nez Perces. This she did quite quickly, to the chagrin of her sister. It was not until the close of Sue McBeth's life in 1893 that the two were reconciled. At Sue McBeth's death, Kate McBeth assumed responsibility for the men's school, along with her women's school, in Lapwai.

Miss Kate proved "inflexible and adamant when a question of right arose and yet she was one of the gentlest and sweetest of Christians" (Morrill and Morrill 1978, 360). Her more kindly and inclusive manner helped heal some of the breaches in the Christian camp. The death of Archie Lawyer just weeks after the death of Sue McBeth and Robert Williams's death a year later also contributed to the community's ability to mend some fences. By 1896 Mary Crawford had joined her aunt and assumed the care of the women so that Miss Kate could attend solely to the men's school. A women's mission organization in the East sent funds to build houses for student pastors, and the school took up its final residence in Lapwai, where it became Miss Kate's work to encourage the ministers to pursue the missionary journeys for which their training had prepared them. In her twilight years Kate McBeth served not only to train men for ordination, as her sister had done, but was the friend waiting at home to advise, console, and pray for the native ministers going out to "heathen tribes." Her more benign manner seemed to diffuse many of the battles her sister had encountered while allowing her to continue to train and nurture native pastors.

It was during Kate McBeth's leadership of the McBeth Mission that James Hayes, Sue McBeth's "shaggy headed, broad shouldered six foot, youngest 'boy,'" did most of his evangelistic work. It is estimated that he preached to twenty-five tribes between the Canadian and the Arizona borders (Morrill and Morrill 1978, 360). It was among the Makahs of the Olympic peninsula, however, that a conflict arose between Kate McBeth's missionary friend Helen Clark

and the Rev. Hayes. Reminiscent of the conflict between Archie Lawyer and
Sue McBeth, even Miss Kate's attempts to smooth the ruffled feathers of each
one could not prevent a repetition of the battle for authority.

Like Sue McBeth, Helen Clark found that her isolated position among the
Makahs had given her the opportunity to expand her authority beyond the confines of her gender. Her encounter with James Hayes challenged that authority.
By his identity as an Indian, Hayes, like Archie Lawyer, was moved to embrace a
more inclusive vision of ministry, which Clark contested. His authority as a minister gave him the power, as it had Lawyer, to move in the direction of his choosing and eventually endorse a church structure to his liking among the Makahs.
He was, however, prevented from doing so until Helen Clark left the Makahs.

In the judgment of most missionaries, Hayes was a model Christian Indian.
Amelia Frost, for example, the missionary among the Shoshones, regarded him
as instrumental in building up the native church. She welcomed his visits, and
he numbered her among his good friends.[6] Missionary journals also touted the
Nez Perce pastor. For example, the September 12, 1888, edition of *The Occi-
dent,* in an article entitled "The Jubilee at Walla Walla," hailed him as "a St.
John, [who] gave the most convincing proof that the blood of these martyrs [Dr.
Marcus and Narcissa Whitman] had been the seed of the church . . . an object
for those to whom seeing is believing." Hayes was an exemplary Christian Indian who delighted missionary personnel, made good copy for missionary publications, and furthered the cause of Presbyterian missions. It was thus surprising to find him at odds with missionary Helen Clark.

Clark was a veteran missionary among the Choctaws and Spokanes before
her missionary career of just over twenty years among the Makahs (Clark n.d.).
By the time Clark arrived at Neah Bay in 1899, her views of Indians were fairly
well established. According to an undated letter to Kate McBeth, probably written before she left Spokane, she had come to the conclusion that "the Indian
needs oversight." To her way of thinking, even the Indian pastor of an Indian
church needed "backing and someone to engineer for him." Like the missionaries studied by historian Peggy Pascoe, Clark's gendered assumptions were that
Indian women were "pure, pious Christian women" at heart, but Indian men—
even Christian ones—were suspect (Pascoe 1990, 122).

On the strength of the reports she had heard about the success of Hayes's
evangelistic trips among various tribes, Clark invited Hayes to visit the Makahs
in 1905. Her expectations of James Hayes were spelled out in a letter to Kate
McBeth. Clark indicated that she was praying that "the Spirit may be poured out
and his services blessed in the salvation of many souls." But she also expressed
her "hope [that] he will not push to baptize any one but those I think fit." Neah
Bay was her domain, and she had strong notions how best to run it.

---

[6] James Hayes had been a favorite of Sue McBeth's. See, for example, her description
of him in Sue McBeth to J. C. Lowrie, November 9, 1880 (*AIC:* 21[D]/329). Amelia
Frost wrote of him in her letter to Mrs. Young, December 6, 1906, copied in Kate
McBeth's hand (McBeth/Crawford Collection, 2).

Upon his first visit to Neah Bay, in 1905, Clark received Hayes cordially, housed him and his co-worker, Nez Perce minister Mark Arthur, and even doctored them with cough medicine when they became ill. The evangelistic meetings were apparently quite successful. Hayes baptized eleven Makahs and made plans to return the next year. He expressed concern, however, over setting up a church. Perhaps all agreed that the Makahs were not yet ready, because they planned for Hayes to return the next year. Clark appeared to look forward to Hayes's return.

If the newly baptized converts did not come out for services during the year, as Clark complained, the Makahs came out in force during Hayes's visit. He seemed to be on good terms with Clark, who bought some whale meat for him to sample. He conferred with Clark over the desire of two young men to attend McBeth's Mission, though the father of one of them was a leader of the Indian Shakers.[7] There was no indication that trouble was brewing between him and Clark, unless the preface of his letter to Miss Kate, "to let you know about my work in this dark land," held multiple meanings.

Despite the large crowds attending his services on his second visit, Hayes baptized only four men, and no church was organized (NBPC n.d., 3). The record of the baptisms, kept by Clark, did not mention the name of the minister. Penciled in by another hand, however, were the words, "John Hanks [one of the baptized in 1905] says Rev. James Hayes was the minister" (ibid.). And then, despite his work, Hayes's name failed to appear anywhere in the brief "Beginnings of Presbyterian Work at Neah Bay," sent in by Clark in 1924 as an introduction to the *Session Book of the Neah Bay Presbyterian Church* (ibid.).

It is difficult to discern from this distance what transpired between Hayes and Clark or why nearly twenty years intervened before his next visit to that part of Washington State. Clark gives some clues in her letter to her friend Kate McBeth. Clark and Hayes, it seems, clashed over their willingness to accept converts who wanted to maintain a foot in both the Indian Shaker Church and the Presbyterian Church. Clark "objected to taking them into church fellowship unless they were willing to give up the Shakers." Hayes was more flexible. Recognizing the interest of the Shakers in the Presbyterian meetings, he even suggested evening services to accommodate those who "have . . . dance about the same time when we have service in afternoon." Although he gave little indication of his thoughts regarding Shakerism, he was willing to allow the opportunity for those in the Shaker Church to join in the Presbyterian meetings. Clark, however, apparently objected to Shakers even attending the church meetings.

---

[7] The Indian Shaker Church is not to be confused with the Shaker sect begun by Ann Lee in the eastern United States and popular from the 1830s to the 1850s. Although characterized by similar active worship styles, the Indian Shakers began in 1881, when John Slocum, a Squaxin Indian, was believed dead and revived. He preached that God had sent him back to lead other Indians to Christianity. For general information on the Indian Shakers, see Mooney (1991), Eells (1985), and Barnett (1972).

Ultimately, Clark refused entry of the Shakers into the church meetings unless they were willing to forsake all association with the Shaker Church. Her intolerance of the expression of cultural differences in worship, combined with her devotion to orthodox Calvinism, set her at odds with the Nez Perce minister (Barnett 1972, 145).[8]

While Hayes also seemed to object to Shakerism as less than the true faith, he found it more compatible with Christian ideals than did Clark. He therefore seemed less offended by it and more willing to embrace those who practiced it, no doubt believing their exposure to Presbyterianism would, in time, win them over. In fact, many Shakers who claimed conversion to Presbyterianism entered the church when Clark's tenure was past, in part through the ministrations of the visiting Nez Perce pastors.[9]

It seems, however, that Clark also felt personally rebuffed by the visiting minister. She accused Hayes of not appreciating her hospitality. She wrote McBeth that although Hayes "boarded with me [he] went out among the Indians whenever asked. He seemed much more grateful for anything they did for him then [*sic*] what I did."

Ultimately, Clark seemed to have had the most difficulty with Hayes's gender. Although he was a "good man," she indicated her trouble with him by claiming that, "unfortunately [he] does not know everything." Helen Clark's struggle "to turn [her] moral influence into authority," in Pascoe's terms, meant setting the terms of Makah church membership; the search for authority assumed "the primacy of Victorian female values and was sharply critical of male privilege" (Pascoe 1990, xvii, 50). Hayes threatened her tenuous position because he had the power—available only to men as ordained ministers—to force her to submit to his version of church membership. To protect her standards for church organization and to prevent loss of her authority in Neah Bay, Clark did not invite James Hayes back. She claimed he was "not suited to these Coast Indians as well as the interior ones."

Further, Clark implied that Hayes's interest in the church was for personal aggrandizement. She attributed his liberal terms of church membership to a concern with making a good impression on his fellow ministers by baptizing large numbers. Like the white men in the church, she complained, he simply "wants to have 'a showing at Presbytery.'" She adopted the position of her

---

[8] Mooney claimed that by 1896 the Presbyterian Church had given "official endorsement" to the Shakers. If their orthodoxy was in question, their "character and actions" were not, for the religion had noticeably beneficial effects, according to the Presbyterians, on the moral improvement of the Indians, condemning as it did alcohol, gambling, and shamanism (see Mooney 1991, 747, 751).

[9] Noted Shaker leader Lans Kalapa (the church session records spell the name Kallappa) joined the church March 7, 1925. His brother, James Kalapa, came forward May 29, 1927, following an evangelistic meeting led by Nez Perce pastor James Dickson and Spokane pastor Daniel Scott (both schooled at McBeth Mission). He did not join the church officially, though, until October 24, 1937. On the influence of the Kalapa brothers at Neah Bay, see Barnett 1972, 63-65.

benefactor, Mrs. Caroline Ladd of Portland, who, she reported in a May 12, 1902, letter to McBeth, did "not desire [the mission] to go into the hands of the men."[10] For Clark, that included Indian men who could, by virtue of ordination, insist on doing things their way.

While Helen Clark praised Kate McBeth's work in training Indian pastors, Clark would not allow the native pastors to interfere with either her understanding of Presbyterian doctrine or her realm of influence at Neah Bay. Although she decried James Hayes's suggestions, style of leadership, and expectations of her, her main concern was with his potential to upset her plans for a church established on her terms.

If Clark won the immediate battle with Hayes, it is not so clear that she won the war. Whatever Hayes thought of her, he did not write it down. Nor did he return to Neah Bay until after she left in 1921. In 1924 the new Neah Bay Presbyterian Church invited him for a visit. Hayes's return to the Makahs was a warm one. As church member Helen Peterson remembered it in an interview with the author on May 18, 1994, they enjoyed Hayes's "jolly" nature, his love of singing and of storytelling. Peterson recalled one story Hayes told with great enthusiasm about a proud moose that was humbled by a wren that took up residence in his nose. Perhaps Hayes saw himself as the wren in Clark's nose!

The ambiguous space where the battle for authority between James Hayes and Helen Clark was waged cannot be understood outside the categories of race and gender. Clark struggled with the same cultural system that the McBeths did, one that allowed her to achieve positions of power because of her race but limited her authority on account of her gender by denying her the access to church office that males of both races possessed. In other words, as a white woman she could wield authority over Indian church members, but she was limited in her authority over Indian ministers. Hayes, schooled by Sue McBeth, had learned to respect the authority and power of women missionaries, even as he learned to maintain boundaries around his own authority. Both McBeths, recognizing his cooperative spirit, had also learned of his intransigence when "'bossed' by a woman." He would not tolerate losing respect among his peers, as Sue McBeth once warned her sister, Kate McBeth. As she put it, "He is a *man* and feels his manhood," so Kate would be wise to avoid testing him. Clark, as the doorkeeper to the Makahs, was able to assert her authority and keep him out. Hayes, however, bided his time until she was gone and then resumed his ministry among the Makahs.

III

If Kate McBeth's tenure as teacher to the Nez Perces brought a respite from the battles over authority in the church, it also strengthened the independence of the native pastors. At her death in 1915, having seen four more Nez Perces

---

[10] References to grandsons Harry and Elliot Corbett indicate Clark's sponsor was Caroline Ladd, although Clark does not refer to her first name.

ordained, her niece, Mary Crawford, also called Maisy, picked up the reins. A gifted musician, Mary Crawford was no less determined than her two predecessors to provide ministers for the church. She arrived in Idaho in 1895. As her Aunt Kate had done before her, she took up the work of the class for women and children to relieve her aunt for the men's school. She continued in that role until her sister, Elizabeth Crawford, took it on after Kate's death so that Mary Crawford could attend to the men's training, though she never completely gave up the children's work. It fell to her to secure the gains of her aunts by diligently guarding against any Indians who might resurrect the "old heathenism" and by defending the school against any white Presbyterians bent on taking the work from the women. As successful as she may have been with the first battle, she ultimately lost the second. And because of that loss, the native pastorate lost as well.

Much like James Hayes and his challenge to Helen Clark, Albert Moore tested Mary Crawford's resolve to keep out all former "religious superstitions" from the church. He went much further than Hayes, however, when he dissolved all distinctions between the Dreamer religion, identified as "ipnu' tsililpt," and Christianity. Willing to grant some cultural similarities, although loath to take advantage of them to encourage Christian conversion, the Presbyterian missionaries drew the line at suggesting that all religions were alike. And Dreamers did not even pretend to be Christians. Moore's assumptions put him outside the bounds of the church as far as Crawford was concerned.

Moore came in to the Presbyterian Church as a young man, having been a part of the Dreamer religion, a mix of Christian and older Nez Perce beliefs that evolved from Smohalla's visions of the 1850s (see Mooney 1991, 716-31; Relander 1986; and Josephy 1979, 424-25). The Dreamer religion had gained adherents during the uncertainties and privations of the treaty era. Like other revitalization movements, it called for rejecting the white man's dress and culture and returning to life as it had been lived prior to his coming. Relying on dreams and ritual practices and ceremonies influenced by Catholic worship forms, Dreamers hoped to rid the land of all white men; its eclectic nature opened Moore to exploring the Christian faith.

For Moore, the teaching of the Presbyterian Church paralleled what he had learned among the Dreamers, particularly concerning morality (Thomas 1970, 64). He discerned no clear difference between them, because both "real Indians" and Christians did not lie or steal, and both rewarded good behavior on earth with the promise of heaven. His confusion was understandable but also expedient. Moore had a thorough enough understanding of Christian theology to recognize differences as well as similarities. Moore had not only joined the church but also had spent three years at a Bible college in southern California preparing to become a minister.

Despite his training, Moore found so many similarities between his old religion and his new that Crawford became concerned that he was confusing the two. When he claimed that Christianity was "just like old 'ipnu' tsililpt,'" and concluded that "we were Christians before the White man came," Crawford bristled, insisting that although they may have acted like Christians, they were not (Thomas 1970, 66). One could not, as James Hayes preached, "go to Heaven without the gospel of Christ and without atonement of Jesus Christ." Despite the similarities, there were definite differences, and to deny them would make conversion unnecessary and Christ insignificant. She offended the minister-in-training by calling the Dreamer religion "savage." He responded by "stepping out" of the Presbyterian Church and the ministry (ibid.).[11]

Crawford was not as fortunate with the men of the Presbyterian board. The vision of native ministry was lost in the wake of the Progressive Era; despite ordaining another four men (two from other tribes), the McBeth Mission in Idaho was closed in 1932. The "mystique of efficiency and progress" (Moorhead 1994, 264-87) took hold within the church mission boards, causing an overhaul of programs and institutions that failed to produce large numbers of converts or church leaders. An economic and religious "depression" assailed the country and all mainline denominations, affecting church membership rolls and the amount of funding for missions (Pascoe 1990, 197).[12] The Indian Reorganization Act opened additional positions of Indian leadership through tribal councils and the Bureau of Indian Affairs. Even tribes such as the Nez Perce, which failed to endorse the act, began to find the era more conducive to the hiring of Indian personnel in a variety of positions related to Indian affairs, draining church leadership pools (Prucha 1984, 2:992). Finally, the Presbyterian Church, in an effort to standardize ordination programs, and thus make the church more efficient and its clergy more effective, began to demand a formal seminary education of its ministers (Bowden 1991, 238).

In Idaho the aging missionary Mary Crawford fought to keep open the beleaguered school that her aunt had begun. Blaming low salaries and low morale among the Indians for the lack of students, Crawford's umbrage was exacerbated by having received word of the closing of her school while she was on furlough in the East. Neither Crawford nor the native pastors she trained could stand against the changing tide.

Where once missionary women and native pastors could bolster each other's positions in the church, the onset of the Progressive Era, followed on its heels by the Great Depression, subdued their independence and reduced their involvement in church leadership. Mary Crawford and Perry Ides both fell victim to these tragic events when, in 1925, Perry Ides became the first, and only, Makah minister of the Neah Bay Presbyterian Church. The retirement of Helen Clark allowed Ides—one of the first converts, a trusted translator for Clark and a graduate of the McBeth Mission—to settle into his role as pastor with relative ease.

---

[11] Moore, however, returned to the church in his last years and was buried in the Spalding (Indian) Presbyterian Church in Lapwai, Idaho, in 1965 (see "Oldest Nez Perce Dies at 103," *Lewiston Morning Tribune* [Sunday, October 10, 1965], 20).

[12] Church attendance declined across all denominations and in both Indian and non-Indian churches. For example, Walker (1968, 86, 87) charts the declining church attendance of all Nez Perce churches during this era. It fell off dramatically around 1922 from about 450 to just over 200 only ten years later.

His teacher, Mary Crawford, recommended him over a white minister at Neah Bay because she believed him "far more capable of handling the situation and taking charge of the work at Neah Bay." At his ordination in 1925 he was lauded for "passing a very creditable examination and making a fine impression on Presbytery." Yet despite his many qualifications for leading the church at Neah Bay, it remained a mission church and Ides had to deal with women missionaries throughout his ten years as minister.

Perry Ides asked advice of the missionaries, but he held his own views and apparently ran his own shop. Ides was not adverse to the support of the missionaries who were sent to Neah Bay, but he preferred it when they left him to be the minister of the church while they worked in the community. For the most part, now ordained and free of the more controlling Helen Clark, he set his own agenda.

Ides had the advantage over the visitor Hayes in that, by the time he became minister, Clark had gone and none of the women who followed stayed more than a few years or were able to secure a hold on the community as Clark had managed to do. Ides was also on his home turf; he was one of the people, not an outsider. He thus was able to garner a broader base of support within the community. He was also able to use his authority as an ordained minister to maintain a grip on the operations of the church. In Ides's case, however, his successful assault on the gender issue failed to assist him on the racial issue.

Perry Ides could not withstand the forces of the Board of National Missions, which appointed William S. Thorndike to the Neah Bay church in 1935 (NBPC n.d., 63). As the first male missionary to the mission, Thorndike was also the first ordained minister to oversee the work. The church was not large enough to support two ministers, and the white minister soon dominated. When up against one of the same gender, racial categories became the deciding factor.[13] Ides chose other avenues to continue his ministry to and for the Makahs, but he had learned that while ordination gave him leverage over women, who were not eligible for that office, it did not ensure equal footing with white men who possessed the same title. Even his friend and counselor Mary Crawford could not come to his assistance. She had been forced to retire three years earlier and the McBeth Mission closed. The ambiguous space where roles between women missionaries and native pastors could be negotiated collapsed under the domination of white churchmen.

The venerated missionary statesman Henry Venn claimed that native churches without native ministers would "remain in a dependent condition, and make but little progress in spiritual attainments. The same congregation, under competent native pastors, would become more self-reliant, and their religion would be of a more manly, home character" (Anderson 1967, 98). Mary Crawford made much the same observation, saying that when "you take away the independence

---

[13] In an interview with the author in 1994, Thorndike's daughter, Gertrude Stock, said her father was horrified when he arrived to replace an existing pastor who had not been informed by the Presbytery that he was, in effect, being replaced.

of the Indian ministry and place him under the white man, you will break his spirit." The same could be said of the independent-minded missionary women who, although not themselves ordained, found that as they worked to ordain and empower the native men, their own authority was enhanced. The loss of the mission heralded a loss of their missionary spirit.

When the churchwomen lost power over their mission boards in the 1920s, the church lost one of its greatest missionary arms. When the native pastors of Idaho lost both their teachers and their pulpits, the church lost some of its most faithful and valuable leaders. Despite struggles over limited power, the missionary women and native pastors of the Pacific Northwest used the ambiguous space of the socially and culturally marginalized to forge relationships that benefited both of them. Because they did so, the Presbyterian Church also benefited from their active and capable leadership. Even their combined strength, however, could not guarantee their role in the church when the authority of ordained white male leadership was asserted.

3

"Standing behind the Looms"

American Missionary Women and Indian Church Women
in the Devolution Process

Melissa Lewis Heim

In September 1997, at the fiftieth anniversary celebration of the foundation of the Church of South India, the Indian political leader and Christian P. A. Sangma named empowerment of women as the major goal for the twenty-first century, noting that the Indian church could no longer ignore 50 percent of the population. He also offered a grim statistic; the total number of women in full-time pastoral or evangelistic work had declined dramatically over the previous fifty years (Webster 1998, 51). These developments would probably have dismayed women associated with the American Madura Mission (AMM) in the early years of the twentieth century. American women had worked with Indian women in evangelization, health, and educational endeavors, beginning in the 1830s in Madurai, South India. By the 1920s one hundred Indian women were employed as Bible women evangelizers by the AMM. The Lucy Perry Noble Institute (LPNI), a women's technical school, employed two American women and twenty-three Indians. The Women's Hospital in Madurai maintained 110 beds, usually at full capacity, with forty-three nurses in training, one Indian doctor and an intern, two American doctors and one American nurse, all women (ABCFM 9.10, 1:16 Deputation Survey; Otto 1928). In 1934, on the one-hundredth anniversary of the founding of the AMM, the American missionary board fulfilled a long-stated goal of fostering independent churches by formally transferring power to a representative body called the Sangam, made up of American and Indian members of both genders.

The experiences of American missionaries Gertrude Chandler and Bertha K. Smith as well as Indian church worker Dr. Grace Kennett during this process of devolution of power from the AMM to the Indian Christian Church highlight the complex dynamics and shifting relationships among men and women, both

American and Indian, in the local churches and the mission-founded institutions in the Madurai region. By the 1930s the ideals and goals of the "Woman's
Work for Woman" program that developed in the late nineteenth century, as
well as the achievements of this work in the early twentieth century, were challenged and obscured. The loss of autonomy for American women's mission
boards and economic pressures in the United States, coupled with Indian men's
authority in the newly independent Indian church, restricted the independence
of both American women missionaries and Indian women in the Indian church.

In her 1934 annual letter to friends and supporters in the United States, missionary Gertrude Chandler described a scene where she worked, at the girl's
training school just outside the city of Madurai, in South India. The students
were practicing on large looms, part of the home-crafts program of the school,
and Chandler was giving a tour to a visiting delegation of American missionaries who entered the weaving room and stood behind the looms, watching the
young women at their work. Chandler incorporated this image of support at a
distance in her annual letter. American missionaries, Chandler wrote, are standing behind their "Indian co-workers who are handling the threads with new
patterns in mind." The task of the Americans in South India at this time, Chandler continued, was to "share joy and excitement and be ready to help [Indian
Christians] see where weak and broken threads are and lend a helping hand to
untangle threads that will get twisted and snarled" (ABCFM 16.1.9, 7/24/34).
Chandler described devolution as a process placing Americans in the background,
needing to step back and give support from the sidelines, and Indians in the
foreground, taking a leadership role. But in some situations American women
and Indian women found themselves on the same side, both chafing under the
authority of Indian men in church organizations. In other situations American
missionary women came into conflict with Indian church women. National identity as well as gender and economics affected women's experiences during the
process of devolution.

THE GOAL: INDIAN CHURCH AUTONOMY

In 1934, when Gertrude Chandler wrote the words "standing behind the
looms," American missionaries had been living and working in and around
Madurai, South India, for one hundred years. Developing self-supporting In-
dian churches had been a stated goal of the AMM from its early years. Rufus
Anderson, the Foreign Secretary of the American Board of Commissioners of
Foreign Missions (ABCFM) encouraged AMM missionaries to develop vital,
independent indigenous churches as quickly as possible. His visit to South Indian mission stations in 1855 served to catalyze the AMM to ordain its first
Indian pastor, G. Ryappan Winfred. Two years later American missionary Horace
S. Taylor organized seven Indian churches under his care into an association, or
Sangam, a Tamil name for a renowned literary assembly of scholars and poets
in pre-fourteenth-century Madurai (Heim 1994, 119-22, 124-31). The Sangam
represented for Taylor an essential step forward in Indian Christian autonomy;

by choosing this Tamil name, Taylor and his Indian colleagues situated the new Christian organization in South Indian cultural history. Seventy-seven years later, in 1934, the AMM transferred its authority to an organization also named the Sangam, an association of seventeen women and twenty-five men, all representatives from former AMM churches, Indian ministers of those churches, or American missionaries. Operating under the authority of the Sangam, various councils and executive committees administered all but one of the institutions formerly run by the AMM.[1] The Sangam also assumed the role formerly played by the AMM in relating to the Madura Church Council, the highest ecclesiastical body representing Indian Christian churches founded originally by AMM missionaries. Devolution of power and authority, envisaged by Rufus Anderson and others in the nineteenth century, came to fruition in the twentieth century. But in the process women sometimes experienced difficulty establishing their own authority.

INITIAL STEPS IN DEVOLUTION

In the years leading up to 1934 the AMM tried more than one way to broaden the role of Indian Christians in church and mission work as part of a larger movement toward indigenization in Indian churches (see Harper 2000, 205-20). But even before the turn of the century, the AMM developed a plan to employ representative pastors, who would make yearly visits to all the congregations in a certain area and report at the annual mission meeting (Chandler 1909, 371). At first the AMM chose the representative pastors, then the local church union took over that responsibility. Worried that local groups were "passing the appointment around" as an honor rather than choosing the most able pastor, the AMM assigned the General Church Union the job of choosing representative pastors. Although this devolution plan offered increased responsibilities and a broader scope of work for Indian pastors, the pastors remained clearly under the control and direction of the American missionaries. Indian pastors made their reports at specified times in the AMM meetings and did not participate in appropriation decisions (Fleming 1916, 227-29). It is also important to note that Indian Christian women were not eligible for ordination at that time, so the representative-pastor plan by definition excluded a significant segment of the Indian Christian community as recipients of devolved authority.[2]

Another devolution plan, which involved representative groups at the church, region, and district levels, offered more opportunities for women's involvement. This plan, which also involved ecclesiastical organization, began in 1910

---

[1] A separate College Council exercised authority over the American College and communicated directly to the ABCFM (see editorial, "Madura Enters a New Century," *The Missionary Herald* [March 1934], 75).

[2] The Church of South India (CSI), a union church successor to the Sangam, did not approve the ordination of women until 1982. In 1997 about forty ordained women served full-time in the CSI (Webster 1998).

with the formation of the District Conference (Fleming 1916, 230). Under the District Conference, the thirty-three churches of the AMM, each with its pastorate committee, were organized into five circles, each led by a circle committee. Church members donated money not to their local churches but to their circle. The circle committees, made up of all pastors in the area, all missionaries, including wives, and representatives elected from each church, made decisions formerly under the purview of the station missionary. The AMM appointed the chair of the circle committee for as long as the AMM contributed 50 percent of the funds used by the District Conference. When AMM donations dipped below 50 percent of a circle's total operating budget, the District Conference took over the authority of appointing the circle committee chair. The District Conference, from the beginning, directed all pastoral and evangelistic work, as well as all elementary education in the AMM area (Fleming 1916, 232-33).

In its first year of organization, the District Conference had twenty-eight members: nineteen Indians, mostly pastors, and nine missionaries (Eddy 1910, 67). Responding to concerns about developing a clerical bureaucracy and autocracy, the AMM made a "special provision" for more lay representation beginning in 1912. In that year District Conference membership grew to thirty-five, with roughly one-third each from pastors, missionaries, and Indian laymen (Fleming 1916, 232).[3] Although women were not present in 1912, the lay representation provision did not rule out participation by Indian laywomen. Several years after its establishment in 1910, the District Conference changed its name to the Madura Church Council (MCC). This body, representing the Indian churches that had grown out of AMM evangelization efforts in the nineteenth century, was made up of pastors and Indian laymen, and, at least by 1929, laywomen (AMM, May 1929). When the Sangam was established in 1934, its Constitution provided that twelve out of a total of about forty Sangam members would be representatives from the MCC. At least two of the MCC representatives had to be women (Madura Mission Sangam 1934). In both of the major institutions created for devolution, women held representative positions, but the MCC received no financial support from the American Board, while the Sangam oversaw institutions still receiving some American funds.

ECUMENICAL STEPS FOR CHURCH UNION

Roughly concurrent with these developments, the AMM and its member churches were embarking on a church union initiative with other missionary groups and their related Indian churches in South India; American missionary women and Indian church women also participated in ecumenical steps. In 1905 local church councils of the AMM and its affiliated ABCFM Jaffna mission churches joined in a federation with the local councils of the London Mission Society in South Travancore. By 1908 these two groups had joined with the

---

[3] Fleming uses the term "laymen," but it remains unknown at this time whether any Indian Christian laywomen were included.

churches associated with two other missions in Vellore to form the SIUC (South India United Church) (Grafe 1990, 73-74). These initiatives, with many fits and starts, culminated eventually in the establishment of the Church of South India in 1947. While the story of church union in South India lies beyond the scope of this essay, it is important to note that the process of devolution took place during the same time period and that women also played a role in union initiatives, just as they did in devolution. In 1934, the same year as the Sangam foundation, American missionary and Indian church women organized the Women's Conference for Church Union, held at the LPNI and hosted by Gertrude Chandler. Fifty-five women from the five constituent members of the SIUC attended. Gertrude Chandler gave an enthusiastic report to Mabel Emerson at the American Board in Boston. The meeting, Chandler wrote,

> did nothing but strengthen the feeling that Union is possible and lots of controversial points will soften down as soon as we are working together. Meanwhile it is good for the women to know what different groups are doing in different places. It gets their courage up. (ABCFM 16.1.9, 11/7/ 34)

KENNETT, CHANDLER, AND SMITH: INDIAN/AMERICAN RELATIONS, FINANCES, AND GENDER DYNAMICS IN THE PERIOD OF SANGAM AUTHORITY

By virtue of its Constitution, the Sangam offered women an official role in decision making. Nine Indian Christian women and eight American missionary women deliberated, delivered reports, and voted side by side with their male colleagues in the Sangam. But women's membership in the Sangam did not assure smooth sailing for traditional areas of women's work in Madurai and the surrounding district. During this devolution period the work of women's institutions and the evangelization work performed by Bible women came under challenge. Indian physician Dr. Grace Kennett of the Women's Hospital in Madurai, and American missionaries Miss Gertrude Chandler of the LPNI and Miss Bertha K. Smith, leader of Bible women in Aruppokottai, encountered those challenges. These three women also all served on the first Sangam. Their experiences and the institutional problems encountered in their work offer a lens through which to understand the dynamics of gender in a time of shifting power in South Indian churches and Christian work.

Kennett, Chandler, and Smith were associated with institutions that represented the three major areas of women's work in the AMM: health, education, and evangelization. Each of these fields had blossomed in the late nineteenth century, nurtured by the influential mission philosophy Woman's Work for Woman and the formation of independent, but denominationally based women's mission boards. Large numbers of single women joined their married missionary colleagues in broadly based initiatives to improve indigenous women's economic, educational, social, and political status in society (Robert 1997, 125-37).

Dr. Grace Kennett and the Woman's Hospital

In the AMM the first American woman doctor, Pauline Root, arrived in 1885 and soon set up a woman's dispensary in Madurai, serving many Muslim and Hindu women in addition to Christians. The Women's Board of Missions (WBM) subsequently funded the building of a hospital, which opened in 1893. On Dr. Root's retirement the WBM provided a replacement, Dr. Harriet E. Parker, who oversaw the erection of an annex with room for fifty women patients, operating rooms, and an outpatient area (Chandler 1909, 342-46). Grace Kennett, one of the Indian women serving on the 1934 Sangam, had been among the first orphans taken in by Dr. Harriet Parker and cared for in a small dormitory that came to be called the Bird's Nest (Wilder 1961, 255). After completing her primary and secondary education in the AMM girls' schools in Madurai, Kennett studied medicine in Madras. She later described her initial fear at starting a course of study with male students.

> For an Indian maiden to delve into anatomy, physiology, medicine, and a few other things right along side of the men was a shocking idea to many people—but I survived. Not only did I learn to be a doctor, but I completely recovered from the fear which I once had of the masculine gender. Men can no longer scare me, for they are only human after all. (ABCFM Biographical File, 33:22)

Ultimately, it was conflict with women, not with men, that resulted in Kennett's departure from the Women's Hospital in 1940, just a few years after official devolution.

In 1918, when Kennett finished her medical degree, she had returned to the Women's Hospital in Madurai and worked with her mentor, Dr. Parker. In the years after Dr. Parker's retirement in 1934, tensions developed among the new Canadian missionary physician Dr. Isabella Mary Roberts, American missionary nurses Olive Nelson and Kay Hardeman, and Indian women physicians Kennett, Dr. Gnanam Samuel, and Dr. Zeline Pandian. Nelson accused Dr. Samuel of treating some nursing students harshly, and Roberts suggested that Kennett used outmoded medical practices and that she was "overtired." The disagreements among the Women's Hospital staff taxed the new structures created by devolution. The Hospital Council, a committee of the Sangam, first considered the dispute. Dissatisfied with the deliberations of the Hospital Council, Dr. Roberts appealed to the Sangam. Opinions varied widely among members of the Sangam, and they appointed a special committee. Eventually, Dr. Roberts enlisted the aid of a prominent British resident of Madurai, who cabled the American Board in Boston, charging that the Sangam "is determined to force Roberts and Nelson out of mission." The American Board supported the Sangam, and a compromise was reached, whereby Dr. Roberts and Miss Nelson took six months leave and Dr. Samuel, after six months leave, took another job. Shortly after the return of Dr. Roberts and Miss Nelson, Dr. Kennett resigned. She and

Dr. Zeline Pandian later opened their own maternity hospital in Madurai, independent from the Sangam. Although the Sangam had not endorsed Dr. Roberts's side in the controversy, neither did they force her resignation. Apparently, Dr. Kennett and Dr. Pandian preferred a completely independent hospital rather than one under the authority of the Sangam, even with its devolved power (see Banninga n.d.).

Gertrude Chandler and Financial Retrenchment at the Lucy Perry Noble Institute

In addition to medical work, teaching held an important place in the Woman's Work for Woman endeavor. Missionary Gertrude Chandler taught and managed educational institutions in a variety of circumstances throughout her long tenure with the American Board. She was the daughter and granddaughter of AMM missionaries, and her fluency in the Tamil language allowed her to begin work without delay when she joined the mission in 1908. She taught a kindergarten class at Capron Hall, the AMM's primary, secondary, and Normal school for girls in the Madurai city. In 1931, in the devolution period, Chandler took over as head of the LPNI.

The LPNI had grown from a Bible school for teachers at Capron Hall and for Bible women (ABCFM 9.10, 1:7, 8/4/25). From its 1892 beginnings in Madurai, the work was so successful that the AMM acquired thirty acres three miles north of the city at a place they called Rachanyapuram (the place of salvation). They built a Bible school for women, a practical education school for young women, a day school for children, and a dispensary. The LPNI also served as a refuge for Indian women who were recent converts. Its founder, Eva May Swift, was an energetic visionary who sometimes offended some of her mission colleagues. James Dickson characterized Swift as difficult to work with because she wanted to control everything. "She has a fine head piece, and we all admire her," Dickson wrote in a letter to the American Board in Boston, "but [we] avoid working with her whenever possible" (ABCFM 16.1.11, 2/25/24 WBM). Despite difficulties, Swift built up the Institute. A 1924 report listed three schools associated with the LPNI: a Bible school focused on the training of Bible women; the Academy, consisting of eight grades of study for young women at least fourteen years old (some were as old as forty), combined opportunities for learning an employable skill and earning money with the practice of what was called home management; and a third school that served the children of students and employees (ABCFM 9.10, vol. 81 WBM). Sally Bradley, a missionary in 1938, compared the work of the LPNI to that of the 4-H in the United States. It taught "how to do farm and home chores in the best possible way" and encouraged the students to take their newly learned techniques back to their villages. Activities included spinning, weaving, batik, embroidery, homemaking, helping with the rice harvest, as well as "book study" (ABCFM 16.1.9, November 1936).

As head of the LPNI during the period of devolution and financial retrenchment, Gertrude Chandler struggled to maintain the school's programs and personnel. Income came from tuition, government grants, and the sale of items made by the students; the largest funding source for the LPNI, however, was the American Board, which by this point included the Women's Board of Missions. Under the new structure of devolved authority, the Sangam determined the relative appropriations for the bodies under its purview: the Madura Church Council, Pasumalai High and Training School, Capron Hall High and Training School, Pasumalai Seminary, LPNI, Albert Victor Hospital, Hospital for Women and Children, Christian Economic Improvement Association, and the Advisory Committee for Work for Women (Madura Mission Sangam 1934; ABCFM 16.1.9, vol. 33).

Appropriations decisions by the Sangam serve as an illustration of gender issues in devolution. In 1939 the Sangam considered placing the LPNI under the MCC, in effect cutting its budget by over 50 percent (ABCFM 16.1.9, 3/7/39). Earlier, all institutions had been under Sangam authority, and Indian workers at institutions had enjoyed a higher pay scale because of mission board funds. All church workers under the MCC and dependent on church support were paid on a lower scale (ABCFM 16.1.9, 12/10/39). The proposal to transfer one of the major institutions dealing with women's education and outreach to the MCC suggests that a majority of Sangam members assigned a lower priority to women's work. Even three years earlier, in 1936, during a period of severe retrenchment, the LPNI had taken "a heavier portion of the cut than should have been allowed," according to Mabel Emerson at the American Board in Boston (ABCFM 16.1.9, 4/6/36). American funds were sharply curtailed throughout the depression years of the 1930s. The Sangam even considered closing the LPNI in 1934. In a public printed letter to friends in the United States entitled "Learning to Walk Alone," Chandler described the situation using familial imagery. She compared the LPNI to a little toddler, trying to walk independently of the "mother" Sangam.

In September 1934 we were told that we must learn to walk alone, depending on our own strength and gradually letting go of the hand of the Madura Mission Sangam. We kicked off rather bravely . . . but bumps and bruises [followed]. . . . Now we are feeling very uncertain about forward steps.

Chandler went on to explain that the Sangam "decreed" that funds from the American Board should be reduced 50 percent and that the LPNI should try to become self-supporting within three years. "I pled for a five year plan which would give us a much more natural growth in what I believe is the right direction," recounted Chandler, as she continued her familial imagery, "but this was like a wail in the night and roused no one in the face of all the cuts every institution was getting" (ABCFM Biographical File 13:30).

In her public letters Chandler did not raise the question of relative appropriations, presenting instead a picture of cost-cutting across the board, with all institutions suffering to a similar extent. However, in more private correspondence she expressed concern about how some members of the Sangam assessed the relative importance of the women's educational initiatives at the LPNI. Chandler reported "there is a small group of Indians who look upon [the LPNI] as less necessary to the life of the Mission than the Trade School [at Pasumalai] and they cannot conceive of closing down long established work in favor of newer experimental work" (ABCFM 16.1.9, 11/7/34). Chandler did not cite a bias against women's work per se, but the Trade School only trained boys and men and the LPNI served only girls and women. Some male missionaries did see bias in the Sangam actions. John J. Banninga, a Sangam member himself, advised Gertrude Chandler that she should resist disproportionate cuts to the LPNI budget. "Don't let the Sangam continue to give you so much smaller a proportion of the Board appropriations than the other institutions get," he cautioned, while on furlough in the United States, "I think we should insist that they go back to the 1929 ration and that all institutions get from the present appropriations what we then got" (ABCFM 16.1.9, 12/17/35). The Sangam also monitored the number of students the LPNI accepted, insisting that Chandler only admit the number budgeted for. Chandler complained to Boston that she had to turn away thirty students above the expected number, "even though I knew I could get a government grant for them" (ABCFM 16.1.9, 5/27/36). Government grants did not always follow the timetables of the mission institutions, causing a shortfall in income—and the Sangam's authority over the LPNI budget restricted Chandler's ability to maneuver.

Gertrude Chandler expressed great concern about the financial health of the LPNI in the 1930s. She cited increasing debt as a heavy burden. "I go on piling up debts for yarn, for school supplies, for books, and little can any of you imagine what a horror it is to me." She went on to explain that she was raised from childhood "to hate the word 'debt'" (ABCFM 16.1.9, 8/20/35). At one point she apologized to Mabel Emerson, her main correspondent at the American Board offices in Boston, for sending so many letters with a grumbling tone. "In the midst of most encouraging things, I just have no money" (ABCFM 16.1.9, 6/9/35). Chandler attempted a variety of measures to increase revenues for the LPNI. When she went on vacation to Kodaikanal, in the hills west of Madurai, Chandler took along items made by the students to sell at a special shop she set up. This selling of handicrafts became such a regular part of Chandler's time in Kodaikanal that she appreciated greatly her vacation to a colleague's "isolated hut," calling it the best rest she'd had in a long time. "To be able to go off anywhere without having to sell my Rachanyapuram wares was bliss." But Chandler could not forget the need for raising money. She reported to Mabel Emerson in Boston that despite sales nearly double those of the previous year, she still was going to find it difficult to find sufficient funds to last through even the first half of the school year. Chandler also noted that the LPNI was allowing some American College women students to rent rooms at Rachanyapuram in order to raise some more income (ABCFM 16.1.9, 5/27/36).[4]

---

[4] See also G.C. to MEE, 7/16/34, ABCFM 16.1.9 where Chandler suggests renting to college students "living with me or on my compound."

Gertrude Chandler's most ambitious plan to raise money involved a change in mission policy. Chandler wanted to move out of the mission bungalow on the LPNI compound and live in the dispensary/nursing home, a smaller building on the compound. She hoped then to rent out the bungalow and put the money in the LPNI budget. Mission policy dictated that any funds gained from missionary residence rental go to the House Fund, which was used to repair the residences. An examination of the decision-making process shows how power was shared among individual missionaries (in this case, a single woman, Gertrude Chandler), the Sangam, and the American Board. Chandler made her proposal to the Executive Committee of the LPNI. From there the proposal went to the LPNI Council, and then to the Sangam, which approved it. But ultimately, because all buildings remained the property of the American Board, its approval was needed also. The American Board at first cabled a refusal, but Secretary Alden Clark was present in Madurai at the time and gave his assent. Finally, the proposal received official sanction at the American Board Prudential Committee meeting as a "very special emergency measure for one year only" (ABCFM 16.1.9, 1/26/36, 2/7/36; 3.4, Box 3:14). So, for at least a short time, the women's practical education offered at Rachanyapuram received a modest infusion of money. Despite Chandler's creative schemes, financial problems continued to plague the LPNI.

Bertha Smith and Devolved Authority to Indian Pastors

While Gertrude Chandler worried about paying the bills at Rachanyapuram, Bertha K. Smith worried that devolution threatened the Bible women's work of evangelization in Aruppukottai. Smith had joined the AMM in 1917, and by 1924 she was working in Aruppukottai, a town about thirty miles south of Madurai. When the plans for devolution were made, Smith objected to the placement of Bible women's work under the Madura Church Council, which was the highest ecclesiastical body representing churches in the Madura district. Under the devolution plans, the MCC exercised authority over local church life, making pastoral appointments and conducting ordinations. The MCC also had responsibility for primary education and evangelization. Smith wanted the Bible women's evangelization work to fall under Sangam authority rather than MCC authority. She also disliked the committee work required by the new system. "I realize that in future in one sense the work is no longer mine, but I will be trying to carry out the wishes of a committee and so the responsibility will be shared" (ABCFM 16.1.9, 1/3/34). She feared that her goals for the work might not be the same as the committee's goals. And her fears were partly realized when, four years later, a survey committee recommended that Bible women change their focus from evangelizing Hindu women to working with Christian women who were already in the church (ABCFM 16.1.9, 11/17/38).

Despite concerns, Bertha Smith did participate in the new plan for devolution, serving as superintendent of women's work on her local council committee, but she was a reluctant group member. After the first two organizing meetings, Smith reported to friends at home, "I hope I can get along without any more meetings for awhile now. I feel that I would rather do something than talk so much about it" (ABCFM 16.1.9, March 1934). Pastor Samuel Joseph helped to smooth the transition, for Smith wrote enthusiastically, "no missionary could be nicer to me than he has been." Smith had to change her method of accounting when she had to report to the church council rather than to the mission. Formerly, she had kept four separate accounts, one for each school she oversaw and one for the Bible women. Under the MCC she had to combine the three schools into one account, but still keep the Bible women's account separate. "It has taken me some time to get on to their way of doing things, but they have all been very patient with me and I have been learning" (ABCFM 16.1.9, 6/19/34).

Bertha Smith encountered new difficulties with the MCC system after her supportive Indian colleague, Pastor Samuel Joseph, retired in 1935. Catherine Quickenden, a former co-worker in Aruppukottai, understood how much Smith would miss him.

> Poor Bertha is losing her last special Aruppukottai friend this month I fear—Rev. Samuel Joseph—they have worked together very closely these last two years and she has enjoyed the work with him. Now he must retire. . . . He has been in Aruppukottai over twenty years. . . . It will be difficult to fill his place. (ABCFM 16.1.9, 3/30/35)

Bertha Smith clashed with the new pastor, Rev. Edward Paul. Under the old system, when Smith reported to the AMM, Smith could have worked around the pastor or even ignored him to a certain extent. But since Smith's Bible women's work was connected with the MCC, she was linked more closely with the local church structure. Pastor Edward Paul was a member of the Women's Department Executive Committee, as well as chair of the South Local Church Council. "I have been subject to petty persecution now for this last year," Smith reported to the American Board in Boston. She charged Paul with incompetence, "Everyone knows that he is utterly unfit to be a pastor" (ABCFM 16.1.9, 6/30/37). Smith attributed her problems to her objections about the MCC overseeing the Bible women's work. "Indians object to my frankness in expressing my opinion" (ABCFM 16.1.9, 12/22/37). Smith had expressed her opinion vociferously about a "terrible situation" between one of the men teachers at the boarding school and some of the students. Improper behavior was implied, but the problematic relationship remained unarticulated in her letters to the American Board. As Smith recounted the situation, she, acting as manager of the boarding school at that time, had requested the MCC to send a committee from Madurai to address the situation, but they "refused their aid." She consulted with the Boarding School Committee, whose members said the teacher should be transferred by a date six months in the future. Bertha Smith then resigned as manager because, in her words, "I refused to be responsible for the spiritual lives of those under such circumstance." When the teacher did leave, Smith also found fault with his replacement, characterizing him as a man "who had failed to make good in two other places." When she complained to the South Local Council, the chairman promised he would be transferred, but he never was because, according to Smith, his father was on the Executive Committee (ABCFM 16.1.9, 6/30/37).

Eventually, in 1938, Smith wrote an open letter to all pastors in the MCC and members of the Sangam. She charged that pastoral and other appointments in the MCC were made for "electioneering ends, and not for spiritual ends." She also charged that it was impossible to dismiss permanent church council agents (including Bible women) regardless of conduct, and that it was also difficult to transfer agents. Smith lamented that no one took responsibility for bad agents; some teachers did not keep registers properly or did not get reports in on time, some supervised poorly, but those in charge did nothing, according to Smith. "All abdicate responsibility. . . . Local Council Chairmen, pastors, agents, managers all say 'our hands are tied'" (ABCFM 16.1.9 Open Letter, 1938). Smith stopped attending church for over two years because of her objections to Rev. Edward Paul. Tensions grew so strong that Bertha Smith did not want to leave on her furlough, for fear that the Sangam would not approve her return.

Before devolution, Bertha Smith's status would have been discussed by the AMM, the local missionary body, and ultimately decided by the American Board in Boston. Under the new system Smith was employed at the will of the MCC, under the authority of the local pastor. Smith eventually decided to resign from the MCC, and the Sangam voted in the September 1939 meeting to transfer her to the authority of the LPNI Council and to have her live at Rachanyapuram until her furlough (Madura Mission Sangam 1934-39, September 1939). Smith found useful work at the LPNI, but some of her actions concerned Gertrude Chandler. Chandler felt that Smith had a "complex against Indian men." She reported that Smith "has already angered two of our helpers here and will not do anything with them—so there you are—how long can it continue?" (ABCFM 16.1.9, 11/2/39). Apparently the situation improved after Smith's furlough, for she remained in mission work until 1961. Despite her long tenure, Smith's early problems with the MCC organization and personnel highlight some difficulties with the transfer of power experienced by an American woman.

Devolution and Its Effect on Bible Women

Devolution posed additional problems for Indian women. American missionary women described the difficulties faced by Indian Christian women in church work and evangelization. Writing in 1925, Eva Swift expressed concern about the effect of devolution on the work of Bible women in the villages. While the Bible women were nominally under the direction of the church council and the local Pastorate Committee, Swift charged that Indian pastors exercised the most control in practice. Bible women's pay came from the MCC, but local pastors actually distributed the money. Swift warned that Bible women were "in danger of lapsing into a sort of personal attendant upon the Pastor and his family." Even when pastors had the best of intentions, Swift continued, it was difficult for them to give the needed guidance and support. "I know of Bible women who live entirely alone in a village where there are no other Christians." Swift underscored "the comfort or help or uplift that comes to the woman who works as a member of a group which meets for report, discussion, prayer, and continued Bible study" (ABCFM 9.10, 1:7, 8/4/25). Some AMM women missionaries had overseen such Bible women's groups, but when responsibility for all church work was turned over to the MCC, many Bible women were left without adequate support, according to Swift. Swift sat on the MCC for several years, but her assessment remained negative concerning the progress of women's work:

> I feel that the work for women by women has not only made little advance during these years, but that as to the Bible women's service, it has actually lost ground. . . . I feel that, as regards the women, a false step was taken when the Pastor was made the paymaster, and the women in so many villages were placed, practically, under his authority. (ABCFM 9.10, 1:7, 8/4/25)

Increasing the sphere of authority and decision-making power for pastors and for the local church councils and the Madura Church Council represented progress in devolution. However, Indian Bible women did not participate directly in that devolution. The power exercised by American women missionaries in directing Bible women was not devolved to the Bible women but instead to the Indian pastors and to the church councils. Under devolution, Indian women exchanged leadership and support by foreign (American) women for control and maintenance of traditional cultural assumptions by Indian men.

Gertrude Chandler, writing thirteen years after Swift's pessimistic assessments, still saw problems for Indian women in church work such as Bible women's evangelism. As the AMM turned over decision-making authority and financial responsibility to local councils and ultimately to the MCC, Indian women church workers lost financial support and moral support from American sources. Chandler considered it "almost impossible" for Indian churches to support women church workers on a fair salary. "They need some security, for the demands on them from even male relatives . . . and their families, are terrific." Chandler contrasted the work situation for Indian women with that of American mission women. The Indian women had more difficulty traveling and had not the "background and resources of good health to carry them through long periods of intense nervous strain" (ABCFM 16.1.9, 7/9/38). Chandler cited "two bad health breakdowns" of Indian women leaders in the Arcot Mission as a cautionary incident. There was still an important role to be played by single American women missionaries, Chandler concluded.

> The place and influence and possibilities of service for the unmarried woman in society is not yet well enough established. . . . The unmarried Indian woman in rural areas is up against terrific odds and she needs the actual presence of her sisters from the West for moral support. (ABCFM 16.1.9, 7/9/38)

Chandler's phrase "sisters from the West" highlights the gender solidarity expressed by many American women missionaries toward indigenous women (Singh 2000, 227-30; Hunter 1984, 189-204). They worried that devolution weakened the sisterhood. Bertha K. Smith, as we have seen above, also expressed concern about the effects of devolution on women's work. As early as 1932 Smith was worried about women's work in Aruppukottai coming under the control of the church council. She feared that the MCC would assign other aspects of church work a higher priority in appropriation decisions (ABCFM 16.1.9, 1/20/32).

The challenges faced by women's institutions and by those involved in evangelization work during devolution stemmed from economic problems of the Depression years in the United States and from disagreements between individual missionaries and the new MCC/Sangam power structure. Perhaps some of those challenges can also be linked to the effects of the merger of the women's board with the general Congregational mission board, but a process of professionalization, secularization, and modernization was at work even before the merger that contributed to a decline in American grassroots support for the woman's missionary movement (Hill 1985). In a printed letter to friends in the United States, Gertrude Chandler lamented the loss of women's sponsorship of Bible women:

> When I think of the good village homes built by the Women's Board of olden days and know that some of them are standing vacant and getting beyond repair, I feel sad but am helpless to do anything about it. (ABCFM 16.1.9, 8/8/36)

This nostalgic tone of loss and decline is echoed in another letter of Chandler's, written upon her arrival back at the LPNI after furlough in the United States. She described the buildings as "pathetic" and predicted that the Assembly Hall could fall down in a big rain. "Poor Miss Swift would die on the spot, I think, if she should see these buildings which used to be spotless and such a joy" (ABCFM 16.1.9, 11/2/39). By invoking the name of the founder of the LPNI, Eva May Swift, Chandler was lifting up for herself and for the reader of her letter one of the giants in Woman's Work for Woman in the AMM. Chandler's words implied that the great accomplishments of the earlier generation were under challenge in the new order.

Sangam minutes record an amendment that suggests that others may have shared Chandler's concern for women's work under the new structure. The amendment provided that each local council was to appoint a superintendent for women's work and an Advisory Committee on Women's Work (ACWW) consisting of one delegate from each local council and one from the women's institutions (Capron Hall, the LPNI, the Women's Hospital, and the Christian Women's Association). The committee was also empowered to "co-opt" two additional members. The Sangam would appoint a convenor of the committee from its membership. The advisory committee was charged to promote and review all the women's work under the purview of the Sangam and the MCC. It was to meet twice a year and report recommendations, as appropriate, to the Sangam, the MCC, or to any of their subordinate groups (Madura Mission Sangam 1934-39, January 1934). After four years the committee reported to the Sangam that it had "tried to guard the funds definitely intended for the uplift of women," but still the number of Bible women employed had to be reduced because of financial constraints. The committee tried to end its report on a positive key, noting that the numbers in three of the local councils had been increasing slowly after the reduction (Madura Mission Sangam 1934-39, January 1938). But the fact remained that women's work experienced difficulties during the period of devolution.

Under devolution, representation on the Sangam ensured that Indian women's voices were not entirely silent, and women's institutions like the LPNI, Capron Hall, and the Women's Hospital offered not only educational opportunities for Indian girls and women but also opportunities for leadership positions. But Depression-era financial pressures and a diminution of American women's influence in mission administration in the wake of the union of the Women's Mission Board with the American Board resulted in the constriction of women's work in India. Also, traditional cultural expectations for women in India threatened their work.

In 1934, in her reflection on devolution entitled "Standing behind the Looms," Gertrude Chandler had described the task of American missionaries as one of support as Indian Christians took up the threads of the loom with "new patterns in mind." In 1997, as P. A. Sangma's speech suggests, the pattern of full participation of Indian Christian women in the life of the church had yet to be woven.

4

Susan Beamish Strachan *(1874-1950)*

Mission Entrepreneur, Educator, and Leader

Christina Tellechea Accornero

A simple beginning marked the life of the woman who became the co-founder and co-director of the Latin America Evangelization Campaign (LAEC), later known as the Latin America Mission (LAM), and the leading Protestant seminary in Central America, the Latin American Biblical Seminary. In 1874 Susan Beamish was born in Ireland to English parents. The Beamishes had been Protestants in England for many generations but took advantage of a land grant in the seventeenth century and planted their Protestant family in the heart of Catholic Ireland. Susan and her seven siblings grew up more than two hundred years later in an English ghetto of sorts, despite the two centuries of family residence in the County of Cork. They attended the Anglican school of Christ Church parish.

One of many women who were fully committed to the missionary cause in the early twentieth century, Susan Beamish led a life of piety and devotion and became one of the leading women in evangelical missions. A closer look at her life reveals a woman who grew to be a creative and significant leader. As a person called by God to the mission field in Latin America, she took the initiative to establish, direct, and nurture a small mission organization, care for her family and others, and promote her husband as a traveling evangelist. She was an exemplary steward of the resources of the organization, especially in her care for the people of the LAM. Susan was the manager and administrator of the LAEC, in a position that was very unusual for a woman of her time. Her husband, Harry Strachan, was the recognized, visible leader who traveled extensively and kept out in front the evangelistic priorities of the mission. It was Susan, however, who dreamed big dreams—and then implemented them for the supporting ministries. In response to the needs around her, she established the Latin American Biblical Seminary and opened a hospital and an orphanage. She also edited *The Latin American Evangelist,* or *The Evangelist,* as it came to be known, a magazine that supported Harry's deputation trips to the United States and Canada.

MISSIONARY TRAINING IN LONDON

Susan Beamish spent four years at the missionary training school Harley College in London, where she studied nursing and grew spiritually and as a community leader. She was part of the growing movement of unmarried British women who undertook pioneer missionary work during the 1890s. During her second year at school she met a Canadian-born young man from Aberdeen, Scotland. His name was Harry Strachan. Harry left school for one year due to his father's death but found himself back at Harley and in an Africa prayer group with Susan. Gradually they became acquainted and formed a friendship based on their common interest in moving toward missionary work in the Congo. The unreached of Africa were a central mission focus for the Guinness family, founders of Harley and of several faith missions.

Just before graduation day Harry proposed marriage to Susan and told her of his confirmed call to the Congo. Susan's response was that she was flattered, but she had just received word that she did not qualify to go to the Congo and that the Lord was calling her to Argentina instead. As Susan went through her training for Argentina, Harry struggled with God for understanding. The months passed and Harry was to begin his senior year at Harley. Just a few weeks before Susan was due to sail for Argentina under the Regions Beyond Missionary Union, Harry's inner struggle was at last resolved. To his great shock, he too was blocked by a physical exam and denied entrance to the Congo.

EARLY YEARS IN ARGENTINA

Susan headed for Argentina after a long farewell to her family and Harry. In her first year she was not asked to use much of her nurse's training and found herself teaching children. She soon encountered the realities of life for women on the mission field in Latin America. According to Latin American tradition, women were to be good wives and mothers to large families. Her frustration grew as she thought about the potential for conversions in her area, and she began to question her role and her assignment in the mission. She was putting first and second graders through their English classes—was this a part of missionary orientation? If she were married would her assignment be any different? If her hostess were typical, it would just mean trading teaching for housekeeping, with extra pastoral responsibilities thrown in. Susan could not, however, deny her passion for the missional cause. She did not want to put limits on what God could do through her, but she had to respect the culture. She dreamed of going beyond her expected role as wife and mother, because she saw in Argentina great ministry potential. She said, "We have no excuse. There are open doors, people willing to hear the gospel and this can yield a large harvest" (LAM, Box 58:13).

Harry finally finished his studies in London and arrived in Argentina in 1902. They had six months of getting reacquainted, and then Harry left to study Spanish in Las Hores, a town a few hours away. They spent the Christmas holidays together and began to plan for their marriage. In that same year Susan celebrated her twenty-eighth birthday and was baptized by immersion. She had been sprinkled as an infant, but her observations since her arrival in Argentina had convinced her otherwise. She saw the superstitious and almost magical connotations of infant baptism in the folk religion of her Roman Catholic neighbors and was convinced that somehow the rite of baptism needed to become a more vivid testimony of the new birth in Christ.

The Strachans were married on June 15, 1903, embracing the traditions of Argentina. After the wedding the Strachans visited with friends from the Christian and Missionary Alliance Church in Gualequaychú and then moved into their new home in Buenos Aires. In November 1904, after finishing their language studies, training, and year of apprenticeship, they had a new home and place of service in Tandil. Harry was thirty-two and Susan was thirty years old. Tandil, in the pampas region of Argentina, was to be their home for the next fourteen years. A Protestant witness in Tandil had been initiated by a Plymouth Brethren missionary named Owen in 1883. This emphasis was maintained subsequently by Baptists and independents, until in 1903 the Regions Beyond Missionary Union had assumed responsibility for the work. Now it was up to the Strachans to carry it on.

From a strategic point of view, Tandil was the place where three major activities began and where priorities were set. The first of these projects was the development of an evangelistic campaign strategy for Harry's ministry. Their steps were seen as "traditional," beginning first with the local congregation and concentrating on prayer and Bible study. They were getting reports from back home about the Welsh revival and longed to see similar fruits in their own congregation. As the response grew, they rented a local theater and began prayer meetings.

As they looked at Harry's ministry potential, they saw fourteen other towns that could be reached by train. Harry organized a laymen's League of Evangelism, mobilizing the members of their congregation. All the while Susan supported his evangelistic vision but started to long for children. Her conflict grew within as she thought of other missionaries who put "the work" first and the requirements of many mission boards that the children be sent to boarding schools when they came of age.

Susan was thirty-six when she gave birth to their first son, Robert Kenneth. Beginning a family thus became the second major project launched by the Strachans in Tandil. In little more than a year Kenneth was followed by Harry Wallace and two years later by Grace Eileen. Susan had her hands full, managing the church when her husband was away on evangelistic trips and directing the primary school that operated on the premises.

The tormenting questions returned as Susan tried to choose homemaking as her primary task. "Is it really my first duty to stay at home and dedicate myself to my children? Or should I feel obliged, rather, to give myself first of all in support of my husband's ministry, like Maria Hudson in China, leaving the children to the care of others in a boarding school?" God had called her to Argentina even before she had known she was going to be Harry's wife. Did God have something different in mind for her—some future for which the past was simply preparation? (LAM, Box 59:2).

The third project of the Strachans turned Susan's thinking around and showed her how God intended to use her gifts. As she followed the news from home and around the world about the progress of World War I, Susan learned that women were being mobilized to fill the vacancies in wartime industries and elsewhere. She had unbounded faith in women as she continued to read of the debates over the rights of women throughout the Western world. Her Irish fire and crusading spirit were frequently touched by the struggle being waged for women's suffrage in England and in North America; she was moved to begin discussions of organizing a Christian women's league.

Her concerns about women in Latin America first surfaced in conversations with fellow missionaries. Missionary women—most of them wives—were tolerated rather than welcomed at the annual assemblies and conferences of the faith mission agencies. When any discussion finally came to a vote, most of the wives voted with their husbands. Not wanting to make themselves a determining factor in the decision-making, they also sacrificed being heard as resources of ideas and insights.

In September 1916, during the annual meeting of the Evangelical Union of South America (EUSA), formerly the Regions Beyond Missionary Union, some of the women wanted to organize a formal protest with the EUSA London office. Others felt that such action could be interpreted as spiritual rebellion and preferred simply to raise the issue in one of the plenary sessions. Susan spoke up, "Rather than make it an EUSA issue, why not attack the problem at its roots and in its broader dimensions?" she asked. "We are not the only ones who are having problems about their [sic] role as women. The indifference and discrimination is fairly widespread in the Argentine Church. All Christian women need direction and encouragement." She proposed, therefore, that the women—as many as wanted to—organize themselves, along with sisters from other missions and churches, in a women's league for promoting Christian ministry among Argentine women (LAM, Box 61:5).

Thus, the League of Evangelical Women in Argentina was formed, according to its charter, "to better fit ourselves, by cooperation, for the work to which God has called us in this country and to promote the organization of a National League of Evangelical Argentine Women." It began with Susan and a partner, Zoña Smith of the Disciples of Christ, first as an English-language league on September 15, 1915, and later was succeeded by a Spanish-language league, La Liga. The objectives of the women's league were (1) to promote spiritual life among women; (2) to inculcate evangelical teaching in their homes; (3) to evangelize their neighbors and acquaintances; and (4) to contribute to the improvement of moral and social conditions in their communities (LAM, Box 65:23).

As its first general secretary, Susan became the driving force and imagination behind the formation of La Liga. She served from its inauguration on May 24, 1917, until a year later, when she moved out of Argentina. For the next fifty years La Liga was a significant factor in developing women leaders in Argentina. Through organizing La Liga Susan learned that God had given her remarkable skills and capacities for mobilizing women. It was no longer a question of whether she should devote herself to her family or to her ministry in mission. God expected her to do both. Nor was it a choice between doing her own thing and supporting her husband's ministry. She knew that God would tell her how to balance her priorities. When the Strachans departed Argentina, Susan left behind her a monument to her capacities for organization, mobilization, and witness.

NEW BEGINNINGS IN MINISTRY

For five years after Gracie's birth, Susan was in poor health. After ten years in Argentina the family needed a furlough. It was too risky to try to cross the wartime Atlantic, so the EUSA urged the Strachans to take a few months in the United States and to seek medical help there. It was finally decided that Susan needed surgery and that Harry would go to Canada to deal with the mission board. They were not in agreement with Harry and Susan as to the next steps of the ministry. The Strachans eventually decided to cut loose from the EUSA because the missionary society was disintegrating (Roberts 1993, 32).

As they were waiting for a response from the executive director in London, Harry was asked to speak at two different gatherings. In these meetings at two Presbyterian churches he met some key people who would become friends and supporters of the Strachans' future ministry. Their formal letter of resignation to the EUSA was dispatched to London and accepted in July 1919.

One year later, while waiting in the Bible House in Panama for a steamer to Venezuela, their call was confirmed. After long sessions of prayer, a program for reaching the entire Spanish-speaking continent with the gospel emerged. After traveling the continent for sixteen weeks, they independently came to the conviction that the base of operations would be in San José, Costa Rica.

The new work in Costa Rica became all-consuming for the Strachans. Susan worked long hours to get out the first issue of the "little mission magazine" with which she and Harry hoped to maintain contact with supporters in the homeland. By the end of 1921 the first issue was off the press and on its way to friends, family, and others whom they hoped would subscribe. Susan's major responsibilities at that time included the publication of *The Evangelist,* and later, an evangelistic paper in Spanish called *El Mensajero Biblico* (the biblical messenger).

The first issue of *The Evangelist* described the field, the people, the language, the religion, the missionary situation, the missionary forces and policy, and their difficulties (LAM, Box 41:11). Her editorial duties were undertaken concurrently with the management of a downtown church, the mission, the Bible Institute, a hospital, and a home for children and orphans.

THE BIBLE INSTITUTE OF COSTA RICA

On their trip of continental exploration Susan and Harry had seen a number of Bible institutes struggling to prepare preachers for the small evangelical churches and their evangelistic challenges. One of Harry's goals in his campaigns was to conduct on-the-job training in evangelism in order to prepare young men for the ministry.

But what about the women? In Argentina, Susan had learned that the women were the strength of the church. She was convinced that women needed training, too. In surveying their rented quarters one morning, Susan noted that there was enough space in the backyard to build two or three rooms—adequate for a classroom and dormitory. Once the landlord had given his consent, all she needed was the money to build. And, of course, there was the additional cost of board for the girls (Roberts 1992, 59).

By the time Harry returned from Guatemala and El Salvador, Susan had the plans sketched out. Harry agreed, and the project began. Months later, when Harry left for Colombia, Susan and her co-workers began the task of teaching eight young women from Central America. Thus began the Girls' Institute, the forerunner of the Bible Institute and the Latin American Biblical Seminary.

Harry returned after six months of continuous campaigning to find Susan dreaming of yet another project. The first short term of the Girls' Institute had gone well, and interest among potential students exceeded the capacity of the patio classroom. One evening after supper Susan took Harry on a stroll past a lot and shared her idea. The lot could be used to build their own Bible institute and campaign headquarters. The four recent major campaigns showed the need for more formal training of the young men who were feeling called to full-time service. It would cost at least twenty-five thousand dollars, so they agreed that Harry would take an extended deputation and fund-raising tour through the United States.

In 1922 a separate account was opened for the building fund of the institute with five dollars given by a businesswoman in the United States—she promised five dollars a month to help support a student. The work began under the careful management and prodding of Susan. By February 1924, when Harry returned, the foundations had been laid and the brick walls of the first floor were already up. By July they had raised twenty-five thousand dollars. Their first student graduated in 1927 (*LAM* 1929). A 1929 report written by Susan, who was the director at the time, states:

> The Bible Institute of Costa Rica has the largest student body of any training seminary in Latin America. The thirty-seven men and women enrolled this year come from nine different republics: Bolivia, Peru, Colombia, Panama, Costa Rica, Nicaragua, Honduras, El Salvador, and Guatemala. The teaching and missionary staff count up seven other nationalities, so that it may rightfully claim to be the only International Institution of its kind in Latin America. (*LAM* 1929)

In 1941 the school was renamed the Latin American Biblical Seminary. Publications of the seminary included *Vinculos,* aimed at the seminary's alumni; "ID," produced by the school's Committee of Missionary Activity; *Discipulo,* a short-lived seminary publication; and "ECOS," a one- or two-page newsletter for students consisting largely of announcements (LAM, Box 19:2-3).

By 1966 the seminary had grown to include fifty-nine students representing twenty-three evangelical organizations. The Caribbean Bible Center was developed in Sinceléjo, Colombia, in 1953 to provide additional theological training for lay people and a facility for Christian camping and conferences. The center was founded as a memorial to Robert C. McQuilkin, founder of Columbia Bible College and longtime friend of the Strachans. A Bible education correspondence course was initially based in LAM's Communications Division and transferred to the center in 1967. An extension program was also developed in 1967 (LAM, Box 1:14).

THE ORGANIZATIONAL STRUCTURE
OF THE LATIN AMERICA MISSION

The lines in the early days were fuzzy between the Bible Institute, the LAEC, the missionary staff, and the Strachans. For the most part, Susan was the manager of them all. She was co-director of both the field office and the Bible Institute, but in reality she functioned as the only director. Harry spent up to six months at a time on campaigns and for the most part came home to find things moving quickly under Susan's direction. Susan, according to her son-in-law Dayton Roberts, was basically a woman of action. The institutions she founded, the ministries she managed, the magazines she published—all bore witness to her executive capabilities and to her gift for dreaming dreams and then giving them the feet and hands to make them effective realities (Roberts 1993, 55).

As a missionary leader she also developed skills in personnel and public relations. She used *The Evangelist* to express the needs of the ministry and to gather the prayer partners. For example, the need for a large tabernacle in San José was first put before people in the fall of 1927. By the end of 1928 the building was virtually finished; on May 5, 1929, it was dedicated. That same year Susan and Harry announced a five-point program of advance that included the tabernacle, an evangelistic campaign in Chile, the construction of the Clínica Bíblica Hospital, the evangelistic occupation of Guanacáste Province on the Costa Rican coast, and the construction of a missionary home adjoining the chapel in the city of Herédia (Roberts 1993, 50).

On January 12, 1939, the LAEC changed its name to Latin America Mission, Inc. The mission expanded its work into Colombia in 1937. Key institutions that emerged in Colombia included the Association of Evangelical Churches of the Caribbean, the Evangelical Missions Officers Council, and the Evangelical Confederation of Colombia (which largely replaced the Evangelical Missions Officers Council in 1950). They were dedicated to coordinating efforts and minimizing overlap and competition among evangelical mission agencies (LAM, Box 58:9).

The mission was administratively restructured in 1971 with the formation of CLAME, the Comunidad Latinoamericana de Ministerios Evangelicos (Roberts 1991, 145). CLAME (in English, the Community of Latin American Evangelical Ministries) became the umbrella organization of which various LAM divisions became autonomous members, along with the U.S. branch of the mission. In addition to decentralizing the mission, the major consequence of this restructuring was the redistribution of authority into predominantly Latin American rather than expatriate missionaries' hands (LAM, Box 70:2).

Pretiz and Roberts report that virtually all of the member entities of CLAME passed through some kind of crisis experience during the early years of their autonomy. They think, however, that nearly all of the ministries emerged stronger because of the crisis. The crisis fell into the categories of legal structuring, ideological conflicts, and transfer of properties. Roberts thinks that the formation of CLAME also caused a massive emergence of new, mature, Latin American leadership with a new sense of fiscal responsibility and advances in relations among personnel (Pretiz and Roberts 1997, 28).

STRUCTURAL CHANGES IN BICULTURAL ORGANIZATIONS

The issues of restructuring for LAM, a bicultural organization, were deeply rooted in the styles of operation prevalent in both the United States and Latin America. The board was challenged to consider the implications of stewardship for the people in many different ministries throughout Spanish-speaking countries. Asking questions about different management styles opened up difficult issues of paternalism, hierarchy, colonialism, and corporate control.

Changes began to occur first at the death of Harry Strachan and then later as the leadership responsibilities passed from Susan to their son Kenneth. At its October 1944 meeting, the Board of Trustees of the LAM appointed Kenneth deputy general director. He left for the LAM offices in the United States and, as soon as possible, changed his title to co-director with his mother. They worked out a simple division of labor—Susan continued to edit the magazine and to correspond from the field with donors, and Kenneth assumed responsibility for the home base activities in the United States. Together they served in the Field and Inter-Field Councils (Roberts 1993, 71).

Harry and Susan Strachan had had an understanding with each other and had worked out a co-directing relationship, even if it was not official or evident to the public. Susan deferred to her husband as the evangelist and man in charge of the operation. She was only visible when Harry was on the road. She became known as the director of the Bible school and other ministries over the years, but she always took a back seat when Harry was around.

When Kenneth took over the leadership after Harry's death, the North American board and the leaders in Costa Rica began shifting to an all-male leadership model. As co-director, Kenneth started challenging his mother on issues of leadership. He and his mother had a longstanding disagreement about Latin leadership and reorganization. He coined the term "Latin Americaniza-tion" and initiated a process of moving toward full Latin leadership against his mother's wishes (Elliot 1968, 94). By the time of Susan's death in 1950, Ken had three close colleagues prepared to lead—Dit Fenton, Dayton Roberts, and Dave Howard (ibid., 125).

REFLECTION ON SUSAN STRACHAN'S ROLE IN THE LATIN AMERICA MISSION

As a historical narrative, the story of Susan Strachan, interwoven with that of LAM, provides a fascinating and instructive case study for the role of women in evangelical mission leadership. Susan Beamish Strachan was an intelligent, cre-ative woman who courageously faced the tensions between the people (mission personnel) and product (goals and programs) of mission. She challenged the attitudes, theories, and hierarchies of her day with grace, confidence, and strength. She led her family and LAM as a woman, with a female perspective on how people should be nurtured and equipped. She brought to the mission the nurtur-ing and caring personality of a woman and a mother who knew that the evange-list must be trained, but also transformed from just taking the word to people to a mindset that considered people's physical, emotional, and spiritual needs as well. She determined to set goals, to seek the fullness of her calling, and to walk with other women and men on a journey with God. Her daughter, Gracie, well described her uniquely female, holistic perspective on the mission of the church:

> Mother demonstrated in her life that evangelism requires support and en-hancement. She exemplified the way God's people respond to the needs of the world. Her life also made a statement about her role as a woman. Somehow, there never appeared to be any contradiction between her ex-ecutive and family duties. Whether we, her children, were an integral part of the Mission or the missionaries became, in effect, an important part of her family, was not clear. It was evident, however, that there was plenty of love to go around.
>
> I think Mother's life tells us something: that evangelism never stands alone. Alone, evangelism is vulnerable to distortion or suffocation—it often becomes either an unworthy kind of proselytism, or is easily snuffed out in favor of other priorities. But when evangelism is a part of the total mission of the church, surrounded by compassion and service and train-ing for life, then it is vital and enduring. It is meant to be a part—not the total—of the Christian task. Evangelism is the priority of mission but it cannot, must not, should not stand alone. (LAM, Box 53)

5

Missionary Women and Holiness Revivals in China during the 1920s

Kevin Xiyi Yao

The decade of the 1920s was a turbulent time in China, during which the Protestant missionary movement and Chinese churches underwent tremendous changes. While the missionary forces and churches experienced significant growth, they were severely tested by the waves of anti-imperialist campaigns in Chinese society and the conflicts between the fundamentalist and modernist camps within churches and the missionary enterprise. Another significant development of these years was massive evangelical revivals that shook the missionary community and Chinese churches.

In China the influence of holiness teachings was felt among certain sections of the Protestant missionary forces long before the 1920s. To surrender oneself to God was a powerful missionary motivation for obeying the Great Commission, especially among the China Inland Mission (CIM) missionaries. However, most scholars agree that "the first revival to gain nationwide publicity in China and international repute outside China" was the Manchurian revival of 1908 (Bays 1993, 162). The central figure of this revival was Jonathan Goforth, a Canadian Presbyterian missionary. But it was in the 1920s that waves of revivals swept across the Chinese churches and Protestant missionary community; these revivals helped change the character of Chinese churches forever.

Among the most widely known revivalists in China of the 1920s were several missionary women. By leading nationwide revival events, they gained unprecedented recognition and influence domestically and internationally. Their leadership added new features and flavors to revival movements traditionally dominated by men. This paper focuses on two prominent American missionary women: Grace Woods and Ruth Paxson. Their ministries in China, their holiness message, characteristics of their revivalist activities, and their unique contributions to evangelical revivals and churches in China will be examined. This study aims to demonstrate that a small group of missionary women played the leading roles in revivals in China of the 1920s. Their holiness message and spirituality deeply shaped these revivals, their ministries constituted a unique part of the conservative reaction to the modernist movement, and they exerted important influence on the growing Chinese evangelical churches.

GRACE WOODS AND THE SHANGHAI REVIVAL

The Shanghai Revival of 1925 has not received significant attention from China mission scholars. However, this revival was very important because it was the only massive revival initiated by foreign missionaries in the 1920s. It was also a milestone in the transition from missionary-led revivals to Chinese-led ones.

The leading figure of the Shanghai Revival was Grace Kemp Woods, who spent from 1919 to 1926 in China. Raised in a Baptist family, Grace Kemp was deeply influenced by the holiness tradition and particularly its practical piety for missionary service. In April 1919 she left her home in New Jersey to visit the mission fields in the East—Japan, China, India, and Burma. From 1919 to 1921 she traveled widely in Eastern Asia and visited numerous missionaries, mission organizations, and conferences. In the summer of 1920 she witnessed the founding of the fundamentalist Bible Union of China and got to know Henry Woods, a conservative Southern Presbyterian missionary involved in literary work. Woods, missionary to China from 1883 to 1928, was chief spokesman for the Bible Union at its founding stage. The Bible Union of China was founded by a group of conservative missionaries to fight modernist influences in the mission field. From its founding in 1920, it attracted national and international attention. During the late 1920s and early 1930s, it declined and eventually disbanded.[1]

After a short trip to the U.S. in 1921, Kemp visited India and Ceylon and then returned to China. In 1923 she married Henry Woods in Shanghai.

While helping her husband with his monumental work of compiling a four-volume Chinese Bible Encyclopedia reflecting conservative views, Grace Woods acquainted herself with the situation and needs in the mission field and missionary circle in Shanghai. In a Sunday morning service Charles Rankin, a lawyer and doctrinally conservative missionary, delivered a sermon. According to Grace Woods's own account, his words on the horror of hell and terrible condition of lost souls had a shocking impact on her and intensified her anxiety and concern for lost souls and the need for worldwide revivals.

As a result, on January 1, 1924, Grace Woods organized a prayer meeting for a worldwide revival. Among the attendees were some of the best-known conservative figures of the Protestant missionary community in China: J. W. Lowrie (chairman of the China Council of the Northern Presbyterian Mission), Jennie Hughes (founder of the Bethel Mission in Shanghai, an independent evangelical

---

[1] For a study of the Bible Union of China, see Yao 2000, chap. 3.

mission enterprise for evangelistic, medical, and educational work), D. E. Hoste (director of the CIM), and Ruth Paxson. It was at this prayer meeting that a World-Wide Revival Prayer Movement (WWRPM) was launched. The purpose of the movement was "to further the work of the Holy Spirit in prayer and intercession for revival in the Body of Christ and the salvation of sinners" (Woods 1936, 46). Grace Woods was appointed chairperson of the movement, and an executive committee was formed.

Although the committee soon became defunct, the movement remained a loose network run by Grace Woods herself. By organizing regular prayer meetings and distributing evangelistic literature, the WWRPM expanded its influence among missionaries not only in China but also worldwide. After she moved back to the United States in 1926, Grace Woods continued to run the movement from her home in New Jersey and played a significant role in mobilizing and rallying the evangelical forces in North America.

Grace Woods realized that

some of us might be skeptical about the possibility of a revival of prayer in our day. . . . Even thoughtful Christians are liable to think that in our day, prayer is useless; action and thought alone will help. Take for instance the China situation. In the bedlam of anti-foreign feeling and the advancement of Bolshevism . . . prayer cannot help; so the practical man speaks. (Woods 1927, 71)

Her strong holiness conviction and her experience with the WWRPM reinforced her view of the importance of prayer and practical piety. She once summed up the spirit behind the WWRPM as follows:

Prayer changes everything, and to this means of liberating His blessing for the world need we must give our all—"workers together by prayer." He is looking for Intercessors. O! let us not fail HIM. He waits to be gracious and to "open the windows of heaven and pour us out such a blessing that the WORLD shall not be able to contain it."
World-wide Revival; this is what we need,
World-wide Revival; for this, O God we plead,
Send it, Lord; send it! Before it be too late,
To Save the countless millions, who for The Truth still wait. (Woods 1927, 9)

For Grace Woods, what the missionary movement and native churches needed were not human projects and debates but prayer and divine intervention for a spiritual revival and renewed missionary enthusiasm. This motivation was actually behind Woods's other major initiative, the Shanghai Revival of 1925.

When Grace Woods visited Japan in 1919, she came into contact with the Japan Evangelistic Band (JEB) and its chairman, A. Paget Wilkes. She attended a missionary conference at which Wilkes gave a series of speeches on personal evangelism. Deeply impressed by these speeches, Woods concluded that "this was what the Church needed—a consciousness of the supreme importance of the evangelistic note, individually applied!" (Woods 1936, 51). She was instrumental in having Wilkes's lectures published as *The Dynamic of Service* and distributed them widely among missionaries in different countries through her WWRPM network. In 1924 she extended an invitation to Wilkes to speak to the annual missionary gathering at Kuling, the great summer resort in central China where missionaries spent their vacations.

Paget Wilkes (1871-1934) was theologically shaped by Wesleyan holiness teachings. Arriving in Japan in 1897 from Great Britain, he had joined the JEB, a conservative missionary organization founded by a British missionary, Barclay Buxton, and quickly became its major spokesman and leader. Both Wilkes and Buxton were connected to the Keswick Convention in England and championed the "victorious life" in the mission field. Under the leadership of the two men the JEB became a stronghold of holiness mission and conservative causes against modernist influence. Wilkes, especially, gained a reputation as "the best loved and most hated man in Japan" (Stewart 1957, 69), because he was loved by conservatives and disliked by liberals.

Essential to Wilkes's theological thinking was the "second blessing of the Holy Spirit." He once summarized the JEB teachings:

> We may state it briefly thus: being wholly sanctified is the completion of the work of grace done in the heart at conversion, and is generally a second definite experience. It is received by Faith, and is not by mortification, or by works, or by growth, or by consecration. This second work of grace is twofold: first a cleansing of the heart from indwelling sin, and secondly an incoming of the Holy Ghost making the Lord Jesus all in all to the believer.
>
> Before the Divine Spirit enters in all His fullness . . . we believe that we are "sanctified by His Blood." . . . It is then, and then only, that the Holy Spirit can take complete control and keep us from falling. We further believe that there is no state of grace from which we cannot fall . . . and that there is no such thing as sinless perfection (so called) this side of the grave. But we do believe that the Lord Jesus is made unto us sanctification, living His life in us, and producing the same nature as He has in Himself. (In Stewart 1957, 73-74)

For the most part Wilkes's teachings were in accordance with the classical Wesleyan view of sanctification, which tended to have a more positive view of human nature than did the Keswick spirituality.

Grace Woods echoed Wilkes's missionary theology, even though they held different views on the so-called second blessing. Grace Woods had expressed her concern that Wilkes's theory of entire sanctification "smacked of human 'perfection,' or, as some expressed the experience, 'eradication.'" From her background in the Reformed rather than Wesleyan theological tradition, Woods believed this teaching was "not scriptural" (Woods 1936, 58). Nevertheless, she was deeply impressed by Wilkes and his fellow missionaries' efforts to live out their teachings in Japan. She was convinced that Wilkes had a lot to offer to the missionary community in China and could stimulate a spiritual victory and renewal. As a devout believer in holiness teachings, Grace Woods stressed practical piety and missionary sacrifice over theological differences. She once stated: "God is greater than the difference of opinion held by many good and faithful servants of His, who do not see eye to eye on all the doctrinal constructions placed on certain portions of His Divine Word" (Woods 1936, 58-59). Therefore, in setting up the Shanghai Revival, Grace Woods was determined to invite Wilkes to come to China. Along with Wilkes, J. Russell Howden, a prominent speaker at the Keswick Convention in England and a member of the CIM Home Committee, was also invited.

In her efforts to bring Wilkes and Howden to China, Grace Woods cooperated with the Milton Stewart Evangelistic Committee financed by Milton Stewart and headquartered in Shanghai; the Bethel Mission headed by Jennie Hughes and Mary Stone (1873-1954), who was one of the earliest Chinese women medical doctors and spearheaded numerous medical and evangelistic enterprises; and such prominent conservative missionaries as D. E. Hoste, J. Walter Lowrie, and Ruth Paxson. Despite initially declining the invitation, Wilkes finally agreed to come to Shanghai in June 1925. But the planned missionary gathering could only take place in Shanghai instead of Kuling because of the outbreak of anti-imperialist movements in many major cities in China. The large number of missionaries who already lived in the Shanghai area combined with the intense political situation, which had forced hundreds of missionaries to evacuate from inland China, created a large audience for the upcoming revival meetings.

The revival conference officially started in the Union Church on June 28. Paget Wilkes, J. Russell Howden, and others spoke daily. Their speeches attracted a large crowd, and the church often overflowed. Most of the audience were foreign missionaries, but some Chinese Christians also attended, and the attendance of Chinese Christians grew steadily as the conference proceeded. The organizers of the conference tentatively planned a ten-day event, but the reaction to the conference was so enthusiastic that the conference for missionaries was extended for another two weeks.

After three weeks of the missionary conference, the organizers of the event decided to conduct a conference for the Chinese audience. Leland Wang was invited to be the interpreter for Wilkes and other speakers, and Dora Yu was asked to help run the conference. By late July J. B. Thornton, an American missionary from Japan, had taken over the role of major speaker. After both Wilkes and Thornton returned to Japan, different pastors from local Chinese churches were invited to address the daily meetings. Leland Wang and Dora Yu became increasingly prominent by preaching and presiding at the conference. Prayers, confession, and testimonies occupied almost half of the day. Many Chinese Christians eagerly shared their stories of God's transformation of their lives. Theft, covetousness, and other sins were confessed, and restitution was made. The conference eventually came to an end on September 1.

The essential messages of the revival conference were the conviction of personal sins and call for repentance and total surrender to Christ. They made a significant impact on the conservative missionary community and won a great deal of sympathy and support from them. Thornton was so impressed by the conference that he told Grace Woods: "These meetings are not a conference; a conference is dependent upon a human leader. This is a REVIVAL. I have never in all my experience seen anything like it. . . . A conference is dependent upon a speaker, these meetings are independent of any one!" (Woods 1936, 111). The Kuling branch of the Bible Union of China designated August 25 as a day of fasting and prayer that the revival "may go throughout the land and that the Spirit of God may prevail over the disturbed conditions" (ibid., 91). Similar actions of fasting and prayer for victory were also taken in other summer resorts such as Pei-Tai-Ho, Kikungshan, and Mokanshan.

The Shanghai Revival's impact on Chinese churches cannot be overestimated. Not only were a large number of Chinese Christians attracted to the meetings, but also the revival was instrumental in the founding of the famous Chinese evangelistic group, the Bethel Band. Methodist holiness missionary Jennie Hughes, the founder of the Bethel Mission and the Bethel Band, was inspired by Wilkes's message and his work with the JEB (Woods 1936, 86). Among Wilkes's audience was Andrew Gih, a young evangelist associated with the Bethel Mission and one of the future key members of the Bethel Band. Wilkes had said to his Chinese audience: "China must be evangelised, not by missionaries but by you. How many of you will devote your lives to preaching the Lord Jesus Christ?" (in Stewart 1957, 82). Gih was deeply stirred. "Mr. Wilkes led us to expect great things from God." He continued:

> He showed us from his experience in Japan that the Holy Spirit can enlighten the minds and convict the hearts when the Gospel is heard for the first time. We were given a vision of the need and the possibility of working together with God carrying revival fires all over China, and we have found it blessedly fulfilled. (In Stewart 1957, 82-83)

Gih acknowledged Wilkes's role in inspiring Chinese evangelists like himself and thus contributing to the emerging revival movements led by Chinese Christians. In a sense the Shanghai Revival was a transitional event between missionary-dominated revivals and Chinese Christian–dominated ones.

Grace Woods had always been an ardent champion of holiness piety in the forms of prayer, fasting, and revival. Not so much interested in defending orthodox doctrines, she was more enthusiastic about the teachings of spiritual victory than theological debates, and she cherished the value of missionary unity. Not surprisingly, her first impression of the founding of the theologically conservative Bible Union in 1920 was rather negative. She felt sorry that "a cleavage, deep and wide, was made between the two factions" and believed that "all these differences would disappear under the beneficent influence of a heaven-sent revival!" (Woods 1936, 24, 25). Obviously, she had the hope that a spiritual

revival would re-unite the missionary community on an evangelical basis. However, as the WWRPM and the Shanghai Revival unfolded, it quickly became
clear that the theological orientation of Grace Woods's causes were evangelical
and conservative and were at odds with the liberal and social gospel model of
mission. However, Grace Woods and other holiness teachers held several key
beliefs: the authority of the inspired word, belief in the supernatural power of
divine intervention, and a mission centered on soul-winning. These beliefs were
shared by fundamentalists with a Reformed background. Naturally, the WWRPM
and the Shanghai Revival received the warmest welcome and applause from the
fundamentalist camp. No matter how Woods felt about the fundamentalist movement, her cause was inevitably inclined to the fundamentalist side.

On the other hand, the liberal missionary circles in China watched the Shanghai
Revival with suspicion. Grace Woods pointed to the liberals' negative reaction:
"Shanghai had many 'superior persons' who snickered at the methods used. . . .
Very foolish and absurd, no doubt said the superior persons of that day" (Woods
1936, 95). In the midst of the fundamentalist-modernist controversy of the 1920s,
Woods found that her revival movement sided more and more closely with the
fundamentalist cause. It is not surprising to read Grace Woods's favorite stories
about how some philosophically minded modernists who had dismissed the
concept of a personal God and the supernatural Christ were reconverted by the
Shanghai Revival and reestablished their relationship with their personal savior
(ibid., 98-102). Indeed, the holiness teachings and revivals advocated by Wilkes
and Woods were more piety-oriented, more experiential, and less ideological,
doctrinal, and confrontational than the Calvinistic fundamentalist position. Nevertheless, as modernism posed a growing threat to certain traditional beliefs, the
fundamentalist and holiness teachers often found each other natural allies.

RUTH PAXSON AND HER HOLINESS TEACHINGS

Ruth Paxson was among the most prominent and influential missionary revivalists in the 1920s and 1930s. She arrived in China in 1911. In her early
years as a missionary in the country, she was affiliated with the China Continu-
ation Committee (CCC) and the YWCA. In 1914 the CCC sponsored a series of
evangelistic meetings for Chinese women, and she was among several missionary women speakers and began to emerge as a powerful evangelist. In 1919 she
joined the newly founded Chinese Home Missionary Society, which was designed to evangelize some remote provinces in China. Rejecting the growing
modernist tendencies of the YWCA, Paxson later left the organization and established herself as a popular speaker and organizer of numerous evangelistic
and revival meetings among foreign missionaries as well as Chinese Christians.
She was also invited to speak at the Keswick Convention in England. She
authored several major works, such as *Life on the Highest Plane* (1928), *Rivers
of Living Water* (1930), *Called unto Holiness* (1936), and *The Wealth, Walk,
and Warfare of the Christian* (1939). Most of these works were collections of
her speeches and lectures at various revival and spiritual training events. These

works, in which Paxson systematically laid out her message of revival, enable us to explore her theological thinking and holiness message.

Essential to Ruth Paxson's message was a dualistic view of Christian life. In her opinion there were only two kinds of Christians: carnal Christians and spiritual Christians. A carnal Christian was someone living in sin and under the power of the devil, and a spiritual Christian was someone living in holiness. Throughout her works Paxson always made a sharp contrast between the two kinds of Christian life. She repeatedly said:

> The carnal man is under the power of the law of sin. It operates in his life bringing him much of the time under its dominion. But there is another and higher law at work in the believer and as he yields himself to its mighty power the spiritual man is delivered from the law of sin and death. (Paxson 1928, 1:203)

Corresponding to the conflicting ways of Christian life, there were two kinds of people in the world: natural humans and saved humans; there were two spheres: the kingdom of Satan and the kingdom of God. Paxson insisted on no compromise and no middle ground between the two sides.

According to Paxson, one of the basic tenets of the gospel was "the spiritual nakedness of the natural man and his inability to stand in the presence of God unless clothed in the garment of His Son's righteousness" (Paxson 1928, 1:142). She declared that sin was a "God-ignorant, God-defying and God-displeasing" attitude (ibid., 2:220). For her the essence of sin was evil in one's personal morality or lifestyle rather than corporate evils in society, and the manifestations of sin were strikingly individualistic. In her own words, "worldliness is 'the lust of the flesh,' 'the lust of the eyes,' and 'the pride of life'" (ibid., 2:198-99). Sin can manifest itself as "temper, anger, fretting, worry, murmuring, pride, selfishness, malice, worldliness, unfaithfulness, evil speaking, bitterness, jealousy, envy, quarreling, hatred" (ibid., 2:192).

In contrast to the natural humans and carnal Christians were believers who were completely transformed by God's grace and filled by the Holy Spirit. These spiritual Christians had their sin crucified and cleansed. Thus they totally yielded every aspect of their life to God and led a life in the higher plane and holiness. "Holiness is, then," Paxson declared, "a heart of pure love for God. It is Christ, our Sanctification, enthroned as Life of our Life. It is Christ, the Holy One, in us, living, speaking, walking" (Paxson 1930, 34). She always insisted that sanctification had to be thorough and complete. The thoroughness of sanctification was powerfully illustrated in Paxson's concept of "habitual victory." Through his or her identification with Christ, she believed, the believer was given victory over sin. "He who has given victory over one sin can give victory over all sin; he who has kept from sin for a moment, can with equal ease keep for an hour or a day" (Paxson 1928, 2:201-2). "Real victory makes a change in the innermost recesses of the spirit that transforms the inner disposition and attitude as well as our outward deed and act" (Paxson 1930, 23). Therefore, in Christ the victory over sin is habitual, not intermittent.

The role of the Holy Spirit was essential to holiness teachings, and Paxson's theory shared this trait. As was typical for a Keswick teacher, she insisted that "to be spiritual . . . one must be filled and be kept filled with the Holy Spirit" (Paxson 1928, 3:16). In explaining the manifestation of the in-filling of the spirit, Paxson carefully distinguished herself from Pentecostalism. According to her interpretation, "To reproduce the life of the Lord Jesus in us in a growing perfection is the mission of the Holy Spirit. . . . The Spirit-filled Christian is the one who is most like his Lord" (ibid., 3:17). The supernatural power given to believers enabled them primarily to serve in mission instead of possessing extraordinary ability such as speaking in tongues. In other words, the hallmark of a spirit-filled believer was his or her perfect moral behavior. Paxson's shunning of the pentecostal emphasis on manifestations of the Spirit reflected the growing tension and division between the classical holiness tradition and its growing pentecostal offspring. In fact, Paxson warned against "a spectacular manifestation of so wonderful an experience" (Paxson 1930, 80).

Typical of evangelicals, Paxson stressed the individualistic nature and personal manifestation of sin. She firmly believed that "sin is the cause of every bit of the suffering and sorrow in the world" (Paxson 1928, 3:188). Therefore, all problems in social structures and international relationships were reduced to the mere outcome of individual sin. Paxson's solution to social problems was equally typical of evangelicals. Since sin was the root of all social injustices and evils, victory over sin would naturally and eventually lead to the elimination of these injustices and evils. Each individual's relationship with God had to be readjusted before social relationships could be readjusted (ibid., 3:221).

Paradoxically, Paxson often implied that, in reality, contemporary societies were so corrupt and evil that any efforts at social reformation were hopeless. Behind this pessimistic social view were her dispensationalist convictions. True to dispensationalism, her view of history was anti-humanist and anti-evolutionary. For her, historical change was not a natural process of human endeavor but was subject to divine intervention, and human societies were never in progress but in retrogression. In her view neither the reform of the world nor the conversion of humankind was in God's plan (Paxson 1928, 3:188-89). This conviction actually implied that her advocacy of personal conversion as a precondition for social improvement would not result in any significant social reform.

It was no wonder that Paxson was very critical of the social gospel. In China of the 1920s and 1930s, the popularity of the social gospel was growing. The social gospelers' denial of the total corruption of human nature and reconfirmation of humanity's ability to redeem itself were at odds with Paxson's view of history and society. Paxson's criticism of the social gospel also reflected her generally negative view of modernism. Her firm belief in biblical authority and the supernatural and her preoccupation with personal sanctification made her a natural enemy of liberal theology and the modernist mission approach. She often complained about "the apostasy in the pulpit" and listed "religious decadence" along with "moral deterioration" as "two outstanding marks" of "the last days" (Paxson 1928, 2:215, 3:300). According to her, the rise of modernism was in fact a part of Satan's plot against the coming reign of God, and modernists were no other than Satan's tool (ibid., 2:144).

Not surprisingly, when the founding of the Bible Union of China in 1921 started an unprecedented wave of the fundamentalist offensive against modernism in China, Paxson immediately joined the fundamentalist camp. She was one of the early leading figures of the Bible Union. In her ministry she frequently defended the fundamentalist attack on modernism.

However, Paxson's holiness message was not completely compatible with fundamentalism. Many of the fundamentalists in China were missionaries with Reformed backgrounds. With their strong emphasis on correct ideas, clear-cut confessions, and orthodox doctrines, they tended to be very dogmatic and polemical. In contrast, the holiness tradition stressed the experience of in-filling of the Spirit and victory over sin. A deep inner spirituality and sacrificial piety were major parts of the tradition. Usually spirituality and piety are less controversial and divisive than rigid dogmas.

Despite her support of the fundamentalist cause, Paxson had mixed feelings toward her many fundamentalist comrades, particularly those with Reformed backgrounds. While endorsing their defense of "fundamental truths," she regretted and criticized their extreme dogmatism, intolerant militancy, and lack of deep spiritual experience and consecrated life:

> You and I may be separate and yet not be holy; we may be orthodox and yet not be spiritual; we may be "dead to sin" and yet not be "alive to God." We may have cut ourselves loose from every form of worldliness but in so doing have become critical and self-righteous. We may be loyal defenders of the faith, yea, ready even to lay down our lives for it and in so doing become bitter and unloving. We may be faithful in the fulfilling of every obligation to God and have given ourselves in self-sacrificing devotion to His cause and yet have no warm glow of love in our hearts. (Paxson 1928, 2:132)

Here she not only highlighted the differences between herself and certain fundamentalists, but she also pointed to the kind of help holiness teachings could give the fundamentalist movement in its search for a more solid spiritual foundation or source.

In Paxson's opinion, some fundamentalists' tactics in fighting modernism were simply too negative, acrimonious, and polemical. Within the fundamentalist camp in China she was the major voice for a more positive and constructive approach. At the opening convention of the Bible Union in 1922, Paxson delivered a lengthy speech entitled "Orthodoxy and Spirituality." In it she called for combining a firm stand for orthodox doctrines with a deep spirituality and a loving and constructive attitude. Endorsing the Bible Union's agenda, she warned against "unloving or unholy suspicion," "self-righteousness," and "unnecessary separation," and urged her fellow missionaries to "practise the love we preach and yet protect the church from those who proclaim another gospel" (Paxson 1922, 29, 30, 31, 32).

Ruth Paxson's holiness teachings were largely in accordance with the Keswick tradition. She represented the mainstream of the holiness revival movement in China. Through her extensive evangelistic ministry she exerted tremendous influence on the theological thinking of many Chinese revivalists and evangelical churches. Many leaders of Chinese evangelical churches accepted her views on sin, sanctification, and social reform.

CONCLUSION

In her monumental work on American women in foreign missions, Dana Robert points out that evangelical faith missions and holiness missions gave missionary women opportunities to go beyond the traditional roles of women in educational and medical services, to engage in direct evangelistic activities, and even to take on leadership roles (Robert 1997). The cases of female missionary revivalists in China support her conclusion. During the 1920s, for the first time in Protestant mission history in China, missionary women took initiating and leading roles in massive revival movements and commanded national and international attention equal to any male mission leader of the day. The missionary community immediately recognized this unprecedented phenomenon. A male missionary in China declared that "we men have failed. Now the Lord is showing us what He can do through women" (quoted in Monsen 1986, 111). It was even said that "the revival in China was a women's movement" (ibid., 109). It was not a coincidence that missionary women could dramatically rise to national prominence through evangelical revivals. The spontaneous, individualistic, and interdenominational nature of revivals made it possible to bypass the established mission structures controlled by men. That Woods, Paxson, and other women missionaries all carried out their ministries largely independent of traditional mission societies, and on an interdenominational basis, testifies to this point.

At the core of Woods's and Paxson's revivalist teachings was the emphasis on the sinfulness of human nature and the importance of conviction of sins, and a thorough transformation of one's life by the Holy Spirit, or sanctification and "victorious life." The movement combined the classical Wesleyan with more Reformed Keswick holiness teachings. In addition, most holiness teachers found the pentecostal understanding of the Holy Spirit unacceptable.

Woods's and Paxson's holiness ministries appealed to foreign missionaries as well as Chinese Christians. Their holiness teachings made a deep and long-lasting impression on emerging evangelical Chinese churches. As a result, many prominent Chinese Christians such as Dora Yu, Leland Wang, and Watchman Nee all came under their influence by attending their evangelistic gatherings and reading their works. Woods's and Paxson's major themes such as conviction of

sin, repentance, spiritual rebirth, and an evangelism-centered mission approach
have been accepted and integrated into the theologies and vocabulary of Chinese evangelicals. As missionary women, Paxson and others provided Chinese
Christian women with role models and directly contributed to the rise of a generation of Chinese women evangelists (see Leung 1999).

In the 1920s the holiness revivals belonged to a larger conservative movement in China. Like the fundamentalists, holiness teachers like Woods and Paxson
were appalled by growing modernism in the mission field. They also shared
many theological and missiological beliefs with fundamentalists. Generally
speaking, the holiness revivalists supported and endorsed the fundamentalists'
fight for the "fundamental truths." In return, most fundamentalists held very
favorable views of the evangelical revivals across China.

However, within the conservative camp, Woods, Paxson, and other women
missionaries demonstrated interests, tastes, and ethos different from the fundamentalists from Reformed backgrounds. Instead of investing most of their energies in fighting a doctrinal war, they concentrated on cultivating a conservative
or evangelical spirituality and revitalizing the missionary community and
churches with this spirituality. In other words, while fundamentalists engaged
in polemical battles with their modernist foes, Woods, Paxson, and other holiness teachers pursued a more experiential and practical approach to confrontation with the modernist tide in the mission field.

6

Dora Yu (1873-1931)

Foremost Female Evangelist in Twentieth-Century Chinese Revivalism

Silas H. L. Wu

Dora Yu[1] was hailed as "the foremost" Chinese evangelist during the early decades of the twentieth century. She was the first cross-cultural Chinese missionary in modern times—and a woman—who devoted herself to full-time ministry, "living by faith." She was the first Christian woman who founded a Bible school (known as the Bible Study and Prayer House) dedicated to the training of Chinese woman workers for full-time ministry. Being recognized as a world-class Christian leader, she was the first and only Chinese—again a woman—to be honored as a keynote speaker at the International Missionary Meeting at the 1927 Keswick Convention. She was the only first-generation revivalist through whom major Christian leaders were produced who carried on the revival movement in its second stage. Among the latter, Watchman Nee was her most important fruit; his influence on the Christian Church in China was profound and far-reaching. It was at Dora Yu's 1920 revival meetings held in Fuzhou that Nee's mother, Lin Heping, experienced a powerful spiritual quickening, which in turn led to Nee's own strong conversion and his consecration to full-time ministry, also "living by faith."[2]

Although Dora Yu was a pivotal figure in the history of modern Chinese revivalism, her life story and her spiritual ministry are unknown even among scholars in Chinese church history. Dora Yu's life story in relation to Watchman

---

[1] Rev. Sung Oak, a doctoral candidate at Boston University School of Theology, generously shared his rich Korean sources on Yu Lingtsu (Dora Yu), for which I am indebted to him.

[2] For the 1920 revival meetings conducted by Dora Yu and Lin Heping's conversion, see Lin Heping (1943, 11). For Nee's conversion, see Lin Heping (1943, 20-21); for his personal testimony, see Wei Guangxi (1980, 6).

Nee's 1920 conversion has been circulated widely among evangelical Christians in China. However, regarding her pre-1920 years, there is only the traditional story of her dramatic turnabout in her voyage to England to attend medical school. It was said that when her vessel was passing through the Mediterranean Sea, "there, God met her, calling her to abandon her career and return to China to preach Christ to her people" (Kinnear 1978, 29-30; Lee 1981, 11). About five years ago, this touching story, like a colorful bubble, was pricked as a result of my discovery of Dora Yu's personal testimony under the title *God's Dealings with Dora Yu* (Yu 1916).

In her testimony she avoided mentioning anything about herself and other matters regarding *who, where, when,* and *what*—facts that historians would consider essential to any history. Instead, her testimony stressed "God's dealings" in her life, internally in her spirit and soul, and externally in her environment through God's "instruments." In her testimony she did reveal that she had attended medical school for eight years yet failed to mention the name of the school, its location, or the names of her medical professors. She also spoke vaguely of someone who seemed to have cared for her throughout her lonely years (her parents died two years after she entered medical school). Yet, she only referred to that person as "my friend," without revealing name, gender, or position. She also revealed that in 1897 a missionary friend asked her to go with her to Korea, yet she failed to say *where* in Korea and under *what* foreign mission's auspices. After six years in Korea she returned to China to serve God full-time and established perhaps the first Chinese faith mission, yet she failed to tell us in which city she started her work.

Despite these historiographical dilemmas, the discovery of Dora Yu's 1916 testimony was an important breakthrough in my search for the historical Dora Yu. Even though her testimony provides us with few historical facts, it nevertheless does offer certain clues enabling us to flesh out her shadowy identity. Her testimony, for instance, tells us that her first trip to England was made in 1913, when she was already forty years of age. This invalidates the legend about her abandoning the voyage to England for medical school at a young age.

The story of Dora Yu sheds much light on the pioneering missionary work done by American women doctors, on the origins of western women's medical schools established in China, on the role of female Chinese medical students and their functions in the mission churches, and on the unique role of Bible women in mission churches in China and Korea. Her story also raises an important gender issue in missiology: Why were the major Chinese revivalists before 1927 predominantly women, and why after that date did female Chinese revivalists suddenly recede into the background in the next stage of Christian revivalism in China? After 1927, one observes a marked shift of gender selection in China's revival movement, which was taken over by a new generation of male evangelical revivalists such as Watchman Nee, Wang Mingdao, John Sung, and Leland Wang.

THE EDUCATION OF DORA YU

Dora Yu's original name was Yu Lingzhi, but its romanized spellings vary widely. In the 1896 graduating class roster of the Soochow Hospital Medical School, for example, its spelling was Yui Ling Zse (Ling Tsu is another variation). Her English name, Dora Yu, was known only in missionary circles. She was born in 1873 in Hangzhou at the American Presbyterian Mission (North) compound where her father was studying to be a preacher. Her only sibling was a sister three years older.

Her grandfather was a rich man who lived in the countryside (probably in Zhejiang) and owned hundreds of acres of land, with a large house complex, the wall of which was a mile long. A great fire burned down virtually the entire property, sparing only the house itself. Her grandfather died before the Taiping Rebellion (1850-64). However, her father, who was a physician serving in the imperial army and militia forces, was taken prisoner by the rebels. Her father gained the favor of the Taiping officials because of his medical expertise. Later, still fearing the Taipings, he managed to run away from the camp. He then wandered to Hangzhou after the rebellion was over. It was in Hangzhou that he heard the gospel and became a Christian some time between 1865 and 1870. He must have been influenced by the woman whom he later married, and by her mother, both of whom had been brought to Christ a few years prior to his marriage at the age of forty. Dora Yu testified in 1916, "As I look back now I praise God for the privilege of being brought up in a Christian home" (Yu 1916, 2).

When Dora Yu was two and a half, her father was appointed pastor in a small village, one that consisted of only twenty-four families, in the vicinity of Hangzhou. It was there that she developed a deep love of nature. Two years later her father was transferred back to Hangzhou. There she attended the mission's day school where, she said, she was a slow learner compared to her sister. But in prayer life and in simplicity of faith her experience was far better. "As far as I can remember," she said, "I scarcely ever forgot to pray since I knew how to pray by myself; Christ was a very real Person to me, and I loved Him. My sister had such a fear in the dark, but I used to say to myself, 'If Jesus is here, why should I fear?' And I was never afraid" (Yu 1916, 3).

It is significant that at such a young age, Dora Yu recognized Christ as a "Person"—not a "power" or any abstract entity—and that in her testimony she frequently referred to her intimate dialogue with God, whose will she frequently disobeyed. This point is the key to understanding the many seemingly esoteric, mystical, and riddle-like episodes in her testimony. It is essential for us to see that the Dora Yu story involved the interaction of two parties—Dora Yu and God. The same principle must be applied to our understanding of the Christian revival in China, in which Dora Yu played a pivotal role along with her fellow revivalists. As George M. Marsden has pointed out:

The history of Christianity reveals a perplexing mixture of divine and human factors. As Richard Lovelace has said, this history, when viewed without a proper awareness of the spiritual forces involved, "is as confusing as a football game in which half the players are invisible. (Marsden 1980, 229)

In 1888, when she was fifteen, Dora Yu was sent to an unspecified location by her parents to attend medical school for eight years. The school was attached to the Soochow Hospital. The history of Dora Yu's medical school reveals much about the dedication and sacrifice of the female medical missionaries who were sponsored by the Woman's Board of Foreign Missions of the Methodist Episcopal Church, South (MECS). At first, Dora Yu was one of the three "native nurses" who constituted the medical class within the Soochow Women's Hospital (Mary Black Memorial Hospital). The Soochow Women's Hospital was attached to the Soochow Hospital (the General Hospital), which was established in 1883 by W. R. Lambuth, M.D., and his brother-in-law, W. Hector Park, M.D., in order to preach the gospel through medical services. In 1884 the two American physicians established a rather small-scale Soochow Hospital Medical School [for Men] (*Second Annual Report* 1885, 5, 33), which graduated its first three medical students in 1888. One was Dr. Yang Wei Han, who, during the early years of twentieth century, was Dora Yu's close co-worker in her ministry.

The establishment of the Soochow Women's Medical School in 1888 was closely related to the establishment of the Soochow Women's Hospital. The latter was established to strengthen the function of the General Hospital by reaching out to the upper-class, shut-in Chinese women. Under strong Confucian tradition, upper-class Chinese women secluded themselves in the deep precincts of their living quarters. It was considered a serious breach of social decorum even to allow their faces to be seen by men on the street. Direct contact between the two sexes was taboo in the upper-class society. For this reason it was impossible for these shut-in women to be seen by American male doctors. Therefore, in 1886 the Woman's Board of Foreign Missions of the MECS sent its first woman medical missionary, Dr. Mildred Phillips, to Soochow in order to prepare for the establishment of a hospital for women. The latter was completed on October 25, 1888, and was named Soochow Women's Hospital (Mary Black Memorial Hospital).

At the same time Dr. Phillips organized the three native nurses including Yu Lingzhi, into a medical class (see Campbell 1893, 20; *Woman's Missionary Advocate* 1894, 296). Dora Yu referred to this in her testimony as the "medical school." After Dr. Phillips's marriage in December 1892 (Campbell 1893, 20; Fearn 1939, 28; Cannon 1926, 101), the Women's Hospital was temporarily under the supervision of Mrs. Campbell until Dr. Anne Walter's arrival in late 1893. Earlier in 1893 Anne Walter received her M.D. from the Woman's Medical College of Pennsylvania, where pioneering female medical missionaries were produced (see Robert 1997, 162). Anne Walter sailed to China to be in charge of the Women's Hospital in Soochow in the place of Dr. Margaret Polk, who was one of her warmest friends, and a fellow graduate from Pennsylvania. As soon as she arrived in Soochow, Walter chose Ling Tsu for her personal nurse. She said that Ling Tsu "was with me continuously, accompanying me everywhere until the very day I left Soochow [in early 1896]" (Fearn 1939, 18, 30). Anne Walter married a fellow physician in Soochow, Dr. Fearn, and they moved to another city not far from Soochow and devoted themselves to medical service there for forty years.

It was during Anne Walter's tenure as the head of the Women's Hospital and its Medical School that Dora Yu completed her medical education. According to the *Woman's Missionary Advocate* (October 1896, 108), she was one of two women who graduated on June 20, 1896, from the very first woman's medical college in China.

THE BEGINNING OF DORA YU'S MISSIONARY CAREER

During her medical school years Dora Yu had developed an intimate relationship with Mrs. Josephine P. Campbell (1852-1920). Mrs. Campbell, daughter of Bryant L. Peel, a Texas lawyer, had married Rev. A. M. Campbell of North Carolina in 1878. When she was about thirty, her husband and two young children (one boy and one girl) suddenly died. It was under the influence of two close friends, Laura Haygood and Dora Rankin, both pioneer China missionaries of the MECS, that she decided to go to China to devote her life to missionary work. Mrs. Campbell's misfortune was matched by that of the young medical student Dora Yu. Two years after entering medical school, she lost both her parents. Mrs. Campbell took care of her like her own child. In missionary circles she was considered Dora Yu's unofficial godmother, although Dora never publicly recognized that relationship.

By this time Dora Yu had fallen in love with a certain Chinese gentleman "out of my own choice." They planned to marry in 1892. However, shortly before the wedding she strongly felt the need to break the engagement so that she might serve God with undivided love. It is highly possible that her decision was influenced by such prominent single American woman missionaries as Dora Rankin, from whom she had adopted the English name Dora. She later mentioned how her "missionary friend" (Mrs. Campbell) rendered her spiritual help at this time to guide her through the crisis.

In 1897, a year after Dora Yu's graduation from medical school, the Woman's Board of Foreign Missions of the MECS decided to send Mrs. Campbell to Korea to start the mission's women's work there. This decision came about partly because the Woman's Board was motivated by its increasingly strong desire to match the male-dominated General Board by sending out its own female missionaries and partly in response to the appeal of Prince Yun, a young Korean reformist politician.

While Yun was in political exile in Shanghai, he attended Young J. Allen's Chinese-Western School. There he was converted under the influence of Allen, one of the most prominent American missionaries in China. Later, Prince Yun went to America to study first at Vanderbilt University in Nashville, Tennessee, and then at Emory College in Georgia, both of which were strongholds of Southern Methodism. It was mainly through Prince Yun's enthusiastic appeal to the Southern Methodist leadership that the MECS decided to send its first missionary, C. F. Reid, to Korea in 1896 to test the waters for opening a new mission field. According to *Woman's Missionary Advocate* (November 1896, 142): "On the 9th of August Rev. C. F. Reid, for ten years the faithful, devoted, and beloved pastor of our Central and Trinity Churches in Shanghai, under the appointment of Bishop Hendrix, left with his family to open the new mission of our Church in Korea." At that time Korea was still under the jurisdiction of the Central District of the China Mission. The following year the Woman's Board of Foreign Missions of the MECS decided to dispatch its own women missionaries to Korea. The choice was Mrs. Campbell who, Dora Yu said in her testimony, "asked me to go with her to Korea." She did not mention, however, the name of the city to which they went.

Before her departure to Korea in 1897, Dora Yu had the opportunity to speak to the students at the elite school known as McTyeire School for Girls, a school for China's upper-class girls established by the Southern Methodist Mission in 1892. There she had a touching encounter with a seventeen-year-old girl from Fuzhou named Lin Heping, who was studying English in preparation for going to America to study medicine. Lin was so impressed by Dora Yu's spiritual dedication to Christ that she insisted that Dora accept a gift of a gold ring as an expression of her deep admiration (see Lin's autobiography [Lin 1943, 16-17]). Lin Heping was none other than the future mother of Watchman Nee. Shortly after this, Dora Yu left for Korea, where she became one of the two female pioneers who opened up women's work for the Southern Methodist Mission in Korea from 1897 to 1903.

Dora Yu described her six years in Korea as one of "wandering in the wilderness," comparing her own miserable experience to that of the Israelites in Exodus. During these years of "wandering," she suffered serious health problems and torturing pains in her soul because of her falling under the spell of the "world" (a code word referring to human lusts and pride; see 1 John 2:15-17). At the beginning she was "absorbed in the study of the language," which she found a more difficult task than she had anticipated. Although she was one of the two representatives of the Woman's Board of the MECS, during the first four or five years of her mission work in Korea she was always referred to as Yu Ling-tsu siautsia (Miss Yu Ling-tsu) or Yu Xiaojie (Miss Yu) or Yu Yishi (Dr. Yu). She was not considered a missionary or worker. Rather, she was always listed in the mission record as a Bible woman, financially supported by the Tulip Street Society of Nashville under the supporter's name, Johnetta Dodd.[3] It

---

[3] For her titles, see *Woman's Missionary Advocate* (February 1898, 237); Campbell's letter to the *Advocate*'s editor, Mrs. Butler (January 1899, 207); and *Korean Repository* (October 1897), 4:400.

was only in March 1902 that she was recorded for the first time as one of the two "foreign workers" (Campbell being the other).[4]

In addition to her work as a Bible woman, Dora Yu was burdened with other heavy duties as well. As the only physician of the mission, she alone had to attend to Korean female patients and to be the school physician after the Pai-Hwa School (Carolina Institute) was established. She also took charge of the industrial department of the school, teaching the "slow-learning" Korean girls (those taken from poor families) the art of embroidery. She was also a translator and compiler of textbooks, using what was available in Chinese as a source (Yui 1901, 29). After the school chapel was established, she took the major responsibility of giving sermons on Sunday to female audiences and conducting in-house Bible studies with the school workers (servants, doormen, and so forth). In addition to receiving daily Korean women visitors, she also participated in door-to-door visitation in the neighborhood to spread the gospel. During the last years of Dora Yu's stay in Korea, her workload tripled while her health steadily worsened. In 1903 Dora Yu and another Bible woman at the Cha-kol Chapel of the Pai Hwa Girls' School visited 2,540 women in the district of the capital city where the school was located (Campbell 1903, 41-42). In her 1903 annual report, Campbell said of Dora Yu's labor:

> Miss Yui [Yu], our little missionary from China, has entertained with gospel teaching 925 women and 211 children. She has had one very devoted pupil, who seems very much in earnest, one of our nearest neighbors. (Campbell 1903)

In the same report Campbell also recorded her sorrow regarding Dora Yu's returning to China for good:

> Two incidents have arisen to bring sorrow to our hearts, the first being the necessity of Miss Yui's [Yu's] returning to China on account of ill health. We will sadly miss her in the work, for she had a good command of the language, and her whole desire was and is to serve her Lord. (Campbell 1903, 42)

There was evidence, however, that Dora Yu's departure was not caused solely by her ill health. She also had suffered extreme emotional strain for some time because she was tempted to yield to a persistent suitor's pressure to get married. The latter was a powerful, high-ranking official in the Korean court (see Wu 2000, chaps. 8-9). No wonder that she revealed in her testimony that she relied heavily on bromide (a strong sedative drug) at night for two years and that

---

[4] See *Woman's Missionary Advocate* (August 1902, 60; May 1903, 409). She was once again called a Bible woman shortly before her return to China (December 1903, 215).

sometimes she felt so depressed that Satan even suggested that she end her misery by suicide.

In her testimony Dora Yu revealed that sometime in the summer of 1902 God wanted her to return to China because he had work for her to do. She refused to respond to God's calling because she was unwilling to give up her own "thing," a word she does not define, but which undoubtedly refers to her ambition to maintain her prominent position in the mission. After much suffering under "God's dealings," she was compelled to return to China for good in September 1903.

DORA YU AS HOLINESS EVANGELIST

After Dora Yu returned to China, she settled in a city located somewhere between Soochow and Shanghai, where her sister's family lived. Abandoning her original plan to serve the Lord by teaching English or practicing medicine part-time, she responded to God's call to serve him full-time, "living by faith." She established what might be called the first Chinese faith mission, following in the footsteps of Hudson Taylor as well as those of an increasing number of faith missions from America (see Robert 1997, 192-98). This might have been one of the factors that caused her to foster a close working relationship with the China Inland Mission (CIM) in her ministry. It was also at this juncture that Dora Yu began to read the writings of major Keswick speakers, such as Andrew Murray and G. Campbell Morgan, as well as those of D. L. Moody, leading evangelist/revivalist of his day in America. The messages delivered at Keswick in England and at Moody's Northfield conferences in America shared an emphasis on the "necessity of Spirit-filled lives of holiness." Both places featured a type of "American Wesleyan/Holiness spirituality" that had been "shorn of the troublesome feature of perfection" (Bundy 1993,118). While Keswick influenced Yu's pursuit of a life of holiness, Moody's emphasis on the necessity of "power from on high" influenced Yu's own pursuit of power through experiencing "the baptism of the Holy Spirit" as essential equipment for effective revivalism.

In her preface to *God's Dealings with Dora Yu,* Yu stated, "No one knows the true innermost experiences of our lives, the deep-seated sins and weakness which God's grace alone can overcome." Her lifelong practice of dealing with sins indicates that she, as a Southern Methodist missionary, must have already subscribed to Wesleyan Holiness theology before encountering the Keswick spirituality.

For her, the greatest joy in reading those books was to find others who seemed to have experiences similar to hers in their lives. From 1904 to 1908 Dora Yu became increasingly prominent in leading revival meetings in the Shanghai/ Soochow region. She termed her experience at that time as one of being "beside the still waters"—alluding to Psalm 23.

Her spiritual experience during this period was very much influenced by the ministry of Andrew Murray, whose devotional classic *Abide in Christ* was influencing evangelical Christians worldwide as they sought to deepen their experience of the "indwelling Christ." Dora Yu wrote in her testimony:

"Abide in Me and I in you" [John 15:4] is a wonderful truth! Christ and I are to change places; mine is to "sit with Him in the heavenly places." "Your life is hid with Christ in God." While down below, "it is no longer I that live, but Christ liveth in me." "For me to live is Christ." What a life of freedom, what a life of victory to have Him as our Lord and all in all! (Yu 1916, 30)

From 1907 she stressed how to follow the Spirit and deal with sins through confession and restitution. She also experienced "being refilled with His Spirit" (Yu 1916, 35-36).

By 1908 Dora Yu's ministry had attracted national attention, and she began to accept invitations for revival meetings outside the Shanghai/Soochow area. It was in that same year that the Bible Study and Prayer House was established in Shanghai (see *Chinese Recorder* 1916, 326-27). She conducted Bible readings in three languages: Chinese, English, and Korean. Weekly prayer meetings were held in the house as well.

In 1909 her revival ministry spread to the southern provinces. Unable to speak the southern Chinese dialect, she delivered messages in English with a western missionary translating them into the southern dialect. By then the tight schedule and fast pace of the revival meetings nearly caused a mental breakdown accompanied by physical exhaustion. She was invited by her CIM friends to Yentai (Chefoo) to rest for ten weeks at CIM's newly completed Missionary Home.

In November 1913, shortly before the outbreak of World War I, Dora Yu was invited, under the auspices of the CIM, to visit England. She returned to Shanghai in December 1914 by way of America. She "thanked God" for the many "dear people" who

were giving themselves unreservedly to God's working in fashioning their lives into the image of His dear Son, so that the world may, in its midnight hour, have a glimpse of this beautiful Life, which creates a deeper hunger and longing in those who come in contact with them, to live a higher life. (Yu 1916, 49)

Here we can observe Dora Yu's internal spiritual dynamic through two small windows: "midnight hour" (referring to endtime theology) and the longing for "a higher life." Both of these reflected Keswick influence on her. Many western missionaries in China at that time were helping the new Republic of China in its social and educational reforms. A smaller number of western as well as Chinese missionaries such as Dora Yu, Ruth Paxson, and some of the CIM missionaries promoted spiritual growth and God's kingdom through "intercession and evangelism," following the watchword coined by Paxson: "power through personality by prayer" (*Chinese Recorder* 1914, 671-81).

At the same time Dora Yu felt deeply saddened by "the general Christian atmosphere," in particular by the rising menace of "higher Criticism" advanced by some prominent American "modernist" theologians. By the 1910s Yu had also begun to warn Christians in China of the danger of overly emphasizing spiritual gifts, referring to tongue-speaking and divine healing. Her warning was undoubtedly directed toward the rapid spread of pentecostalism. Her view, however, was balanced. She said: "The gifts of the Holy Spirit are necessary in His service, but may be dangerous if not controlled by the Life and Love of Jesus Christ. Many have shipwrecked their usefulness by laying too much stress on gifts only" (Yu 1916, 47). She strongly stressed the importance of internal growth in life through the subjective experience of Christ's death and resurrection. "There must be pruning in order to bring forth abundant fruitage. So it is absolutely necessary for us to subject ourselves to the power of the Divine Life now in us, to put off 'the old man' and his doings in order to let Christ's life manifest itself through us" (Yu 1916, 45).

After her return to China, Dora Yu was led in 1916 to move her ministry training center, the Bible Study and Prayer House, to the suburban town of Jiangwan, three miles south of Shanghai. She also set up a Bible school with an initial enrollment of twelve women students. The goal of the Bible school was "to help those who are already the Lord's and have some knowledge of His Word, but need a deeper work of the Holy Spirit to lead to a practical living out of the Truth, so as to equip them more fully for the great service of leading others to Christ." Yet, it was "not to take the women out of their Church, but to render such service as shall enable them to become better prepared workers in the missions that have nurtured them." Her 1916 testimony was published as a thankful note to acknowledge "God's dealings with Dora Yu." She urged her readers, "May I ask you . . . to pray that His purpose may be fully wrought through this place and through me, helping to hasten the completion of the Body of Christ, and thus hastening the coming of our Beloved Lord Jesus Christ?" (Yu 1916, 52-53).

Dora Yu's revival ministry continued, but it became increasingly cooperative in nature with leading contemporary revivalists, notably Ruth Paxson of the YWCA, whose Chinese assistant and translator was Christiana Tsai, who would later author the best-selling *Queen of the Dark Chamber.* During the period of the Intellectual Revolution, around 1919, "liberal" Chinese Christian leaders were busy dealing with the challenge of China's new deity, "Mr. Science," and the rising tide of anti-Christian riots. Some attempted to harmonize science and the Bible; Dora Yu's revival ministry went on with little publicity, and yet it yielded important fruits. A new generation of young evangelicals was destined to have a far-reaching impact on the spiritual landscape of the Chinese church in the ensuing decades.

Peace Wang (Wang Peizhen) was a prominent female revivalist of the new generation (for her biography, see Chen 1974). Born in 1899, daughter of a district magistrate, Wang was converted at a revival meeting given by Dr. Mary Stone (Shi Meiyu), M.D., while attending the Mary Vaughan Girls' School in

Hangzhou. However, it was at one of Dora Yu's revival meetings in 1919 that Wang decided to dedicate herself to full-time ministry. Nearly repeating Dora Yu's own experience, Wang decided to dissolve her engagement to a Mr. Xu, a famous engineer from a very wealthy family. With the consent of her fiancé, one of her first cousins was offered to be Mr. Xu's bride in her stead, thus saving her angry parents from an otherwise great embarrassment.

Wang subsequently enrolled in the then-famous Jinling Women's Theological College in Nanking, where she became acquainted with another newly converted young woman named Ruth Li (Li Yuanru). After her graduation from Jinling, Peace Wang maintained a close co-worker's relationship with Dora Yu and was no less powerful in her evangelistic/revivalist ministry. In the spring of 1925, when Wang was invited to Yentai (Chefoo) to conduct an evangelistic meeting, she spoke to an audience numbering over a thousand, including top theologians and missionaries. One short-statured young man, twenty years of age, named Li Changshou (Witness Lee), was converted and immediately "consecrated" himself to God. Later he became Watchman Nee's close co-worker and carried on Nee's worldwide ministry among the local churches.

From 1920 to 1927, amid China's social unrest in general and mounting anti-Christian riots in particular, Dora Yu continued her training ministry at Jiangwan and her twice-a-year summer and winter prophetic conferences. Also during this period, two major revivals broke out: The Fuzhou Revival of 1923 (Wei 1980, 31-32) touched off through the students of Trinity College as a result of Ruth Lee's visit, and the Shanghai Revival of 1925 resulting from the visit of Paget Wilkes. It was through these two revivals that major Chinese male leaders emerged for the next stage of Christian revival in China.

As for Dora Yu herself, the ever-increasing enrollments at the Bible school made it necessary for her to expand the training facilities in Jiangwan. A new Bible school and new chapel were built under her personal supervision, seriously affecting her health. In late 1922 she began to suffer "violent palpitations of the heart," from which she later recovered miraculously.

In 1924 Dora Yu joined Mrs. Henry Woods of the American Presbyterian Mission on a committee of leading mission leaders in her World Wide Revival Prayer Movement. She was the only Chinese member on the committee. In 1925, in the wake of the May Thirtieth Incident, Dora Yu participated in the bold evangelistic campaign under the auspices of Mrs. Woods's committee. This event was known as the Shanghai Revival, which was conducted by the famous British evangelist Paget Wilkes, founder of the Japan Evangelistic Band. Dora Yu wrote:

> In the summer of 1925, when the tide of anti-Christian agitation was at its height, God, through the instrumentality of Mrs. H. Woods, the founder and chairman of the World-Wide Revival Prayer Movement, [wrought] a mighty revival in Shanghai, and . . . I have met many who testify to the mighty power of the Holy Spirit. (Yu 1927, 69-70)

At the Shanghai Revival young evangelists emerged, such as Andrew Gih (Ji Zhiwen), who later became the leading member of the Bethel Evangelistic Band.

In the winter of 1926 the Northern Expeditionary Army under a Nationalist-Communist alliance reached the lower Yangtze region. Dora Yu testified to the horror of war "with experiences that cannot be easily forgotten." Southern soldiers occupied her Bible school and threatened to burn it down because they believed that it was connected with foreigners. In the spring of 1927 Communist elements within the Expeditionary Army looted Nanking and killed foreigners, including Nanking University vice-president J. E. Williams. As she later lamented in her testimony, some Chinese Christian "modernists" collaborated with Communist elements in their acts of violence.

In the summer of the same year Dora Yu was invited a second time to England, where she was honored as a keynote speaker at the Missionary Meeting of the Keswick Convention. Her speech touched upon the central issue of church unity, very much in tune with the convention's watchword, "All One in Christ." When she was introduced as "a representative of China," she corrected the introduction, saying, " I am not here as a representative of China. I am a representative of the Lord Jesus Christ. I belong to a heavenly city." She strongly appealed to the mission leaders to use their influence to stop the "modernists" from coming to China to undermine the pure faith of the Chinese Christians. Rev. W. H. Aldis, home director of the CIM, who was then presiding over the conference, reported in *China's Millions* (September 1927, 142): "The other [address was given] by a Chinese lady, Miss Dora Yu, who held the great crowd spellbound as she poured out her soul in impassioned words." More details on her speech were reported in the July 28, 1927, edition of the British evangelical journal *The Christian* in a special column entitled "Insidious Influences in China":

> After a season of prayer on behalf of the Chinese and Christian missionaries, an address that stirred the great audience was given by Miss Dora Yu of Shanghai. . . . Miss Yu said . . . "There is reason for grief, however, since Modernism has crept in and is making headway." . . . Miss Yu affirmed that the need for the Church in China today is to have Christ Jesus lifted, and to have the Gospel of Christ preached in its purity. Many of the leaders of the Chinese church do not know what it is to be "born again." . . . From this point Miss Yu's address developed into what was a stirring call for consecration. She spoke with great fluency, and her illustrations were homely and forceful. Some did not hesitate to say that hers was one of the most helpful messages of the Convention. (23)

While in London, Dora Yu received the hospitality of the CIM. At the same time she kept close contact with some of the upper-class Chinese then residing in England, including the heirs of the Sincere Company (Xianshi gongsi)—China's Bloomingdales in Shanghai—Mr. and Mrs. Wenhui Ma. She was indeed the woman apostle of the upper-class Chinese both at home and abroad. Her affiliation with upper-class Chinese believers had nothing to do with her preference for the lower social classes; rather, it was simply a reflection of the prevailing mission strategy to break the social barrier that secluded the shut-in, upper-class people, particularly women.

After she returned to China in 1928 her ministry waned as her health steadily worsened. However, a new generation of Chinese Christian leaders took the torch of China's revival movement from the hand of Dora Yu. When she died in 1931, an even greater movement of Christian revivalism had begun in China.

CONCLUSION: REVIVALISM AFTER DORA YU

Dora Yu's story bears great historical significance for the theology of Christian spiritual growth and for woman's role in missions. Her own experiences as depicted in *God's Dealings with Dora Yu* shed much light on both issues.

In terms of spiritual theology, Dora Yu's experiences underwent two distinctive stages. Before her return to China in 1903 her views were ambiguous regarding the twofold ministry of the Holy Spirit as Life and Power, and the relationship of these features to Christian sanctification and evangelistic ministry. After 1903 Dora Yu's spiritual journey entered a new phase in which the influence of Keswick spirituality was clearly discernable regarding major issues such as progressive sanctification, premillennial eschatology, and Christian unity. She was frequently referred to as a "Spirit-filled" woman, but she was clear that the baptism of the Holy Spirit was helpful only for spiritual empowerment. For pursuing a life of holiness, she stressed the importance of constant dealings with sins, not just by confession, but by total reliance on God's grace through intimate union with the indwelling Christ (cf. Walter Sloan's "Introduction" and "Preface" in Yu 1916, esp. p. 30). With respect to pentecostalism, she warned Christians about the great danger of overemphasizing gifts while neglecting the pursuit of the "life and love of Christ."

Keswick spirituality also influenced her fellow revivalists. In the 1910s Paxson recommended a series of articles published in the *Chinese Recorder* promoting Keswick writings by Andrew Murray, R. A. Torrey, and Arthur T. Pierson. She herself became a prominent Keswick speaker and author in the 1920s. Christiana Tsai was first converted at a revival meeting conducted by American evangelist Samuel Dickey Gordon and then became a close co-worker/translator of visiting American Keswick speakers. Dora Yu's intimate connection with the CIM, whose leaders occupied concurrently the Keswick presidency in the early decades of the twentieth century, led to her invitation to speak there.

Dora Yu's story sheds much light on women's roles in missions in the early twentieth century. Her earlier participation in Southern Methodist mission work fell into the category of "woman's work for woman." Whether serving in medicine, education, or evangelism, her work was confined to the realm of women and children. Her status in the Southern Methodist system was simply as a Bible woman. After having returned to China in 1903, Dora Yu severed financial ties with Southern Methodism and began her own full-time ministry, "living by faith."

The 1920s were an era of momentous changes in all aspects of Chinese life. Pertaining to Christian revival in general and Dora Yu's spiritual ministry in particular, two major developments occurred. First, a new generation of dynamic evangelists emerged. Second, a marked shift in gender leadership occurred after the epic year 1927. Thereafter the first generation of female revivalists waned rapidly. In 1931 Dora Yu died, and Christiana Tsai became nearly blind. At the same time major young female evangelists suddenly stopped their public ministries and willingly receded into the background. A generation of male Chinese revivalists supplanted the women who had pioneered the way. Reasons for the shift are not entirely clear, but they were part of a turn toward fundamentalism and against the ministry of women in 1920s evangelicalism.

Having received initial Bible training under Dora Yu, Watchman Nee soon came under the strict discipline of Margaret E. Barber, an independent faith missionary in Fuzhou. Through Barber, Nee was introduced to the writings of John Nelson Darby. Darby's view regarding woman's role was "not to teach" to mixed congregations either in local assemblies or in public meetings. Through submitting articles to the *Lingguangbao* (spiritual light) for publication, and through personal interaction with its editor Ruth Li in Nanking, Nee was able to convince both Ruth Li and Peace Wang to subscribe to his view regarding limitations on women's public ministry. When the Nationalist army began killing missionaries in early 1927, Li and Wang escaped to Shanghai, where they, together with two other women and Nee, began the first local assembly in Shanghai. It was known as The Meeting in the Name of the Lord (Fengzhuming juhui).

The strain of "holiness" in Dora Yu's spirituality was drawn upon and transformed by Watchman Nee soon after Nee's conversion in 1920; the aspect of "evangelism by power" in her revivalistic ministry was carried forward first by Leland Wang in the 1920s and then in the 1930s by a new generation of young revivalist evangelicals. Andrew Gih emerged from the 1925 Shanghai Revival as the leading figure of the latter group. Gih became the head of the Bethel Band, which had been founded by American holiness missionary Jennie Hughes and her Chinese co-worker, Mary Stone. Meanwhile, Dr. John Sung (Song Shanjie) returned to China in 1927 after he had experienced a mighty spiritual renewal in 1926 at the pre-Christmas revival meetings conducted by the fifteen-year-old girl-evangelist Uldine Utley (on Utley, see Blumhofer 1999). In the 1930s Sung became "China's George Whitefield." John Sung and the Bethel Band under the leadership of Andrew Gih pushed Christian revivalism to a new height, begetting numerous new babies "born of God." Thus, the legacy of Dora Yu's spiritual ministry was continued and intensified by a new generation of male Christian leaders in China.

PART TWO

EVANGELIZATION, LIBERATION, AND GLOBALIZATION, 1945-2000

7

Queens in the Kingdom

Southern Baptist Mission Education for Girls, 1953-1970

Lydia Huffman Hoyle

The organ played quietly. Little boys entered the sanctuary carrying crowns nestled on satin pillows. As the music grew louder, a stream of adolescent girls entered one by one, slowly walking down the aisle of the church toward the stage. The last few were dressed in beautiful, floor-length, white dresses. Together the honored occupants on the stage and those who gathered below sang emotion-stirring songs. The songs reminded all those present that they had "a story to tell to the nations" and that they should "rescue the perishing." Ultimately, a woman rescued the crowns from the squirming young boys and placed them on the heads of the girls in white. To the girl in the center, she also gave a scepter. These new young "queens" then stepped forward to speak to the men and women of the congregation, quoting scripture and promising to follow God's call wherever it might lead.[1]

During the 1950s and 1960s, this scene was enacted thousands of times in Southern Baptist churches across the United States and around the world. Once a year, churches would gather to honor the achievements of these girls, who had spent countless hours completing "mission" projects. The crowns and scepters represented scriptures memorized, letters written, missionaries prayed for, and service to others rendered by girls in the Girls' Auxiliary (GA). On a deeper level, however, these regal symbols represented much more. They gave evidence of the

---

Bibliographic note: The primary documents used in this essay consist of the publications produced by the Woman's Missionary Union for use by the participants and leaders of the Girls' Auxiliary. These publications, with the exception of *Tell* magazine, were not included in the card catalogue but were boxed and available upon request at the Southern Baptist Seminary in Louisville, Kentucky.

[1] The above picture is drawn from my own observation of these events and descriptions of "coronation services" found in *World Comrades* and *Tell: A Magazine for Girls.*

underlying conflict in the male-dominated Southern Baptist Convention regarding the role and status of women in the church. They spoke to the way in which women and girls were able to exercise power in churches that ostensibly held high a hierarchical pattern for church and family leadership.

It is ironic that although the door to pastoral leadership was virtually closed to Southern Baptist women throughout the twentieth century (see Blevins 1987, 45), girls could nonetheless dedicate themselves to the mission outreach of the church and by so doing become queens in the Baptist kingdom. For Southern Baptists, being a "mission queen" was no small matter. Mid-twentieth-century Baptists viewed missions as the lifeblood of the church. Following the Great Commission of Matthew 28, Baptists understood that their primary calling was to "go into all the world and make disciples." This passage ranked second in importance only to the conversionary text of John 3:16 in the Baptist Bible. In the coronation ceremonies, girls were being recognized as *primary* players in what Southern Baptists believed to be the *central* task of the church—missions.

How was this possible? What made it acceptable for girls to become mission queens while boys in the church could only carry their crowns? The answer is found (at least in part) in the mission-education program. Southern Baptist churches, like other evangelical churches across America, displayed missionary pictures on bulletin boards, collected mission offerings, honored special seasons of prayer, and reserved Sunday evenings for the ever-popular missionary slide show. Baptists, however, went a step further. In the late nineteenth century, Southern Baptists began to provide weekly missions education for their children. Starting at the age of four, children came together to learn about missionaries and to discover how they too could be "on mission" for Christ. For girls, the Woman's Missionary Union (WMU), an independent auxiliary of the Southern Baptist Convention, directed this lifelong mission education. Through the WMU and the mission organizations it sponsored for Baptist females, girls came to understand that the evangelization of the world rested, in part, on their shoulders. Even though the girls could not preach in their own churches, the Baptist commitment to world evangelization made it undesirable to squelch any mission enthusiasm. Baptists accepted the Great Commission given to the apostles as a personal commission to all Christians, regardless of gender. So the girls prayed for missionaries, read mission books, memorized scripture, and participated in mission service; and their female leaders made certain that the church recognized the girls' work. Thus, in a denomination in which women had few or no public leadership roles, missions education provided a way in which Southern Baptist women could train their daughters to lead the church in the fulfillment of its self-ascribed purpose—reaching the world for Christ.

Ann Braude, in a chapter entitled "Women's History IS American Religious History," argues that "in assessing women's involvement in religion, we should not limit our perception of power to those forms that are publicly recognized within religious institutions" (Braude 1997, 91). A study of the GA indeed requires that we expand our understanding of power. It is easy to argue that men "allowed" girls their coronations and women their separate organizations because it pacified them and kept them from seeking recognized forms of leadership. It is possible, however, that in accepting the idea that power can only be exercised through official avenues, we are perpetuating a false belief that further marginalizes women's contributions to the church. Regardless of the intent of male dignitaries within the church, GA girls and their leaders were able to make their voices heard.

HISTORICAL DEVELOPMENT
OF MISSION EDUCATION FOR GIRLS

Although Southern Baptist women were relatively late in establishing a de-nomination-wide women's organization to support the missionary enterprise, they were quick to include children in their vision for mission training. Congre-gational, Methodist, Presbyterian, and American Baptist women, among others, organized between 1869 and 1871 (see Beaver 1980, 92-101). When the South-ern Baptist Convention organized in 1845, there were more than one hundred female mission societies in the churches in the South. The new convention, however, would neither encourage nor endorse a denominational missionary society for women (see Allen 1987, 17-18). In 1892, four years after the WMU first organized, the new president, Fannie Heck, proclaimed, "Give us children of today for missions and we take the world for Christ tomorrow" (see Massey 1990, 21-28). With that "call to arms," Heck began publishing materials for children's missionary education in the adult publication *Foreign Missionary Journal*. Following the lead of Virginia pastor George Braxton Taylor, who led a children's missionary band in his own church, Heck called the children Sun-beams.[2] These mission bands enlisted girls and boys between the ages of six and twelve. At the age of eighteen, Southern Baptist women were eligible to join the WMU, with many churches offering a Young Woman's Auxiliary for its younger members. For Southern Baptist women and girls, therefore, there was opportu-nity for missionary education from childhood to old age with the exception of the early teenage years. This gap was soon filled. At first, the teenage girls' organization was called the Junior Young Woman's Association and utilized the same materials used by the women. In 1913, however, Fannie Heck estab-lished an independent organization for teenage girls. This group ultimately took the name Girls' Auxiliary. Within a year, there were 245 GA organizations in the United States and several others in countries where Southern Baptist mis-sionaries were active.

The WMU also launched an organization for boys ages nine to seventeen called Royal Ambassadors (RA). This group had a mission emphasis but other-wise was something of an extra-Christianized Boy Scout organization with camp-ing, hobbies, handicrafts, and athletics occupying most of the weekly programs. The RA organization never had the level of involvement enjoyed by the GA but

---

[2] For brief accounts of the history of missions education among Southern Baptists, see Warren and Bevington (1990), Massey (1990), and DeVault (1970).

in 1954 included 124,262 boys in 13,977 chapters (Bishop 1958, 1175). The GAs, RAs, and Sunbeam bands shared a mission publication entitled *World Comrades*.

In the 1920s the WMU revamped its mission education structure and the leadership of the GA established guidelines around which missionary societies were organized for the next forty years. GA came to include girls from the ages of nine to sixteen. The younger girls, aged nine to twelve, were considered Junior GAs. The older girls were Intermediates. A manual established the song, watchword, and ideals of the group. More important, in 1928 the national leadership introduced a program called Forward Steps, an individual achievement plan that challenged GA members to give evidence of their knowledge about and involvement in the mission of the church. Through this plan, girls could receive recognition as "maidens," "ladies in waiting," "princesses," and "queens." Further "steps" were later added to accommodate the more ambitious girls, who could become "queen with a scepter" (1933), "queen regent" (1933), "queen in service" (1963), and queen regent in service" (1963). Eventually, in 1953, the GAs established independence from the other children's missionary organizations with the publication of its own mission magazine entitled *Tell*. This magazine became the foundation for the activities and meetings of the growing organization. By 1954 there were 206,709 girls involved in GA, nearly half of whom subscribed to *Tell* (Wells 1958, 561). By 1969 the membership had grown to 381,806 (DeVault 1970, 8).

In addition to the weekly meetings of GA groups and the independent study of girls working on their Forward Steps, there were also large numbers of girls involved in week-long summer camps. The first camp was held in 1919 in Virginia Beach (Allen 1987, 207). By the late 1950s, GA camps were being held in every state, with thousands attending each summer. By 1955 sixty thousand boys and girls participated in RA and GA camps (see Massey 1990, 26). In addition, many states held annual Queens' Courts that gathered girls who had achieved queen rank for theme-based studies.

The rapid growth of the GA organization came during boom years for Southern Baptists. Church membership grew at a faster rate than the population in the majority of American denominations during the 1950s, with Southern Baptists increasing from 7 million to 9.4 million. As Robert Ellwood noted in his study of the 1950s, "It was an age of affluence—sometimes a spendthrift age—in things of the spirit as well as of this world" (Ellwood 1997, 5). Even during the 1960s, when many Protestant churches were in decline, Southern Baptist church membership grew. In 1967 Southern Baptists became the largest Protestant denomination in America (Noll 1983, 464).

The decades immediately following World War II also witnessed the development of a distinct adolescent subculture. This movement, fed by a myriad of media influences, led to a group consciousness and sense of separate identity for America's youth. The division of GAs into Juniors and Intermediates reflected something of this developing separation, as children twelve and under were separated from the teenagers. The movement of adolescent sentiment, however, was away from adult-supervised groups and toward autonomous peer groups (see Strickland and Ambrose 1985). The GA organization did not conform to this broader cultural development. For a time, it flourished nonetheless.

By the end of the 1960s, however, the Baptists saw the need to make adjustments to a new climate. In 1970 the WMU instituted a radical restructuring of the Children's Missionary Organizations. Until this time the WMU had independently planned and organized its mission education program without reference to other denominational enterprises. In 1970 denominational leaders requested that the WMU coordinate its programs with those of other church organizations. As a result, both the age groupings and group names changed. Girls in seventh through twelfth grades took the name Acteens. The younger girls became Girls in Action. The independent steps to achievement remained but took on a new form. Although girls could still become queens, the ceremonies began to disappear. Little girls no longer grew up dreaming of white dresses and crowns. In 1969 there were 381,806 girls ages nine to sixteen involved in the GA. In 1989, although the number of Southern Baptists had grown and the girls' mission organizations now included girls from age six to age seventeen, the number of girls involved in the program had declined to 336,081. Many girls became active, instead, in the rapidly expanding Youth Ministries movement. By the 1960s most churches had volunteer-led youth programs and many were hiring professional youth ministers (see Garland and Fortosis 1991).

QUEENLY TRAINING

One might anticipate that the GA in a Southern Baptist church in the 1950s might have been something of a baptized charm school—preparing young debutantes to fill the role of stereotypical Southern women. The girls would thus be encouraged to become gracious "Southern ladies," perhaps developing their manipulative charms as "Southern belles," but also their rigid backbones as "steel magnolias." In looking at the literature the girls studied, one can clearly see evidence of this type of socialization. The GA manual as well as the monthly magazine *Tell* especially encouraged the girls to exhibit hospitality and grace. In the 1950s there were very few voices in the culture at large calling women to go beyond traditional female roles and practices. Since the loudest cultural voices were emphasizing that feminine fulfillment lay in domesticity and motherhood, such "feminine" ideals were givens. The training, however, went beyond the superficial and expected at some points—affirming the girls' potential to affect their world. It was perhaps significant that women wrote the publications utilized by the GA—women without male supervisors. Unlike many denominational women's missionary organizations, the Southern Baptist women have withstood efforts by the denomination to bring them under its wing. They remain to the present an auxiliary of the Southern Baptist Convention (see Allen herein). Many of the women had, no doubt, been GA queens themselves. While on some level these women taught the daughters of the church the necessity of conformity, they also invested in them the promise of a purposeful, world-changing life.

Perhaps women put hope in their spiritual daughters because their own lives were forcibly domestic and constrained. Although the pictures of women that looked out from the pages of magazines seemed unreservedly happy, the 1950s were years of retrenchment in terms of professional opportunities for women. The postwar ideal, portrayed repeatedly in widely read women's magazines, was a middle-class home in the suburbs headed by a professional male and maintained by a housewife (Halberstam 1993, 587-92). Southern Baptist women, while perhaps finding meaning in the role of homemaker, seemed also to hope for greater things for their daughters. These aspirations were apparent in the writing of the women who led the GA.

The participants in the GA came to understand that they could have meaningful adult lives, in part, through taking roles of leadership in their homes and churches in the present. GA literature, for example, encouraged the girls—especially those seeking queen regent status—to lead their families in establishing devotions in their homes. Through taking this traditionally male initiative, the girls might hope to convert their own families to Christianity.

The girls could lead their churches by keeping the goal of mission outreach at the front of everyone's mind. This came primarily through the annual coronation services. The services, designed by the girls and their leaders, were intended to provide a "worship experience for those who participated and those who observed" (Jones n.d., 4). The coronations were also powerfully symbolic events. The girls who had attained the ranking of queen or greater processed into the sanctuary wearing long white dresses. The ceremony, often replete with flower girls and crown bearers, notably resembled a wedding service. The pure young "brides," however, somewhat like Catholic novices, pledged their commitment not to man but to Christ and his mission. For their dedication the girls received a crown, a cape, or a scepter. They became Baptist royalty. Those present were given the clear message that all Christians should imitate the steps of commitment to the mission of Christ made by these girls.

GA members also learned that they could make a difference in their communities and world. Their monthly magazine, *Tell*, was filled with regular admonitions to the girls to pray, give money to missions, serve, and evangelize. The Forward Steps likewise guided the girls toward activities and studies that would enable them to influence their world in these ways.

To encourage prayer, *Tell* published a monthly list of missionaries listed by birth date. The GA manual encouraged the girls to "hold fast the ropes of prayer" and listed prayer as the first of the five "star ideals" for girls in the GA (see DeVault 1970, 7). The teenage girls were to serve as "God's altars," just as widows had done in the early church.

The call to financial stewardship likewise found a place among the star ideals. With rather amazing frequency, the GA literature called the girls to give a tithe (one-tenth) of their "income" to the church. Much pressure was brought to bear on this subject. Study guides led the girls to study Malachi and Leviticus and to learn that failing to tithe was "robbing God" (*Tell* [September 1953], 21). Program notes called for an annual tithing emphasis during which a GA tither would give a testimony and the program chairman would give each girl a stewardship pledge card to pray over, complete, and return. Mrs. C. D. Creasman, a *Tell* writer, described tithing as the law of God, noting that it should be obeyed out of love for God and a desire to "share in His work" (*Tell* [March 1954], 16). Another writer shared this chart (*Tell* [July 1958], 35):

A Dollar Spent for:		
Chewing gum	lasts	5 minutes
Hamburgers	lasts	5 hours
Box of Candy	lasts	5 days
Nylon hose	lasts	5 weeks
Cosmetics	lasts	5 months
Necklace	lasts	5 years
Books	lasts	5 generations
Bible or for God's service	lasts	for eternity

The constant tithing reminders made it difficult for non-tithing GAs to enjoy their gum.

GA leaders also encouraged aspiring queens to take active roles of service in their communities. The potential recipients of their service were numerous and included the homebound, hospitalized, aged, needy, imprisoned, and orphaned. Each auxiliary was to appoint a community missions committee to provide opportunities for service to the GA participants. In addition, those girls seeking to reach the higher ranks of queen regent, queen with a scepter, and queen in service were required to participate significantly in service to their church and community.

Ultimately, all such service possessed an evangelistic edge. According to the last of the star ideals, each girl was to "accept the challenge of the Great Commission." The GA manual admonished, "The Master did not say 'Wait until you grow up, have finished your education and are ready to sail, then obey my commission.' He wants girls to go all the time—winning the lost about us" (*Manual* n.d., 10). This evangelistic goal was also evident in the GA hymn. This hymn, set to a nineteenth-century melody, was sung repeatedly at weekly meetings and coronation services. It began in this way:

> We've a story to tell to the nations,
> That shall turn their hearts to the right;
> A story of truth and sweetness,
> A story of peace and light,
> A story of peace and light.
>
> For the darkness shall turn to dawning
> And the dawning to noonday bright,
> And Christ's great kingdom shall come on earth,
> The Kingdom of love and light. (*Manual* n.d., 64)

Even as teenagers the girls could become Great Commission Christians. They could come to see themselves, as the *Girls' Auxiliary Leadership Guide* put it, as "the channel through whom God's love can be made known to the world."

In many ways the call to service found in GA literature differed little from the less formal training of evangelical women a hundred years earlier. These were all acceptable ways for women to work out their religion. Not even the most conservative concerned church-goers in 1960 worried about women praying, giving, serving, or evangelizing (as long as they limited their solicitations to women). It was only when these girls took the stage and called others to follow them in following Christ that they stepped across the formidable gender barrier.

Although GA literature and leadership promised the possibility of a world-changing life to the girls in the present, it strongly encouraged them to consider prayerfully the possibility of an even more fruitful future. No girl could escape the GA program without at least contemplating a career in mission work. Each girl was to consider the possibility that she was among the called. *Tell* published accounts of GA members who had received a call. One girl described her experience in this way:

> I answered God's call last summer at Girl's Auxiliary camp in Alabama. It was my fifth and last year to go as a GA camper. . . . This year, at vesper service, in classes, in the missionary hour it seemed the speaker always posed the question, "Is God calling you?" . . . Especially at camp this year did I have this meditation period with God. At first, I thought my mind was wandering because almost every time I prayed about my vocation our Girls' Auxiliary 50th Anniversary song would come into my mind, especially the part: "He has no way but through my life, that his love they all may see." I think the entire hymn served as a call to me from God. Thursday night after I made my decision public at dedication service I know I must have been the happiest person in the world. A joy and comfort completely enveloped me. (Dulin 1963, 16)

Juliette Mather, a long-time national GA leader and first editor of *Tell*, served as a late-life missionary in Taiwan. She said, "Here, we pray that some of you will be chosen by Christ to become real missionaries. . . . If God calls you, will you be listening?" (Mather 1963, 3-4).

The message was also communicated clearly that to refuse God's call was to lose and to follow his call was to win. This point was driven home in a multi-installment fictional account published in the first five editions of *Tell*. This story told of a young couple engaged to be married, Bill and Eva, who were called to the mission field. A few months before they were to depart, Eva backed out. "'B-b-but Eva,' Bill exclaimed. 'What of your own call to the field? What of your promise to God?'" (Palmer 1953a, 27). Eva, though both talented and called by God, refused to go with Bill. In the installments that followed, Bill headed to Nigeria alone—ultimately meeting there the dedicated young missionary Elizabeth. The final episode closes with Elizabeth sitting at Bill's bedside as he recovers from jungle fever. According to the account, Bill gazed at Elizabeth and "started to speak, then stopped again. Strange how attractive she had become of a sudden" (Palmer 1953b, 8). It seems that Eva, by turning from her calling, lost more than a missionary career. She also lost the dedication and admiration of her ex-fiancé, Bill.

Although the missionary life was held up as the ultimate career path, it was not always portrayed in ways that would make it inviting to teenage girls. In the story of Bill and Eva, Bill ultimately determined that Eva would never make a good missionary even after she wrote him, telling of her renewed desire to come to Africa. Bill noted, "She doesn't know what it is to get her hands dirty, to work until she's bone tired, to live in the heat with mosquitoes and bugs and snakes, to ignore a smell that burns her nostrils, and have a poor sick native child vomit on her. She wouldn't last a month out here." While some stories in *Tell* certainly romanticized the missionary life, others served as reality-based dream-smashers.

In anticipation of the potential chosenness of each girl, GA leaders encouraged their charges to prepare themselves for a life of service. *Tell* regularly allotted space to promoting Baptist colleges, the missionary training school for women in Louisville, and the six Baptist seminaries. "Dream now," wrote one *Tell* editor in the June issue for 1953. "It's never too early for you to be working, dreaming, and living so that you will not miss any road signs ahead. School time planned and spent wisely will make this life adventure one of real happiness for you as you help to bring in God's kingdom" (3). Program materials encouraged all girls to gain an education regardless of their career destination. "Knowledge is power, always and everywhere," wrote a *Tell* author. "The one who knows has the advantage over the one who does not know" (Marshall 1953, 16). GA Leadership especially encouraged Baptist education. The requirements for the highest GA rank, queen regent in service, included writing an essay on either "Why I Plan to Attend a Baptist College" or "Why I Do Not Plan to Attend a Baptist College" (*Tell* [September 1963], 25).

As the GA young women sought to have an impact on their world and as they planned for their future, *Tell* provided numerous role models to guide them. Some role models came from the distant past. For example, the May 1953 issue of *Tell* spoke of the Samaritan woman of John 4, calling her "the very first Christian missionary" (25). More often Lottie Moon (sometimes called the matron saint of Southern Baptists) and Ann Judson took center stage. *Tell* writers emphasized the faith and determination demonstrated by these nineteenth-century missionary women in the face of great difficulties and loneliness (see, for example, *Tell* [May 1958], 42-46).

In addition, each issue of *Tell* included an account of at least one contemporary woman missionary. Married and single missionaries frequented the pages at roughly the same rate. (The numbers of single and married women serving the Southern Baptist Foreign Mission Board at this time were fairly balanced.) Frequently the account was in the first person. The girls heard of missionary doctors, nurses, teachers, social workers, and homemakers. Although there seemed to be no great effort to glamorize missionary life, the missionaries usually told stories about people they had reached with the good news. All the stories were success stories.

Beyond these brief accounts in their magazine, the Forward Steps program required additional missionary reading. Missionary biographies were the standard fare. Each edition of *Tell* promoted several books. For the mission-minded GA, there was no shortage of role models.

"ARISE, SHINE, FOR THY LIGHT HAS COME"

The above quotation from Isaiah 60:1 was the GA watchword. But how did weekly mission education affect the hundreds of thousands of Baptist girls who participated? How did the annual gathering to honor these girls change churches? Although it is not possible to draw irrefutable lines between cause and effect, it is easy to distinguish some likely connections. As churches saw their girls take the stage to tell of their commitment to the mission of the church, they had to be impressed by the role of leadership taken by the girls. While groups for Baptist men and boys floundered, girls led the church toward its appointed goal of reaching the world for Christ. Some churches, then, were willing to recognize that those same girls could be called into the ministry. In 1964 a Southern Baptist church for the first time ordained a woman, Addie Davis. Although this act did not precipitate an avalanche of female ordinations, some churches did follow.

More important, however, girls were changed by their participation in mission education. It is clear that many girls did develop leadership skills through their participation in the GA. When asked during an interview with the author on September 20, 1998, to describe the impact of the GA on her life, Beth Perkins, a Southern Baptist missionary since 1984, noted the responsibility and leadership encouraged in the GA. She also remembered that as a GA member (who achieved the top rank), she learned to present herself before adults. Perkins made a missionary commitment as a third-grader at GA camp.

One state WMU president noted, "The first time I was ever president of anything was when I became president of our Girls' Auxiliary—oh, how important I felt! The training I received then was good preparation for my work now. I learned how to preside and worked hard to be a good president" (Kong 1963, 12). Beyond the president, virtually every GA member had some leadership role in the organization. Each Intermediate GA had four officers and as many as ten chaired committees. Except in the largest GA programs, almost every girl had a position of leadership. Other girls' organizations active during this period similarly sought to promote leadership in their members. The International Order of the Rainbow, a girls' group begun in 1922 and affiliated with Masonic Lodges, claimed effective leadership as one of its primary goals.

Significant numbers of these girls also came to believe the repeated messages brought to them by the GA leaders and literature. The GA taught them that they had a story to tell to the nations. This story was not simply left to male preachers to tell. God could and would use girls to accomplish his plan. Every year, thousands of these girls made missionary commitments. In GA camps, conferences, and coronation services, girls came forward to announce their belief that God was calling them. It is impossible to list exact numbers. Some of the girls' decisions were recorded. Others were not. One former GA member reported, "Like most every GA, I felt drawn toward missions" (see Moon 1963, 15). Because the opportunities for ministry were extremely limited for women, it is probable that most Baptist girls who had *any* sense of calling understood it as a missionary calling. Although perhaps only a small percentage of those who made commitments to missions as GA members actually served as professional missionaries, many women missionaries traced their decision to serve back to their days in the GA. In 1975, for example, 58 of the 131 women commissioned by the Foreign Mission Board discussed the impact of the GA on their lives in their applications for mission appointment. According to the International Mission Board's public papers on missionary candidates dated September 1, 1998, even among a recent group of accepted applicants for mission appointment, women in their mid-forties and older frequently referred back to the significant impact of the GA on their commitment to the mission of the church. *Tell* also recorded the stories of missionaries who remembered the significant impact of the GA in their ultimate career choice. The testimony of Mrs. Robert Miller Holland, an appointee to Japan, is representative. "When I was nine years old," she noted, "I went to a GA camp at Otter Creek, Kentucky. There I felt the Holy Spirit speaking to my heart, and I volunteered for missionary service. In the years that followed, this call was the foremost thing in my thinking. Most of the decisions I made about schools, dating, and so on, were considered with this call in view" (quoted in DeVault 1970, 8). The GA organization taught girls about what it meant to be "called." It surrounded them with a culture in which one might anticipate personal divine direction.

While encouraging missionary service, the GA leadership also worked to instill the belief that the missionary life was primarily defined by attitude and lifestyle, not geography or even job title. *Tell* recorded the stories of women who had made missionary commitments as GAs but had gone on to pursue other professions. For example, the story of Sara Frances Anders was told in the August 1963 issue as part of a series entitled "GA Grown Up" (18-20). As a Junior GA, Anders wrote an article entitled "Why I Want to Be a Missionary to China." As an Intermediate, she began a GA group at an African-American church as part of her Forward Steps. Anders attended the WMU Training School in Louisville, Kentucky, after completing college. Ultimately, however, she left the missionary track and earned a Ph.D. in sociology. At the time of writing, Anders was serving as a professor at Louisiana College. The *Tell* author reported this happily, noting the link between sociology and Anders's GA work in the African-American church. There were many ways, it seems, to fulfill a missionary calling .

In a telephone interview with the author in August 1998, Martha Layne Collins, the former governor of Kentucky, reflected on her experience with the

GA. She remembered feeling called to missions. Although her struggle with learning foreign languages, among other things, helped to keep her from ultimately pursuing a missionary career, Collins's GA commitment stuck with her for life. For Collins, that meant participating in local mission work and serving as a GA leader. Although one might reinterpret a call to missions, the sense of the calling was not easily forgotten.

Even for those who participated in the GA without ever sensing a personal call to missions, the annual coronation service may have served as an important coming of age ritual. Like badge ceremonies in Girl Scouts, the coronation services included girls from a range of ages. Thus, long before they became queens, the girls could anticipate and prepare. Ultimately, as queens, the girls moved from being "maidens" to being women. Like the rites of passage seen in more traditional cultures, the ceremonies placed each girl in a transitory sacred state. In the ceremonies they moved from being hearers of the word to preachers of the word.

Mission education for girls did not break the back of patriarchal leadership in the Southern Baptist denomination. Men did and do continue to lead the great majority of churches. Mission education did, however, provide a separate organization in which girls could develop leadership skills and a sense of purpose and calling. It also provided a back door through which girls could enter and lead their churches. In Southern Baptist "democracies," men were the recognized rule makers and idea transmitters. The WMU, however, established a parallel base of power by building an independent auxiliary in which it could make the rules and transmit ideas. These ideas then came to hold sway over entire congregations as men and women gathered to hear the prophetic voice of young queens who called all believers to the mission of the church.

8

Shifting Sands
for Southern Baptist Women in Missions

Catherine B. Allen

The year 2000 was the bicentennial of Baptist women as an organized force in the progress of missions in the United States. In 1800 a group of Baptist women cooperated with Congregational women to form the Boston Female Society for Missionary Purposes. Under the leadership of Mary Webb of Boston, the group created a network of Baptist women with many affiliates in Southern states. The Southern Baptist Woman's Missionary Union (WMU), organized in 1888, in all its endorsed published histories celebrates Mary Webb as a foremother.[1]

Baptist women and the cause of missions have progressed together on parallel, tightly connected tracks for two centuries. Missions enterprises best grew in financial and human measures when and where women were organized to lobby the cause. The more women did for missions, the more they pushed back the cultural confines placed on their faith. Women had more freedom and opportunity to serve as missionaries and as missions promoters than in any other role in the church.

The linkage of women and missions was especially true in the Southern Baptist Convention (SBC) which became the largest denominational missionary-sending force in the world in the late twentieth century. Not coincidentally, the biggest promoter of Southern Baptist missions was the Woman's Missionary Union, an autonomous auxiliary that allowed its billion-dollar-plus fund-raising efforts to flow directly into denominational coffers (Allen 1987, 482-94). The WMU had reached a membership in the mid-1960s of approximately 1.5 million women, girls, and young boys. It was considered the biggest women's organization in the country.

---

[1] See Allen (1987, 16) for the latest of three major WMU histories that link WMU to Mary Webb through women's societies in the South.

The year 2000 should have been a time of celebration of continued progress for women and missions. Instead, for Southern Baptists it was a year of sharp reversal in the opportunities for women in missions. In June 2000 the SBC's annual session adopted a revised "Baptist Faith and Message." Article VI, "The Church," includes the following statement: "While both men and women are gifted for service in the church, the office of pastor is limited to men as qualified by Scripture." For the first time in history, the SBC formally and officially set a limit on what women could do for the cause of Christ, and did so as a test of faith. By year end most of the statewide and area conventions affiliated with the SBC had echoed some form of endorsement of the "Baptist Faith and Message." In the aftermath of debate concerning the 2000 revision of the doctrinal statement, some proponents of the new version touted it as allowing no place for female leadership in church or denomination. Some others seemed to understand the pastoral restriction to apply only to the senior pastor, not to other church ministerial offices. So in practice there may be some latitude as to what roles are completely off-limits to women.

In a 1998 amendment to the earlier "Baptist Faith and Message," the SBC had ruled that the role of married women was to "graciously submit" to the "servant leadership" of their husbands. An interpretative commentary adopted by the SBC along with the 1998 amendment suggested that the role of women in the church was to follow its view of male headship in the family. Southern Baptist Convention Annuals for 1998 and for 2000 spell out the official statements for legal purposes. This same language and philosophy was carried forward in the 2000 edition of the "Baptist Faith and Message."

In the future, missionaries appointed by the two SBC mission boards will have to affirm their agreement with the new statement of faith concerning women. International Mission Board trustees ruled in 2001 that its appointees must sign an affirmation that reads in part: "I agree to carry out my responsibilities in accordance with and not contrary to the current 'Baptist Faith and Message' as adopted by the Southern Baptist Convention" (Associated Baptist Press report, January 25, 2001). Missionaries employed by most of the Baptist state conventions will also be required to comply. Not only must missionaries personally harmonize their beliefs with the statement, but they must be willing to work in an administrative setup that believes in divine appointment of male leadership over females. The same ideas must be taught and practiced in field witness and ministry. The same will be true of denominational employees other than missionaries, as well. The six Southern Baptist seminaries will teach and mold students along the same lines. Several of the seminary presidents have been quick to go on record as aggressively teaching the newly articulated limitations on women.

While individual Southern Baptist congregations are not usually required to comply with the "Baptist Faith and Message," the document will overrule the way their financial gifts to the denomination are used. It will determine whether a church's members are permitted to serve in elective posts or appointive posts— such as in missionary roles. Now that the SBC has spoken, it remains to be seen what shape the missionary enterprise will take. Many indicators are already obvious. In effect, the two SBC mission boards, the International Mission Board (IMB) and the North American Mission Board (NAMB), had already been sculpting their policies along anti-woman, conservative lines for sixteen years. Many changes, some subtle and some well publicized, had already decreased the involvement of women in missions. Until now, nobody within the SBC has taken an honest count of the cost.

The changes took place within the context of what has often been termed the conservative takeover of the SBC that began in the late 1970s. The women's issue was a thinly disguised thorn in the flesh of conservatives. Once the takeover was clearly completed, with avowed conservatives in a majority of trustee and top management posts, the conservative interpretation of biblical references to women was made church law. This paper traces how the fundamentalist takeover damaged the historic linkage between women and missions in the SBC, especially through attacks on the position of the WMU.

THE 1978 FORWARD STEP FOR WOMEN

The Missions Coordination Subcommittee of the SBC Inter-Agency Council believed that the changing roles of women in American society would and should change the opportunities for women to serve more flexibly and fully within missions. Leaders on this committee, which I chaired, believed that the cause of missions would be advanced if the growing numbers of young women seminarians were encouraged to take posts in missions. Many of the young women were chafing at the customary confinement of women in the church. Some were ordained or seeking ordination, interested in pastoral roles, and vocal in their demands to be accommodated.

The leaders of eleven SBC agencies co-sponsored the first and only Consultation on Women in Church-Related Vocations in September 1978. Eager seminary students, WMU leaders, and missions leaders quickly snapped up the three hundred seats in the consultation. Sarah Frances Anders, professor at Louisiana College, provided documentary evidence that opportunities for women to serve in denominational posts were already in decline. Women involved in missions expressed their frustrations. At the end, seminary presidents and mission board executives affirmed and encouraged women in missions. (Findings of the Consultation on Women in Church-Related Vocations were given limited circulation. Complete files of the consultation may be seen at the Southern Baptist Historical Library, Nashville. Extensive files are in the Hunt Library and Archives of Woman's Missionary Union, SBC, Birmingham.) It should be noted that this, the most public and aggressive Southern Baptist encouragement for women to have complete freedom in ministry and missions, came from the missions establishment. Furthermore, the WMU took the bold step in 1983 of helping to organize the Southern Baptist Women in Ministry. The new organization openly espoused women serving in nontraditional pastoral roles involving ordination, as well as in traditional missions and church staff roles.

116   *Catherine B. Allen*

Although no direct link has been documented between the progressive Consultation on Women in Church-Related Vocations and the subsequent conservative swing of the SBC, surely the two movements influenced each other. In the following year, 1979, an organized conservative effort to stack boards of trustees became evident at the SBC annual meeting.

FUNDAMENTALIST ATTACKS
ON WOMEN'S LEADERSHIP IN THE SBC

At the SBC session of 1984, the widely known evangelical theologian Carl F. H. Henry made a rare appearance at the podium. He brought a resolution from the Resolutions Committee that was adopted "On Ordination and the Role of Women in Ministry." Up to that time, resolutions passed at SBC annual meetings had been taken as a barometer of opinion but were not binding. This resolution was in effect taken as law by the two mission boards. The lengthy resolution stated that women were to be under the authority of men, were to fulfill "different" roles from men in public prayer and prophecy, and were excluded from pastoral leadership "because man was first in creation and the woman was first in the Edenic fall" (SBC Annual 1984). In summary, the resolution concluded, "we encourage the service of women in all aspects of church life and work other than pastoral functions and leadership roles entailing ordination."

The resolution led immediately to restrictions on missionary recognition and funding of women at the Home Mission Board (HMB), predecessor to the NAMB. The HMB was the first SBC board to have a majority of trustees selected by the new conservative controllers of the SBC election process. Up to this point the HMB had given funding for at least one ordained woman serving as a pastor, Debra Griffis-Woodberry, at Broadneck Baptist Church in Annapolis, Maryland. Another ordained woman, Janet Fuller, daughter of Baptist missionaries in the Middle East, had a two-year HMB appointment as campus minister at Yale University and four other campuses in the area. In 1985, New England Southern Baptists requested that Reverend Fuller be given permanent appointment. HMB trustees refused, citing the 1984 resolution. The HMB then studied the issue of ordained women until October 1986, when a policy was set not to participate in financial support of any woman pastor. If a woman candidate for missionary recognition happened to be ordained, that fact would not disqualify her for appointment, provided she would not be serving in a pastoral role (James 1989, 27). The reaction of the Foreign Mission Board (FMB), predecessor to the IMB, was more gradual, but it should be noted that the percentage of women among its appointees bottomed out in the year after the resolution.

The SBC voted to set up an office and staff at the HMB to fight the pro-abortion movement. In 1989 the HMB began its "alternatives for life" ministry. By agreement to support all mission board programs, the WMU was pressured to give the new program a platform, though many privately regretted the attitudes it espoused. Workers in the anti-abortion office let it be known off the record that the new SBC leadership actually went beyond opposing abortion in the usual sense. They also opposed the use of birth-control pills and many forms of contraception. The most responsible HMB leader in the office told me in 1992, "Our philosophy about the use of contraception is not different from the pope's."

FORMATION OF THE MODERATE WING

A moderate wing of the SBC began to form in 1984, the same year as the anti-woman resolution. Moderates met for several years in a forum preceding the SBC meeting. Prominent WMU leaders were among the speakers each year, as were leaders in the Women in Ministry organization.

In 1991 a formal group emerged, the Cooperative Baptist Fellowship (CBF). From the outset the CBF acknowledged that the role of women was one of the nonnegotiable dividing lines between the SBC and the CBF. "An Address to the Public" was released in 1992 by the CBF. The following statement was one of six that characterized the moderate movement:

> A literal interpretation of Paul can build a case for making women submissive to men in the Church. But another body of scripture points toward another place for women . . . "There is no longer male or female." . . . We take Galatians as a clue to the way the Church should be ordered. We interpret the reference to women the same way we interpret the reference to slaves. If we have submissive roles for women, we must also have a place for slaves in the Church. (Shurden 1993, 256-66)

In late 1992, Keith Parks resigned the presidency of the FMB after a standoff of more than a year with the board's new conservative majority. Several senior staff also resigned or retired, including the only woman vice-president. Many of these, including Parks, went to work in staff or volunteer posts with the new CBF. Parks said, "The atmosphere created by the convention controversy causes many fine candidates either to believe they cannot be appointed or to decline appointment because they are not comfortable with the present Foreign Mission Board direction" (Cothen 1993, 346).

Although many WMU leaders were visible in the formative days of the CBF, the WMU did not officially state that it would accommodate programs other than the official SBC missions programs until 1993. The WMU began to offer editorial and distribution assistance of literature by contractual agreement with the CBF.

THE FMB ATTACKS THE WMU

Reaction of the FMB to the WMU's new policy was swift. The chair of the FMB trustees, John Jackson, told a newspaper reporter that the WMU was an adulterer, taking other groups into the bed where the WMU had lain with the

SBC boards. His intemperate remarks made headlines around the country. Although several peace conferences between the WMU and the FMB were staged, both sides waged war in the public press and in communications to more than forty-five hundred foreign missionaries. The FMB returned its chairman to another term of office. During an FMB trustee meeting at which WMU officials were grilled, Mike Goodwin, a trustee, stated that he saw in the WMU "a sense of disdain for the SBC as the majority has now voted to be. . . . If you're in harmony with them [the Cooperative Baptist Fellowship] you can't be in harmony with us" (videotape of FMB Proceedings, 1993 [WMU Archives]).

Public sympathy for the WMU was considerable. A group of Baptists in Texas organized a campaign for people to write the WMU of their support. More than ninety thousand letters from churches and individuals were collected in a mobile office in Texas and then presented in eighteen file boxes at the national WMU convention of 1994.

The FMB was soon caught in a secret unilateral attempt to gain legal rights to the name Lottie Moon without the knowledge of the WMU. Since 1888 the WMU had promoted a Christmas Offering, which had come to bear the name of the missionary in China who had suggested it, Lottie Moon. The WMU considered that it "owned" Lottie Moon's name. A barrage of publicity made the FMB back off, and the WMU trademarked the name in 1995. However, the WMU soon granted a license to the FMB for use of the name. A similar agreement was reached with the HMB concerning the Annie Armstrong Easter Offering for Home Missions name.

While the big names of the SBC missions enterprise bickered, the cause they espoused fell from grace in the eyes of most Southern Baptists. A Baptist Press article by Art Toalston entitled "Survey Shows Baptists Waning on Missions, Fearing Apathy," released on February 19, 1993, reported the results of a poll sponsored in 1992-93 by SBC agencies. It showed that Southern Baptist leaders ranked home and foreign missions at the bottom of a list of ministry concerns. Those polled thought that in the future, churches would find it hard to enlist personnel and funding for missions. The biggest issue facing churches would be apathy. What was important to those polled was local witness and intake of new members. Next highest in interest was ministry to families. Church leaders were not highly interested in reaching groups outside the usual church membership or in organized missions.

SOCIAL WORK DEVALUED

The WMU had introduced and popularized social work as an avenue of Christian ministry. This had been done through its voluntary programs in local church units since 1909 and through the WMU's own school for training women for missions and ministry. When the WMU's Carver School of Missions and Social Work was merged with Southern Baptist Theological Seminary in 1963, endowment funds had been entrusted to the seminary to carry out the purposes of the school. This was done through a professorship of social work held by a woman and through various programs. Then, in 1984, Southern Baptist Theological Seminary instituted the Carver School of Church Social Work, with C. Anne Davis as dean (the only woman dean in an SBC seminary).

Social work had long been a favored missions method of women. (In 1999, 44 percent of SBC home missionaries working in social ministry evangelism in the United States were women.) The Carver School granted its first degrees in 1986 and created a stream of qualified professionals, 60 percent of whom were women and many of whom intended missionary service.

Diana Garland succeeded Anne Davis as dean. When she attempted to fill a staff vacancy in 1995, her candidate, David Sherwood of Gordon College, was rejected in the final round of interviews. In a Baptist Press article dated March 21, 1995, entitled "Southern's Mohler Removes Garland as Dean," the fundamentalist president of Southern Baptist Theological Seminary, Albert Mohler, revealed that he turned Sherwood down because Sherwood approved of women serving as pastors. Mohler stated that since becoming seminary president in 1993, he had consistently refused to accept faculty who favored women in the pastorate. He further stated that he wanted to affirm the principle he read in the New Testament of "male leadership in the congregation" (see Ingersoll 1997).

The resulting turmoil led to the simultaneous dismissal and resignation of Dean Garland and the closing of the Carver School of Church Social Work. Mohler stated that he found social work "not congruent" with theological education. Thus ended the only area of SBC theological studies in which women predominated, thereby revealing the first official act indicating the future for women in ministry and missions. Simultaneously, both the major SBC mission boards were downgrading their emphasis on holistic ministry and social work, thus reducing opportunities usually favored by women missionary candidates. The WMU issued a demand to Southern Baptist Theological Seminary for return of endowments entrusted to it. A negotiated settlement led to a transfer of $928,541 from the seminary to the WMU Foundation in 1999. A gag order kept the settlement secret until reporters Mark Wingfield and Bob Allen spotted the transfer in the WMU's public audited financial reports and reported the matter in an Associated Baptist Press article dated February 29, 2000, entitled "Carver School Endowment Funds Transferred from Seminary to WMU."

REORGANIZATION THREATENS THE WMU

The SBC inflicted severe injury to women in missions in 1995 when it reorganized its agencies. In early planning stages the SBC's reorganization committee allowed WMU officials to meet with them. In my interview with her on February 10, 2000, Dellanna O'Brien, executive director of the WMU, said, "Their only question was whether WMU would become an agency under control of the convention. When we declined, we were left out."

Today the WMU continues to have an independent board of directors selected by the state WMU organizations. If the WMU had come under control of the SBC, its trustees would have been selected by the committee process that allows the convention president to select trustees. In the new scheme of agency work for the SBC, WMU's time-honored duties were allocated to other agencies. The Sunday School Board (now called Lifeway Christian Resources) obtained what it had sought for thirty years—full rights to run an educational program and publications for women in competition with the WMU's once-lucrative business of providing missions education materials to local churches. The new women's program produced by the Sunday School Board would not be dedicated to missions in the traditional way, nor would it espouse women's initiatives in church leadership.

The WMU's work of missions education was assigned to the newly created NAMB, which took over a previous men's missions agency and the HMB. The WMU's triumphant work in raising money for the two mission boards was handed over to their unilateral control. The WMU was officially relieved of the channels of service to missions that it had invented and tended with great success for more than a century.

When the denomination reorganization plan was revealed in 1995, it appeared that an angry convention crowd might defeat it. A last-minute compromise restored the WMU to the organization plan, but only as a footnote that recognized the WMU's existence and historic role. The option of whether to recognize or to involve WMU was left up to the mission boards (SBC Annual 1995). According to my interviews with current WMU leadership (conducted in February 2000), the two mission boards have so far chosen to ignore the WMU on all substantive matters.

Less than three months after the SBC reorganization meeting of 1995, the newly renamed IMB sent a letter to every SBC pastor, jointly addressed to the church WMU director. Jerry Rankin, president of the IMB, stated that the SBC had affirmed the WMU "as a valued partner in missions education and promotion" in response to the WMU's appeal to be "included as a respected auxiliary." He then criticized the WMU board for taking a "position to promote a divisive mission program." Rankin was reacting to the decision by the WMU to start assisting the CBF with its literature. In response, Dellanna O'Brien issued a public statement on August 31, which was reported by Art Toalston of Baptist Press in an article entitled "WMU's O'Brien: Rankin Letter Is 'Inflammatory . . . Divisive.'" "We are furious with the letter sent by Jerry Rankin," O'Brien said. She claimed that the WMU had no intention of slackening any support of the IMB, but that it would also be serving the churches who wished to have missions education materials about the CBF.

The eroded relationship between the largest women's group in the SBC and the IMB was evident in the WMU national executive board meeting of January 13-17, 1996. Rankin warned the WMU leaders against self-glorification. He expressed resentment that he had been inundated with hundreds of letters accusing him of undercutting the WMU. Then he carefully outlined three issues that the WMU must settle to the IMB's satisfaction before a working relationship could be restored. The first was the WMU's connections to the CBF. Rankin wanted WMU leaders to cut all ties. The second issue related to the WMU's sympathy with any method of doing missions beyond what his board controlled. Third, Rankin told WMU's key leaders that they must accept the reality of the SBC. "It's getting a little tiresome to talk about politics, power, and control after sixteen years. No matter what your perspective is, this is the Southern Baptist Convention and this is where it's going. I think WMU needs to face this . . . and get on track and work together and support the leadership of the mission boards and what the SBC is doing. You don't have to, but this is an issue that must be faced."

Among many who responded passionately but negatively to Rankin's speech was Mary Humphries, president of the WMU of Texas and a former foreign missionary. She said, "In sixteen years WMU has not moved. I have stayed loyal [to the SBC] because of missions, but in my heart I cannot support the present leadership of the Southern Baptist Convention."

Rankin responded, "I am one of those leaders." He again urged the WMU to "get on track" with the SBC's present stance, or be diminished. "We will be at grave loss by going different directions," he said (audiotape of WMU Executive Board Meeting, January 13-17, 1996 [WMU Archives]). In my interview with her, Dellanna O'Brien recalled Jerry Rankin telling her more than once, "If you would publicly deny the CBF and embrace the leadership of the SBC, and stop emphasizing women, we could be at peace."

THE ORDINATION TREND

A 1996 survey taken by Sarah Frances Anders revealed that 1,160 SBC women had been ordained for ministry. Of these, 65 were pastors or co-pastors, 92 were associate pastors, 233 were on church staffs, 300 were chaplains, 20 were professors, 21 were denominational workers, 12 were campus ministers, and only 7 were missionaries. Six women who had been ordained had died. The facts indicated that women who felt called to types of ministry usually involving ordination were not serving in missionary capacities.

The NAMB found that in the previous eight years, six ordained women had been appointed as primary workers. It was not clear from records whether they were ordained prior to or following missionary appointment. The IMB discovered that twenty-nine of its women missionaries may have been ordained, some perhaps as early as the 1920s, but any such ordinations were carefully concealed until a few incidences were revealed in the 1980s. The FMB got negative publicity in 1989 when it refused to appoint a married couple, both of whom were ordained, when the Baptist association from which they came objected. Later in the year they did appoint an ordained woman, bringing the total then serving to ten. In 1991 eight ordained women were foreign missionaries, but none was officially serving in a pastoral role. Among CBF missionaries, five are ordained women, or 10 percent of the women. In 1997 Sarah Frances Anders's research indicated that eighty-five Southern Baptist women served churches as pastor. Numbers of ordained women were growing, but their status and their practice in the population at large were not proportionately matched in the ranks of the two SBC mission boards.

THE RESULTS OF THE CONTROVERSY OVER WOMEN

A place to measure the impact of sidelining women in missions support can be seen in the Lottie Moon Christmas Offering for International Mission and the Annie Armstrong Easter Offering for North American Missions, originated and promoted by WMU. In inflation-adjusted figures, the offerings have tended to decline in per capita value during the years of the conservative pressure on women. They have declined since the 1984 ordination resolution in actual over-all buying power. On the surface, the offerings maintain gigantic proportions of support for missions. Each provides more than half its mission board's income, with total receipts nearing $150 million per year. But in a no-growth situation, without the traditional loyalty and lobbying of women, the financial future may grow dim.

Assessing the status of women appointed by the IMB must start with its astounding total of appointees in early 2000: 4,766. Of this figure, only 53.9 percent are females. This stands first of all in contrast to the percentage of fe-males in SBC church membership, which has been poll-projected in the 1990s at 57 percent (a decline from an estimated 66 percent in the 1960s). Prior to World War II, women made up 63.68 percent of SBC foreign missionaries. As the war ended, the number of women missionaries rose to 64.99 percent or almost two-thirds of the missionary force. In those days foreign missions was the primary avenue of service for women who felt a divine calling to ministry. Women were welcomed into missions roles. There was a variety of professional opportunities in schools, social work, and evangelism oriented to women and children.

The high proportion of women in missionary jobs continued until 1960, when it dropped to 57.91 percent. For almost twenty-five years, during the intensive "women's revolution" in American society, the proportion hovered at 54 per-cent. Since then, the statistic has slipped as low as 52.5 percent in 1995 and in February of 2000 stood at 53.9 percent.

One factor contributing to the reduced proportion of women among mission-aries is a decline in the percentage of unmarried women in the missionary force. Whereas unmarried women once stood at approximately 14 percent of the SBC foreign missionaries, the number slipped to 8 percent in 1975 and then to 6.65 percent in 1985. The mission board launched strong recruiting efforts for single women in 1985. By 2000, even with the addition of new categories of short-term appointees in the census, the percentage had reached only 12.5 percent.

Another relatively new factor in the percentages is the growth of numbers of unmarried men in the roster. The bottom line is that the percentage of women in the foreign missions ranks has slipped, indicating that foreign missions is no longer the inviting channel of female ministry that it once was.

Examination of job classifications of single (and married) women being appointed for career status indicates the disappearance of roles that once attracted women. In 1997-99 only one woman could be found in the classifications of pharmacist, volunteer coordinator, women's worker, and public-health worker. Several single women were working in mission offices as secretaries or business managers. Some were in categories of evangelism and church development. Another factor in percentage declines of women relates to the increasing appointments of single males, particularly in short-term classifications. In 1970 only 1 percent of unmarried missionaries were single males. Now the percentage is 4.6.

The IMB actively recruits and nurtures potential missionaries. The board posts its personnel needs on the Internet. On one day in the year 2000, 156 positions were posted. Only one specified that a single woman was preferred. Only 26 percent allowed the possibility of a single male or female. Seventy-three percent allowed for a couple, presumably with the husband being the professional worker and the wife being a "home worker."

The IMB changed its mission strategy in the late 1980s. In 1989-90, under the leadership of Keith Parks, missionaries were told of a shift toward evangelism and church starting. Many missionaries felt pressured to reduce their professional tasks such as teaching, nursing, and social work. Enormous protest resulted among missionaries and supporters. The next wave of IMB administrators, starting with Jerry Rankin's presidency in 1993, implemented the exclusive strategy of "evangelism that results in churches." In the climate of the SBC, not many women have interests, training, or qualifications to do this kind of work, which is customarily the domain of male pastors. The IMB, however, insists that none of its jobs requires an ordained pastor and in fact the IMB wishes to discourage missionaries (male or female) from acting in pastorates.

According to a 1992 study provided by the IMB Library, major categories to which women were then assigned included leadership development and education, 164; church program promotion, 58 (including 19 doing women's ministry); media ministries, 34; health care, 65; human needs ministry, 41; management and support, 83. The number of women with specific job descriptions was 621. The total number of unmarried women was 595. These figures indicate that only about 26 married women had their own professional job description. Of a grand total of 116 possible job descriptions operative at the IMB, 51 had no women under appointment. In addition to a small proportion of unmarried women in the total mission force, married women appeared to lack professional status of their own.

In August of 2000 the role of women at the IMB received external publicity when *Christianity Today* devoted its cover story (Zoba 2000) to the issue of women in missions. Some of the same statistics quoted in this article appeared in that story. Jerry Rankin offered a rebuttal to assertions concerning the IMB in a letter to the editor (Rankin 2000). He refused to reveal any percentage figures but pointed to the growth in raw numbers of women missionaries. He sidestepped substantive issues about job descriptions and theological requirements.

In 1990 the FMB management group appointed a task force of women to train and encourage homemaker missionaries to undertake direct evangelism. One missionary wife wrote a home evangelism workbook that was circulated by the board. No sooner had the promotion of evangelistic accountability among missionary homemakers begun than it was reversed. A policy statement concerning married women was adopted by the staff strategy group in 1990 and reported to the trustees. The statement affirmed the role of missionary wives "in their biblical role of Christian homemakers and in their God-called responsibilities as missionaries. . . . Adequate care and attention for children is of primary spiritual importance. This statement will be given full weight in assisting all missionary parents, especially mothers, in defining the use of their time" (Stanley 1990).

In the 1980s and 1990s the IMB had three women serving at the vice-presidential level. By the year 2000 there was no woman at the executive level. One of the vice-presidents retired normally in 1989. The second, who supervised 1,350 missionaries, resigned in protest of board policy in 1992. The third female executive resigned rather than accept a demotion in 1997; the dispute was rooted in philosophical differences with the mission board. However, this executive had been harassed over the propriety of being a woman in leadership even before her selection as area director supervising more than 450 personnel. Some trustees and some men under her management were openly rebellious.

Historical statistics for home missionary personnel are difficult to assess, and it should be understood that during the last quarter-century "home missionary personnel" are usually jointly employed by the national missions agency along with a regional or state agency. Nevertheless, the NAMB in 2000 rejoiced in the public press that it had exceeded its goal of having five thousand personnel in the field by the year 2000.

All the workers, regardless of their support package and supervision, must pass through NAMB scrutiny. Many appointees today serve only two years, and about 35 percent raise their own support. Only 1,765 are considered primary workers, or full-time missionaries paid a full support. Some of these are two-year appointees. Of the 1,765, only 149 are females, or 8.4 percent of the "real missionaries," according to popular understanding. The 149 female "home missionaries" have twenty-four different job titles. More than twenty are church-planting strategists. Eighty-five work in social ministries. The number includes an evangelism specialist, a literacy worker (recently her position was abolished), and several employed to direct WMU work at the state level.

The male "primary workers" have spouses numbering 1,499. They are counted as missionary personnel and may receive some economic benefits. However, they are usually not funded and may be only marginally involved in missionary effort. Most of them are thought to be employed externally to earn family support. One figure published in 1991 stated that 4.3 percent of home missionaries were single women.

The NAMB is authorized by the SBC to certify credentials of persons who apply for posts as chaplains in the U.S. military or in other institutions. Many chaplains consider themselves to be missionaries. As of February 2000, 2,614 chaplains were under endorsement. Of these, 254, or 9.7 percent, were females. To meet externally mandated chaplaincy standards, all of them must be ordained. This situation is apparently creating resistance among the NAMB trustees, and some leaders privately predict that an attempt will soon be made to limit the endorsement of females for chaplaincy.

CBF policies and procedures abolished most of the limits that would discourage women from seeking missionary appointment. However, as of February 2000, only 51 percent of the missionary force was female. While the SBC mission boards would not reveal the percentages or numbers of females in the inquiry or developmental processes, the CBF, on the other hand, acknowledged that not as many women as men are asking about missionary service. The CBF is still a new mission agency in a formative stage. Given its openness to women's service, however, one would expect a higher percentage of female appointments. Further research is necessary into the bigger picture of Southern Baptist attitudes toward women and missions in order to put the statistics in context.

WMU officials in the national office acknowledge a financial crisis because of a reduction in purchases of literature, the income from which has provided the bulk of the WMU's budget over the years. Membership continues a slow but steady decline. Relationships with the SBC mission boards continue to be rocky, and it is doubtful that WMU's historic reason for existence is valid today. In late 2000 the WMU of Virginia declared that it would no longer promote a Christmas or Easter offering exclusively devoted to the SBC mission boards. Instead, the Virginia women listed their own chosen projects and offered local units and churches the option of funding these in preference to or in addition to the SBC mission boards.

The decision of the Virginia WMU represents a stark departure for an organization that once controlled the expenditure of the offerings it raised but then lost control. It seems that in some branches of the WMU system, the women are attempting to reassert strategic and financial control by breaking with their traditions. Since the new offering plan has not yet been tested, it is impossible to predict the outcome.

SHIFTING SANDS: THE GLOBAL IMPLICATIONS

The IMB, once a strong supporter of the Baptist World Alliance Women's Department, which had been nurtured by the WMU, no longer funds the organization. Likewise, the numerous "WMUs" fostered by missionaries in foreign countries have lost their funding and their appointed missionary sponsors. In many countries such as Nigeria, Brazil, Japan, Kenya, Argentina, Indonesia, and the Philippines, the women are continuing their organizations and feel a kinship with their sister organizations in the United States. Baptist women in the Philippines, though stripped by the IMB of their publishing subsidy and missionary worker, have begun appointing their own missionaries in Asia.

It remains to be seen whether the limitations on women missionaries and on women's advancement in field strategies will change the outreach to women abroad. Traditionally, women have been most responsive to Christian outreach, and females make up two-thirds or more of church membership in most countries. Although no official strategy pronouncement has been made, many IMB leaders and missionaries privately say they want to reverse the proportion and make church membership predominantly male. They believe that churches will grow faster if they are seen as male bastions.

Nevertheless, a look at the world map of most profoundly non-Christian areas reveals that women have extremely circumscribed and limited cultural roles in those countries. In historic Asian mission fields, such as China, India, and Burma, "woman's work for woman" was a hallmark of cultural transformation. As a legacy of women's missions, these countries today have female majorities among Christians and large numbers of women in church leadership, including ordained pastoral work.

If Southern Baptists had spent the last thirty years engaging their vast resources in direct service to the needy and desperate women of the world instead of crushing the aspirations of women in their own home churches, the picture of missions would be vastly different. Unless this denomination and others empower women to do their utmost to obey the commissions of Jesus Christ without limitation, instead of enslaving them to an institutionalized male ego, what will become of the two billion non-Christian women in the world?

9

American Catholic "Woman's Work for Woman" in the Twentieth Century

Angelyn Dries, O.S.F.

TWENTIETH-CENTURY MISSION TRENDS FOR CATHOLIC WOMEN

In 1985 the Sisters of St. Francis from Oldenburg, Indiana, wrote anecdotal reflections on changes that had taken place in their work in Papua New Guinea since their arrival twenty-five years earlier. Naomi Frey's observation of the transformations she witnessed indicates something about the comprehensiveness of the work of American Catholic women's work for women in the twentieth century. Frey compared 1960 and 1985:

> Then, women crawled into Church on their hands and knees because it was a Huli custom for the woman to be lower than the man. Now: They each walk in their respective doors and sit on their own sides. Then, women cut off a joint of their finger to prove their sorrow for the loss of a child. Now, they know it is sufficient to cry and wail to show their grief. Then, no adult was literate. Now we see men and women using Huli books in church for morning and night prayers. Then, girls were not permitted to attend school. Now, the children of the first educated boys and girls are in our high school. Some of the women are on the school boards. Then, men and women watched the Mass. Now we have Eucharistic ministers, prayer leaders, song leaders, ministers to the sick, and Church committee men and women. Then, women were seen only in their gardens and at Church. Now, there are women's clubs, and on several occasions, women have led peaceful demonstrations, and taken part in ecumenical services. (Frey 1985)

Frey's observations encompassed social, economic, gender, and religious factors. Indeed, one way to view the entire twentieth century of American Catholic women in mission is to identify some of the larger trends she suggested. First, there were geographical patterns, or areas of the world, where the American Catholic church placed emphasis. Between 1900 and 1920, sisters, while continuing the prodigious works they began among English- and German-speaking communities, and, to a lesser extent, among Hispanic and African-American populations, ministered to immigrants from eastern Europe, Italy, and Sicily. In the late 1920s and 1930s the National Council of Catholic Women began reaching out to Latin American women to convince them that the possibility of democratic republics in the southern hemisphere did not preclude a healthy life for Catholicism, given the experience of U.S. Catholics. Between 1920 and 1950, American Catholic missions highlighted China. For about twenty-seven women's congregations, China was the first context in which an American province or congregation began work abroad. Pope Pius XII's encyclical *Fidei Donum* (1957) prompted an interest in mission to African countries in the late 1950s. Beginning in the early 1960s, a focus on Central and South America was again renewed, this time through the Papal Volunteers for Latin America, lay mission institutes, religious congregations, and more recently, parish and diocesan "twinning." An important sociological study of the change of attitudes and relationship toward ministry in post–Vatican II sisters is Neal 1984. Personal narratives told by key sisters during the 1960s, 1970s, and 1980s are found in Ware 1985. Joseph J. Shields presented a sociological study organized around sisters' appropriation of five theoretical models of mission in the mid-1970s: mission as evangelization, liberation, mutual assistance of local churches, church, and fulfillment (Shields n.d.).

Since the 1980s individuals or groups have tended to provide short-term mission experience in a variety of geographic settings, mainly in Caribbean countries and Mexico. China has gained renewed prominence, especially through the work of the U.S. Catholic China Bureau, whose director for the last eleven years has been Maryknoll Sister Janet Carroll. Another trend in the last thirty years has been that more institutes of women religious are sending sisters abroad. In 1970, 188 women's congregations were sending many members abroad. In 1996, 262 institutes of women were doing so, but sending just one or two from each institute.

Still another way to view the trends of American Catholic women's mission in the twentieth century is to note how missionary women moved beyond the institutional church into social ministries. Many American Catholics thought of themselves as an immigrant church for the first part of the century. But the solidification of the works of mercy and education begun in the nineteenth century gave a substantial and respectable visibility to Catholics in America, serving those beyond the Catholic community as well. The names of well-known women religious leaders of the nineteenth century bespeak the growth of the social mission of sisters: Elizabeth Seton (1794-1821) in education; Alphonsa [Rose Hawthorne] Lathrop (1851-1926), establishing homes for the sick poor and cancer patients; Henriette Delille (c. 1812-62), foundress of the African American Holy Family Sisters in New Orleans, educating and evangelizing slaves. The work of pioneers in frontier education Ursuline sister Amadeus [Sara Theresa] Dunne (1846-1919) and the Sisters of Loretto in the Southwest and Denver preceded the annexation of vast amounts of territory added to the United States in the nineteenth century. Katharine Drexel (1858-1955) almost single-handedly financed the U.S. Catholic evangelization of Native Americans through her contributions to particular missions, through her support of the Bureau of Catholic Indian Missions, and through the Sisters of the Blessed Sacrament for Indians and Colored People, a congregation she founded in 1891. Mother Alfred Moes (1828-99) forged the direction of Rochester, Minnesota, when she established St. Mary's Hospital and its world-renowned Mayo Clinic. Women were the public face of American Catholicism.

Between 1872 and 1922, 167 new congregations or provinces were created as more and more women were attracted to religious life. Growth, however, created a tightened pattern of centralization and bureaucracy, simultaneous with other bureaucratic tendencies in business and in national professional organizations. John Ireland, archbishop of St. Paul, indicated that the vowed commitment the sisters made actually encouraged efficiency: "An organization endures; the individual drops from the ranks. His place is quickly filled; there is no interruption in the task of mercy" (Ireland 1905, 325). While his comment might have held true in terms of continuity for mission, the regularization of sisters' lives demonstrated significant role changes by the second decade of the twentieth century. In foundation and frontier periods sisters assumed a rich variety of interior and spiritual roles: spouse of Christ, sister, mother, catechist, pastoral agent, woman of prayer, worship leader. External or public roles were also multiple: crisis intervener, nurse, educator, house cleaner, real-estate manager, spiritual guide, and fund raiser. Centralization constricted sisters' choices to make them specialists with a corresponding diminution of roles in the process (Dries 1989).

Women's congregations, which had grown by leaps and bounds since 1850, began to feel the effects of the Vatican's codification of law in 1917 and the consequent homogenization of religious life. Much of the language of interiority in sisters' diaries and journals of the nineteenth and early twentieth centuries—affective, immediate, emotive, symbolic, fluid, appeal to inner authority—was overtaken by the language of structure: appeal to external authority, circumscribed behavior, permissions, rank, and order.

By the mid-twentieth century sisters felt the pressures of professionalization in their work and the stress of a lifestyle patterned to some extent on a European monastic timetable. Plans for change bore fruit in 1954, when sisters crossed congregational boundaries to solve cooperatively the challenges of providing a solid college education and an in-depth formation for the young women entering religious life. The Sister Formation Movement (1952-70) proved to be the public vehicle for the reassessment and redirection of the "split-level" lives of women religious across the country. A comparable formation program was started in Peru, under the direction of Gertrude Berg, a Franciscan from Rochester, Minnesota. Sister Formation was the first of several sisters' groups that organized across congregations. Other national groups arose out of the feminist and/or racial awareness of the 1970s, among them the Black Sisters Conference (1970) and Las Hermanas (1971).

According to the U.S. Catholic Mission Association, in 1960 the major American sisters' institutes serving overseas were Maryknoll (555), Medical Missionary Sisters (168), Sisters of St. Anne (163), Marist Missionary Sisters (133), Dominicans (Holy Cross Province) (86), Servants of Immaculate Heart of Mary (85), School Sisters of Notre Dame (82), Religious of the Sacred Heart (81). In 1969, 403 lay missionaries served overseas. (Source: U.S. Catholic Mission Association.)

The number of American Catholic sisters never exceeded the number of clergy/brothers going overseas, probably because of the thousands of women serving as missionaries in the United States. But the longstanding mission funding and mission education organizations were effective because women engineered them, from the mission circles to the Catholic Students Mission Crusade.

"WOMAN'S WORK FOR WOMAN" AS A THEORETICAL MODEL FOR TWENTIETH-CENTURY CATHOLIC MISSIONARY WOMEN

The nineteenth-century notion of "woman's work for woman" was a major justification for women's missions in Protestantism. Several assumptions and tenets lay behind the familiar phrase (Robert 1997, 125-88). Women's work was necessary because men were unable to approach women in certain cultures and because women controlled the home and family, the foundation of society. Backed by a strong biblical orientation, women missionaries, first as wives of missionaries and then as single women, provided social and charitable works, "ministries of compassion," which supported the home as the beginning of social transformation (ibid., 441). The "two spheres" concept predominant in the Victorian period delineated liturgical roles, ordination, and church building to the clergy, and social services and catechetics to women—politics to men and the home to women.

While the phrase "woman's work for woman" was favored by Protestants, Catholics held similar views about women's role in mission, though Catholics tended to ground their perceptions in philosophy rather than in the Bible. These views can be seen, for example, in the classic and popular *Conversion of the Pagan World* (Manna 1921), which averred that women were equal to men in their "sphere of action," underlined the "elevation of women" as a gift of Christianity, and attested that converted women were the foundation of an established Christianity in any country. At the same time, though, Manna had to explain why more women than men served in the mission field. To do so, he outlined a hierarchy of sacrifice in mission to account for the discrepancy of numbers. At the bottom of the pyramid and more numerous were the Protestants, who had not sacrificed as much as the sisters, who were in the middle. At the top of the pyramid, and hence fewer, were the missionary clergy, who required more arduous study and preparation than the sisters (ibid., 168).

A traditional theoretical emphasis placed on women's weakness was also, paradoxically, the locus for a spiritual and apostolic strength, beginning with Mary, the mother of Jesus. As New York Bishop John Dunn, a close friend of Maryknoll, wrote in his weekly mission column in the December 11, 1920, edition of *Catholic News*, "Are men alone soldiers? No. . . . God chose a weak, helpless woman as the Co-redemptrix. After Calvary do we see men? No. But Mary and her companions—weak, helpless, suffering, enduring women—they are the first examples of the Apostolic woman" (19). The delicate woman, bearing the heat and ruggedness of the mission day and thus advancing Christian civilization, was the pervasive message in early twentieth-century mission literature. Women as auxiliary to men, as the Veronicas who wipe the face of Jesus, did not downplay the force of women redeeming women in mission countries (Streit 1927, 77). Without the women, Christian civilization would not be possible, because women controlled the family environment, the foundation of a Christian civilization.

By the time the idea of "woman's work for woman" was waning for Protestants (Robert 1997, 125-88), the idea was popularized for Catholics by the media figure and national director of the Society for the Propagation of the Faith, Fulton J. Sheen, who developed his perspective based on neo-Thomist philosophy. Unlike Protestants, who at first reluctantly supported single women missionaries, Catholics saw celibate women in community as an ideal call to mission life. It wasn't until the 1940s that the number of single lay missionaries grew, supported by papal encyclicals, an ecclesiology of the Mystical Body, and a tradition of strong female saints that allowed for more flexibility of ecclesial and gender roles. While the theological foundations for distinct spheres with corresponding tasks and cultural assumptions continued to be written about, the endemic use of biblical images that influenced the imagination and moved one to action undergirded women's energy for mission.

Could women be missionaries in the classic sense of "converting souls"? Or was their task indirect, chiefly auxiliary, elevating the condition of women? The question was answered in multiple ways by lay women and sisters.

WOMEN AND COLLECTIVE POWER TO AID WOMEN

Having briefly noted some twentieth-century trends and theories about women and mission, we will now examine representative women from four different kinds of organizations—fund raisers, medical missionaries, lay women, and the Maryknoll Sisters' "direct apostolate"—to see their perceptions of women's role in mission and in the process to note how the missionaries both perpetuated and negotiated traditional gender boundaries. In the process we will see how they provided new content for mission theology.

Mission Funding: Clara Westropp (1886-1965)

A longstanding tradition among Catholic women was the lay financial support of mission. In 1822 Pauline Jaricot and several other laity in Lyon, France, began the Society for the Propagation of the Faith, a major funding source for missions all over the globe. In the United States, after government regulations regarding the allotment of Indian reservations to various denominations, the Ladies Catholic Indian Missionary Association was founded in 1875 in the nation's capital, close on the heels of the opening of the Office of the Catholic Commissioner for Indian Missions. Key Washington women, including Eleanor Boyle Ewing (1824-88), whose husband was an Army general, several members of the Maryland Carroll family, and philanthropist Agnes Caldwell, who later provided the money to build the Catholic University of America, were charter members and contributors. Fund raising for missions was often accomplished through *mission circles*. In many ways, the mission circle Clara Westropp initiated looked fairly similar to the circles of thousands of Protestant and Catholic women before her. She is particularly interesting, however, because of her context and the outcome of the circles.

The Westropps were one of the prominent families in Cleveland, Ohio. Henry (1872-1952) served in the Jesuit mission in Pine Ridge, South Dakota, for ten years and then in Patna, India, for forty years. His sister, Lillian (1894-1968), was an attorney and a municipal court judge in Cleveland, a charter member of the Women Lawyers' Club and the League of Women Voters, and an organizer of the Woman's Hospital in the city. In the 1930s she inaugurated a court psychiatric clinic, a prototype for others in the country. Clara Westropp, her sister, studied bank management at the Savings & Loan Institute in Mercersburg, Pennsylvania, before teaming with her sister in 1922 to open the Women's Federal Savings & Loan Association of Cleveland. The company operated throughout the Depression and today continues as the Women's Federal Savings Bank. Clara Westropp's approach to the financial institution was based on the belief that most women had control of the family bankbook and had a voice in family finances. Why not, then, extend that power into the public sector?

In 1935 Clara Westropp organized the Little Flower Mission Circles to support her brother's mission in India. In 1946, along with a friend, Anne Olle, she extended the influence of women's money and organization by establishing St. Francis Xavier mission circles throughout the Cleveland diocese. Groups of twelve women, the number in memory of the twelve apostles and the capacity the living rooms would comfortably seat, assembled monthly for prayer, study, and action. Each circle "adopted" a particular missionary in addition to contributing to the general mission needs. The women collected or made items both for the spiritual and material realms. In 1950, for example, among the objects they collectively sent were 31,786 Sacred Heart badges, 44,305 rosaries, 384 boxes of medical supplies, 10 nurses' uniforms, 8 towels, a box of kindergarten supplies, a typewriter, 14 boxes of toys, and the occasional distribution of fruit and cigarettes ("Five Deanery Mission Circle Report" 1950). Correspondence and an occasional visit from a missionary kept all in touch in an immediate and personal manner.

The circles broadened the housewives' world toward mission realities and moved the household accounts into a new direction for women, since men were usually in charge of finances for organizations such as the St. Vincent de Paul Society or Catholic Charities. By 1960 over three thousand women in Cleveland belonged to mission circles, and by 1965 there were over 465 groups in the diocese. Clara Westropp was responsible for promoting mission circles in Los Angeles, Chicago, and Detroit. The habit of global responsibility laid the foundation for other forms of local church social activism in the 1960s.

We get a glimpse of the mindset of the mission-minded women from the mid-1930s through the mid-1960s through perusal of their scrapbooks. A speech pasted into one of the albums demonstrates the view the women took of their activity. Written in 1944, the talk bears the imagery of the World War and a predominant motif that Catholic Action—that is, mission—was participation in the work of the hierarchy. But one also notices the justification for women to enter the so-called male territory of finance and mission. Anne Olle, a diocesan mission circle leader whose daughter served as a missionary in Alaska, remarked:

> We follow the example of Mary, whom the Pope termed as the first orga-
> nizer and the first president of a Catholic Women's organization. She or-
> ganized the women of Jerusalem, he said, and joined in prayer and study
> with the apostles during the days following the ascension of our Divine
> Lord into heaven and the descent of the Holy Ghost upon the apostles.
> She and the other holy women of Jerusalem didn't presume to tell the
> apostles how to do their work or how to extend the Kingdom of Christ.
> They merely offered themselves as an auxiliary to be of whatever service
> that they would be called upon to do. Holy writers tell us that the apostles,
> despite the dignity of their office, did counsel with Mary and the same is
> true today. (Olle 1944)

While seeming to be passively "totally available" for whatever needs arose, the women in fact gave active direction in the allocation of the money and resources they accumulated.

> The strength and influence of the circles in the diocese led to the forma-
> tion in 1964 of a diocesan mission team to El Salvador. Clara Westropp
> was a guiding light in that development. Between then and 1994, the dio-
> cese sent fifty-eight women and men to serve in three parishes. Two of the
> most widely known women from the group were Jean Donovan and Sister
> Dorothy Kazel, murdered in El Salvador in 1980, along with two Maryknoll
> Sisters. ("Mission to Latin America, A Progress Report" 1969)

Mission circles provided social bonding with other women and gave them confidence they could succeed in financial matters and in organizational skills on a scale larger than the family. Symbolically, the circle gathered women in face-to-face contact and emphasized the personal immediacy of the work. Circles provided insight on how women navigated economic waters and bore out Anne Scott's thesis about women's philanthropy, that women pursue organized benevolence not as an end in itself but as a means for spiritual and human growth. Scott (1991, 23-24) summarizes studies that compare the ways women and men work collectively. Men tend to operate more as individuals and donate larger sums than women, especially to buildings named after themselves. Men's careers "make money," and then some of the money is donated, often as a means to enhance either their career or their public image. Women work in a more personal fashion and frequently direct their efforts toward women and children, seeing their philanthropic efforts as their "career." Abundant examples of the "wise as serpents and simple as doves" approach to economic self-sufficiency can be noted in women's groups, including that of Maryknoll Sister Gabriella Mulherin (1900-1993), who in 1960 organized the Korea Credit Union, which had over a million depositors in 1988.

Medical Missions: Anna Dengel (1892-1980)

Our second example of women's approach to mission seems allied with the more traditional nurturing role for women. Anna Dengel, a truly remarkable trailblazer for American Catholic medical missions, was born in the beautiful Austrian Tyrol. On advice obtained in correspondence with Dr. Agnes McLaren (1873-1913), a Scottish convert to Catholicism, militant suffragette, and financial backer of a small hospital for women in India, Dengel sought to fulfill her dream as a mission doctor (Burton 1946). Dengel remarked, after she received McLaren's letter, "This was the answer to my subconscious desires and aspirations, to be a missionary with a definite goal in view, meeting an unfulfilled need which only women could fill" (Dengel 1949, 15). Dengel received her medical degree from Cork College, Ireland, and after a year's internship in England, she traveled to Rawalpindi, India, to work with the Franciscan Missionaries of Mary at St. Catherine's Hospital. After four exhausting years of house visits, hospital work, and interminable numbers of outpatients, she experienced a kind of dark night of the soul. She eventually decided, after seeking advice from several priests, to found a women's community to provide professional medical care.

Dengel came to the United States to solicit funds for the hospital. Among the persons she met was Michael Mathis, director at the Holy Cross Foreign Missionary Seminary in Washington, D.C., who had sent several temporary lay nurses to Dacca, India. After further meetings between Dengel and Mathis, the Holy Cross father assisted her in putting together a constitution for ecclesiastical approval of the Society of Catholic Medical Missionaries. A woman doctor and two nurses joined her as the first members of the society. While Vatican approbation of the group came by return mail in 1925, the women could not solicit funds or make public vows because church ordinance prohibited women religious from becoming surgeons and obstetricians. In effect, the society was stymied from attending the women it sought most to help.

Years before, Agnes McLaren had made several trips to church authorities in Rome with the purpose of changing the legislation. The restriction did not daunt

Dengel and the women, as long as women in mission countries were served. Dengel interpreted the prohibition in light of the greater mission:

> The members of the Society of Catholic Medical Missionaries at present sacrifice the privilege of making public vows in order not to be prevented from engaging in any kind of medical work, so as to be able to help people especially women in all their needs. . . . All rules, vows, dress, etc., [should] be directed to this. ("First Constitution" 1932, XVIII, Article 7)

Some clergy and bishops, among them Philadelphia's Cardinal Dougherty, who invited the women to establish their headquarters in his archdiocese, argued for the change of canon law. Finally, in February 1936, the decree *Constans ac Sedula* lifted the restrictions, and the Medical Mission Sisters became the first Roman Catholic congregation to work as physicians, surgeons, and obstetricians. In the larger picture of Vatican relations with modernity and with important twentieth-century papal encyclicals on mission, the affirmation was part of a growing professionalization in the field of medicine and a clear stance that a positive relationship could exist between religion and science.

A look at the journal Dengel edited for many years, *The Medical Missionary* (1927-70), and *Mission for Samaritans* (1945), the only book on medical missions written by a Catholic American woman to that time, highlights the relationships she saw among women's health, politics, and spirituality. *The Medical Missionary* generally featured stories about women's health, the conditions under which they lived, the efforts made to treat various diseases, the history of medical missions, and photos or drawings of Hindu, Muslim, and tribal African women. Dengel's writings took the pulse of the women of non-western countries. For example, in the late 1920s, sensing India's move toward independence, she characterized Asia's millions of people as "fermenting and effervescing. The very foundation of the old civilization is being shaken because women have begun to rub their eyes and many from their seclusion look into the great world of the twentieth century" (Dengel 1927, 2).

Motivated by the charity of Jesus, medical missions further provided an infrastructure for social justice. "Relieving suffering in the spirit of Christ," she maintained,

> means serving Him personally. It gives fatalism and superstition a death blow and instills hope and trust in God and man. It brings tidings of peace, breaking down religious prejudice and race hatred. It is a way of bringing together under one friendly roof all classes, all colors and creeds. . . . It helps all, with only one distinction, the neediest receive the most. (in Fritsch 1998, 56)

Social justice theory was never far removed from the "flesh and blood" of real women's experience. Articles in 1960, such as "The Role of the Ashanti Woman," identified the losses and gains women around the world were experiencing in the upheaval of revolution, fading empires, and economic imbalance. The stories always identified particular women as part of Dengel's social analysis.

The covers of the mission magazine in the 1930s especially revealed Dengel's holistic approach to mission. Body and soul, science and mission together alleviated the unspeakable suffering of women. Social analysis, professional medicine, and social justice were right at home with prayer, liturgy, and charity. We see this consistently in Dengel's life, in the advice she gave the sisters, and in the editorials she wrote in the magazine. "As missionaries we must love others body and soul and we must strive for the extension of the Church. The needs of suffering humanity must echo in our hearts. Moral and psychic wounds cannot be touched if we leave the physical suffering untouched" (Dengel 1949, 47). Twenty-two years later these exact sentiments were expressed in the now famous first paragraph from the 1965 conciliar document *Pastoral Constitution on the Church in the Modern World:* "The joy and hope, the grief and anguish of the people of our time, especially those who are poor or are afflicted in any way, are the joy and hope, the grief and anguish of the followers of Christ, as well."

Mission for Samaritans provided a historical, scientific, and theological treatise on the importance of medical missions. Dengel placed Christ's commandment of charity at the root of all mission activity. She defined the medical mission apostolate as "that branch of missionary work through which skilled medical care is given to the sick and poor of mission countries, as a means of relieving their physical suffering and of bringing to them a knowledge and appreciation of our Faith" (Dengel 1945, 1). Among the reasons she gave for medical missions was that they were a "work of restitution as well as of charity. . . . It is the tremendous debt which we, the white race, owe to the peoples subjected and exploited by our forefathers" (ibid., 5). Even were it possible to cure all people of serious illness, the need for social justice remained (ibid., 115).

Dengel viewed professional health care for women among Muslim, Hindu, and Buddhist cultures not as a means to conversion per se but as a witness of the gratuitous love of God. From the inception of her mission vocation as a lay woman, Dengel's immediate identification with suffering women was sparked by the opportunity to bring them the care of Christ. Her ability to be "both/and" made her free to critique the coldness of professionalism and to extend the options for charity. Her spirituality flowed from the liturgy and the gospel, but she felt equally at home with statistics and social analysis.

Lay Women Missionaries: The Grail Movement

Our third case study looks at lay women missionaries and specifically the Grail Movement. Despite the norm that mission service involved joining a religious congregation, a few lay women served as missionaries or evangelists in the nineteenth century. Warm association of young women with sisters in their schools often carried over into lay financial and spiritual support of the sisters' work. In the case of the Sisters of Charity, Bronx, New York, Margaret Wohlfert, a teacher in their school, joined the pioneer venture of the sisters in the Bahamas in 1889 and taught kindergarten.

Limited discussion of the topic of lay missionaries took place at the 1923 Catholic Students' Mission Crusade Convention at the University of Notre Dame. In the 1930s and 1940s a number of college women stood on street corners as lay evangelizers in the Catholic Evidence Guild. One of these evangelistic groups, from Rosary College, Chicago, was an officially sanctioned group of women who spoke about Catholic issues from the back of pickup trucks in rural areas of the southern United States and Oklahoma. The women were trained by Maisie Ward and Frank Sheed in the style of the Hyde Park speakers (Campbell 1998). But generally, lay women saw their mission, if not to become Sisters, then to be good wives and mothers, responsible for the religious education of their families, especially because by the 1920s women's suffrage, birth control, divorce, and women in the labor force were important public issues that threatened traditional Catholic values (Orsi 1999).

The impetus for an explosion of lay mission groups came at the same time as the papal encyclical *Mystici Corporis* (1943). The document solidified a growing theme in European and American Catholicism since the early twentieth century and gave impetus to liturgical renewal, which had been brewing in the United States since the 1920s. With the inauguration of the Catholic Students' Mission Crusade in 1918, the Young Christian Students in the 1940s, and the Christian Family Movement in the early 1960s, lay groups, especially women, freely employed the Mystical Body image as a guiding spiritual principle for mission activity.

The Mystical Body, scripturally based on 1 Corinthians 12, seemed to have a kind of democratic impulse, where each person was important and all were working toward a common goal. The image was a contrast to the prevailing nineteenth-century model of church as "perfect society." In some respects the symbol of the Mystical Body balanced the feelings of fragmentation, isolation, and specialization Americans were experiencing. Theologically, mission could no longer be just the responsibility of experts, that is, official mission congregations, or of clergy. Mission was everyone's obligation by virtue of baptism. All were "full-blooded members" of Christ's body. As a popular mission text expressed it, "No member of the Mystical Body of Christ, whatever his position in it, may feel himself exempt from an active, personal share in the missions. For as St. Paul says: If one member suffers anything, all the members suffer with it, or if one member glories, all the members rejoice with it" (Johnson 1947, 8).

During the 1950s and early 1960s over twenty national or diocesan lay mission groups appeared across the country, many of them appealing specifically to women. Lay missionary associations tended to be stronger in the Midwest, probably due to the area's leadership in liturgical renewal and more recent pioneer spirit, which was not as affected by class consciousness, as was true in the East. In 1956 a Committee for the International Lay Apostolate was formed at the annual Mission Secretariat meeting in order to discuss common interests and problems in the lay mission apostolate. Among the more well known of the mission groups that gathered at the meeting were the Grail (1921) and the Lay Missionaries of Los Angeles, both of which are still thriving, the Women Volunteers for Africa (1956), and the Papal Volunteers for Latin America (1960). While there are incomplete figures for the Papal Volunteers, it appears that by far the majority of the missionaries were women. (For the history and impact of the Papal Volunteers for Latin America, see Costello 1979 and Dries 1998, 189-96.)

We will take a look at the Grail as an outstanding example of lay women's leadership in mission. In 1940 the headquarters for the international Grail movement moved from Holland to the Cincinnati, Ohio, area. Founded in 1921, the women's group had as its purpose to bring spiritual values to people in a "modern" world, a position that clearly envisioned a place for women beyond the home. The group had both permanent members who lived at the Grail houses and women who had a freer association, attending regular programs and "schools" the Grail sponsored. Formation at the Grail emphasized community living and liturgical prayer as a foundation for mission and as a source of renewal of an integral Christian culture. In their three-month school of training for the apostolate, the women reflected on their lives in light of the scriptural readings for the liturgical seasons, attended classes, listened to internationally renowned speakers, gardened together, and informally shared ideas around the dinner table.

In 1950 the women established an Institute for Overseas Service; four years later, thirty-five of the two hundred volunteers for overseas mission were from the United States, with twenty-two more women in various stages of preparation for assignment to Africa, Indonesia, and South America. The women served as nurses and doctors, did social work, and were catechists and agriculturists. Starting with their first national conference in 1962, the Grail's vision for women radically shifted from building a new Catholic culture for modern times toward emphasizing more active involvement in social, political, and economic areas. The group developed catechetical programs, some of which became models throughout the United States. They cultivated ecumenical ties with other women, moving, not without pain, from "religious certainty to religious search" (Kalven 1999, 277).

While the group was feminist or at least "pre-feminist" from its inception, Janet Kalven, a member since the 1940s, reflected recently on the "second wave" of feminist consciousness after 1965, whereby they moved from a hierarchic, top-down model of authority, patterned after the Jesuit manner inculcated from the original priest-adviser to the group. Rather than assuming a model of complementariness—that is, women's "femininity" counterbalancing the "hardness" of the masculine—the Grail after 1965 reflected collaborative, inclusive, and holistic approaches in its life and education models. Grail women saw themselves as agents of social, economic, and religious change.

Maryknoll Sisters and the "Direct Apostolate" of Women

Our fourth case to examine "woman's work for woman" is the Maryknoll Sisters, who probably most represented the public face of American sisters' overseas mission. In the early days of Maryknoll it was not clear whether the women themselves would be sent overseas, or whether their mission was to assist the men through domestic chores at the seminary, editing the group's magazine, *The Field Afar*, and similar activities. At first, the women's leader, Mother Mary Joseph Rogers, stated:

> Our desire is to be so organized that with St. Teresa as our model and patron we may devote all our energies of body and soul to the spread of the foreign mission spirit in this country and to the support of the seminary here. Even our longing to go into the mission field is subservient to this great need. (Rogers 1922, 2:435)

The sublimation of their desire to go as missionaries was a logical conclusion to the "distinct spheres" idea, which Mother Mary Joseph seemed to have held, at least in the early stages of Maryknoll history.

By the time the Maryknoll Sisters went to China in the 1920s, the success of the nineteenth- and early twentieth-century work of American sisters had resulted in institutions of every sort, both in the United States and overseas. Bishop Francis X. Ford in Kaying Province, China, lamented that so many sisters served in institutions. He queried, why not train sisters for "the actual spread of the Faith," the "direct apostolate," "work among women not for the benefit of their bodies or minds, but for their souls?" (in Fedders 1954, 113).

Ford observed that missionaries of the past in neglecting conversion of women had aggravated the traditional apathy of the Chinese themselves for the welfare of their women. Although Chinese etiquette had shaped the pattern, concentration on conversion of men diminished the influence of women on the family. Chinese women, whom Ford saw as "the backbone of idolatry," could also become the backbone of Christianity. Where sisters were direct evangelizers, he maintained,

> a new recognition is accorded to the rights and duties of Christian mothers in safeguarding their children. We may look for numerous examples of truly Christian families, a better instructed growing generation, and a gradual refinement of thought and action. This will not be accomplished overnight, but it is inevitable wherever Sisters work. (in Fedders 1954, 227)

The direct apostolate meant that the sisters themselves would go out to evangelize the women in the villages. The first step was "making contacts," daily visits to people's homes to become acquainted with the women. Instruction of women interested in the Catholic faith came next, with a follow-up after baptism. The sisters were not to "camouflage" their intentions by providing medicines and other "social services" on their visits.

Ford's idea necessitated a departure from standard convent routine of certain times for prayers together, the "great silence" in the evening, and a distinctive form of dress. Sisters were sent out two by two into the villages of Kaying Province, China, where Ford was bishop. Sisters lived with families, taught at night during the catechumenate, and wore a modified habit for travel on bicycle and sampan and for wading rivers. Such customs were contrary to convent living patterns of the time.

Sister Marcelline, from whom we learn much about the direct apostolate, suggested how they were able to keep their religious life without the standard conventual routine:

> The spiritual side of our lives was never lessened, though at times it had to grow strong on the sacrifice of deprivation of Mass and Communion during the prolonged stays in mission outpost. At such times, spiritual Mass and Communion, the divine Office, our Rosary and other spiritual exercises were unfailing standbys for us all. (in Ford 1953, 224)

Actually, the American sisters were following to some extent the evangelistic practice of the Chinese lay virgins and sisters. By 1925, figures show that in Asia, 4,678 foreign women and 15,904 native women were missionaries (Streit 1927, 78). The Maryknoll apostolate, the earlier lay evangelization, and other unordained but immediate leadership in liturgical functions foreshadowed the practice of team leadership in mission, an idea supported by the Vatican II image of church as people of God.

The sounds of the nineteenth century reverberate in the foregoing stories of Catholic missionary women in the twentieth century: women remained committed to "woman's work for woman." While early twentieth-century women who called themselves auxiliaries felt a vital part of the mission picture, the demise of the word *auxiliary* by the 1960s spoke more clearly about women's actual roles. In true incarnational fashion the "real world" of saving souls was a matter of connections: body and spirit, prayer and action, professional life and interior devotion, a conclusion that Dana Robert also reached in *American Women in Mission*. Enough research has been done to indicate that women did not subscribe to the ramifications of supposedly being the weaker sex. As men themselves realized, women redeeming other women did not require passivity but action, thought as well as intuition, domestic, economic, and political *savoir faire*. Furthermore, physical weakness and infirmity, even when present, did not deter women from being apostolic but rather provided an impetus to move beyond gender limitations.

HOW WOMEN NEGOTIATED GENDER BOUNDARIES

Having surveyed four cases, what can we conclude about Catholic "woman's work for woman"? How *did* women negotiate the boundaries between the personal and professional, the individual and community, self-sacrifice and the promotion of independent thinkers? First, they did so through being gathered as women. Women met people literally where they were—in living rooms, *zenanas,*

Chinese homes, and market places. The domestic chores common to women around the world yielded a point of identification with women of all cultures. What varied was the manner in which the work was accomplished. The intersection of common reference points facilitated an extension of God's love, women's emancipation, and economic self-reliance. At its best, collectivity provided a spiritual, economic, and social force without which Christianity is not possible. Living or working side by side, clear goals, and large numbers to achieve a common purpose were assets for women's empowerment. When community structures petrified, often following a period of successful ministry against great odds, individuals lost the range of personal options for development within the structure. Feminist historians can find rich resources for a study of American Catholic missionary women because of their emphasis on communal power, embodiment, and intersubjectivity. With the present reexamination of feminist identity because of globalization and a new category of analysis, "collective identities," American Catholic women missionaries have a wealth of experience to contribute to the discussion. Scott elucidates collective patterns for Protestant women's societies (1991, 175), including those of the home and foreign missions (88-93) up to the 1930s, and illustrates the impact on social justice responses thereafter. Rupp and Taylor also discuss the issue from the point of political impact, particularly in suffrage, labor legislation, and nationalism (1999, 363-83). And Benhabib, after a summary of postmodern emphases, asks whether feminism needs rethinking because of the process of globalization, where, on the one hand, we see deeper homogenization and uniformity, and, on the other, we note cultural fragmentation (Benhabib 1999, 325-62).

Second, women negotiated boundaries through the mindset of flexibility and adaptation, neither of which is necessarily linear in thinking. Perhaps the mission circle scrapbooks are representative of this approach. Scrapbooks are malleable, visual, selective, personal, and collective. The scrapbooks of the mission circles, laden with material that over time appears ephemeral yet fraught with the weight of living memory, somehow seem less threatening, more engaging and usable than some of the theological tomes of the era. Adaptation results partly from a desire for relationships and connections: missionaries, people of other cultures, one another, God, Jesus.

Third, women tended to draw from *multiple* resources for life and mission. In the groups we surveyed, Eucharist, scriptures, professional journals, formal, informal, and alternative education, support from like-minded men, fiscal strategies, enlightened papal documents, and even oppressive legislation all played a role in women's effective efforts in evangelization. As noted earlier, the use of biblical images provided proper sanction in crossing gender boundaries.

Finally, and perhaps most important, American Catholic women were willing to identify and deal with ambiguity and the discomfort they felt in the disjuncture between theory and practice in terms of gender assumptions and mission theology. While Anna Dengel worked within the structures to change church law, the response of the Sisters of St. Joseph to Vatican queries as to whether the sisters were in the operating room (thus putting their vocation at risk if they had to view male bodies) was that Sisters were sometimes "in the vicinity of the operating room." In fact, however, at times they assisted with surgery (Coburn and Smith 1999, 203). Some might call this dissimulation; others would call it healthy mission practice. The management of ambiguity was not simply private and internal. Rather, it manifested a public face. The Sister Formation Conference through its monthly bulletins and national conferences as well as summer sessions of the Grail were examples of the same process. We learn from their open, humble, and intense proceedings how women moved from "frontier" to "institution" and back to "frontier," not just in a physical sense but in other dimensions of their lives. As Janet Kalven identified the dynamic for the Grail, she saw the women shift from religious certainty to religious search, from "feminist actions to feminist consciousness" (Kalven 1999, 217).

In the 1960s *development*, and in the 1980s *inculturation*, replaced the seeming triumphalism of *Christendom* and *civilization*. It is worth noting that some of the discussion of the early twentieth century was not just about the importance of establishing a western culture/church. In 1925 Robert Streit placed the humanist values of civilization as a contrast to a technological world in full swing at the time and suggested that the church act as a conscience of civilization:

> The degree of culture and civilization of a people is not measured by the number of its factories, the bulk of its production or the development of its machinery. It is evaluated on the basis of the religious, ethical, social, and economic principles that govern labor, production and the exchange of commodities. (Streit 1927, 119)

Women missionaries offered alternative strategies and values in the development of individuals and communities in each of the areas Streit identified. In so doing, women created the mission emphasis later named in Vatican II documents and contemporary mission theology.

Although we claim a theology today different from the past, women missionaries still identify with women's suffering. Gender-specific topics remain priorities for women in mission: the rights of women, women's health and education, women and children, the need to strengthen family life, the effects of globalization. Wittingly or not, women's actions always have had political overtones, both in the church and society. It is probable that in the next one hundred years American Catholic women will still see their mission as "woman's work for woman."

10

Empowering Immaculate Heart of Mary Missionaries

Compelling Vision, Collaborative Decisions

Mary Joseph Maher, IHM

Impelled by the cries of God's people[s], especially the poor, the margin-
ated, and the oppressed of diverse countries and cultures, we, the members
of the IHM Mission Province, desire to live in solidarity with them, sharing
their joys and hopes, griefs and anxieties, experiencing together the trans-
forming power of the Gospel.
—Vision Statement, IHM Overseas Missions, 1984

Since 1948 almost two hundred Catholic women—members of the Sisters, Servants of the Immaculate Heart of Mary of Monroe, Michigan (IHM Sisters)—have served as overseas missionaries in Puerto Rico, Brazil, Grenada, Honduras, Mexico, Chile, Nicaragua, Haiti, Uganda, Ghana, Kenya, Zimbabwe, and South Africa. IHM Sisters also responded to urgent requests for short-term service in India and Vietnam, and IHMs assisted in the resettlement of thousands of refugees in the United States.

Although small in number (averaging only thirty a year between 1948 and 1998) and spread out across Latin America and Africa, IHM missionaries were united and energized by a compelling mission vision and a collaborative governmental structure that fostered and supported the mission endeavor. The small IHM overseas mission group earned the respect of international mission-sending societies—as evidenced by the election of IHM overseas mission leaders to the boards of the United States Catholic Mission Association and the African Faith and Justice Network, where they served with leaders of large mission-sending societies (for example, Maryknoll, Missionaries of Africa, Columban Fathers, Comboni Missionaries, Medical Mission Sisters, Society of African Missions, and Divine Word Missionaries).

Reflection on the history of IHM overseas missions reveals several characteristics: (1) an openness to go beyond one's borders, culture, and religious
traditions to respond to human needs; (2) a commitment to live among and to
help empower the materially poor; (3) a willingness and ability to change and
adapt in order to meet new needs; and (4) a conviction that action on behalf of
justice is intrinsic to Christian discipleship and to proclaiming the gospel.[1]

LATIN AMERICA—A FUNDAMENTAL OPTION FOR THE POOR

"We share the life of our people . . . drink their coffee and eat their beans."
This simple statement of Valerie Knoche, IHM, captured her experience and
commitment as a missionary who, for more than twenty-five years, lived among
and worked with some of the poorest people of Honduras. It also expressed the
spirit of all IHM missionaries in Latin America, a group committed to solidarity
and collaboration with the peoples among whom they lived and worked.

IHM missionaries are members of a religious congregation of Catholic women
founded in Monroe, Michigan, in 1845. Their principal work was education.
For a hundred years the IHM Sisters concentrated their efforts primarily in Michigan, providing Catholic education in both parochial schools and their own private schools and college. Although they were not founded to be overseas missionaries, they—like most U.S. non-mission-sending congregations of Catholic
women religious—sent missionaries abroad.

In 1948, at the request of the bishop of San Juan, the IHMs sent four sisters to
staff a school in Cayey, Puerto Rico. By 1972 thirty-four IHMs were teaching
in four parochial schools and at the Catholic University of Puerto Rico. The
quality of education they provided equaled that of their counterparts in the United
States. The IHM Sisters taught their students to speak perfect English, secured
school accreditation from U.S. educational agencies, and offered their students
almost every activity and opportunity that students in U.S. Catholic schools
enjoyed.

The year 1973 marked a turning point for IHM overseas missions—a radical
change in mission vision, priorities, and policies. In January, forty-two IHMs
from Puerto Rico, Brazil, and Grenada (West Indies) met for their first Latin
American Assembly. After days of tense and very difficult discussions, they
made "a fundamental option for the poor"—determining that IHM missionaries
in Latin America would share life with and work among the materially poor. By
June 1973 the number of IHMs in Puerto Rico dropped from thirty-four to nineteen. However, in September, three IHMs who had been in Puerto Rico opened
a mission in the mountains of Honduras. In Puerto Rico itself the IHMs opened
missions in very poor and pastorally neglected areas—Vieques (1973), Culebra
(1976), and Ceiba (1976). In all three the missionaries organized religious education programs, trained catechists, formed Bible study/reflection groups, created special programs for youth, and helped conduct religious services. Beyond

[1] For a comprehensive history of the IHM overseas missions see Maher (2000).

the parish, Helen Smith taught high school classes in Culebra's poor public school and Candyce Rekart taught mentally and physically challenged children in the Ceiba public school.

In Vieques, in addition to pastoral ministry, the IHMs took an active role in the people's "struggle to rid the island of the presence of the United States Navy which occupies 75% of the island and controls the water around the island, thus prohibiting the fishermen from fishing in waters that are most fruitful to their livelihood" (Vieques Chronicles, 1979-80). During the sixteen years that IHMs lived and worked in Vieques (1973-89), all the missionaries in Puerto Rico supported the protests in Vieques, as did the IHM Congregation in the United States. In July 2000 the Diocese of Caguas conferred on the IHM Sisters the first diocesan Medal of Human Rights and Social Doctrine, noting that the Sisters maintained a prophetic witness "by their support of the fishermen and all the peoples who protested against the military presence."

Decisions made at the 1973 Latin American Assembly were indeed a turning point for IHM missionaries. The opening of a mission among the very poor in Grenada less than two months before the meeting anticipated the radical change. In November 1972 three IHMs—the first of eight missionaries—went to the island of Grenada in the West Indies to live among the impoverished local people and to assist them in pastoral ministry. (The mission closed in 1982 due to a lack of personnel.) However, it was the experience of six missionaries from Brazil that directly influenced the decisions. Missionaries from Brazil brought seven years' experience of living among very poor people, speaking their language, respecting their culture, and collaborating with them in nurturing a faith that acted to transform social conditions. In 1965 four IHMs had joined two Catholic priests from the Archdiocese of Detroit to open a mission in Nova Descoberta, an extremely poor neighborhood in Recife, Brazil. The Detroit-Recife Mission Team worked closely with Dom Hélder Câmara, Archbishop of Olinda-Recife, whose commitment to the poor was legendary and who had been a leading figure at the 1968 meeting of the Latin American Catholic Bishops at Medellín, Colombia. There the bishops faced their reality—the poverty, hunger, marginalization, and injustice suffered by the great majority of their people and the Church's complicity in it. The bishops committed the Church to work for the liberation of the poor and for the transformation of society based on justice.

The context of mission in Brazil was already tense because of the military dictatorship established in 1964. It was especially tense in Recife, where Dom Hélder Câmara publicly condemned government abuses. In a written communication to the author dated January 10, 1998, Dorothy Diederichs recalled, "Military police were visible everywhere, persons were imprisoned without justification, torture and assassination were common. Paid informers were mixed among the members of the Church communities. . . . Two American priest friends of ours were expelled from the country in 1968. Padre Henrique, a diocesan priest close to Dom Hélder, was assassinated in 1969. Several pastoral persons from the diocese were imprisoned and tortured. Father Bob Singelyn and I were held at gunpoint and interrogated one evening and released the next morning in 1973."

From 1965 to the present, thirteen IHMs have been missionaries in Brazil. They engaged in a variety of ministries, primarily forming base Christian communities *(comunidades ecclesiales de base)* where the people prayed, reflected on their reality in the light of the Scriptures, and took action to improve the quality of their life (for example, getting water, cleaning up sewage, obtaining health care, and improving education). In addition, the missionaries coordinated pastoral work, started women's reflection groups, organized youth groups, and supported workers' rights and the people's rights to land. Beyond the neighborhood, Patricia McClusky taught in the Recife Catholic Theology Institute and Carol Quigley was a member of the diocesan evangelization team. Ann Nett took leadership in promoting alternative health programs and the use of herbal medicines, and Dorothy Diederichs initiated a reflection-action group for women religious living in small communities among the poor in Northeastern Brazil. Now numbering over three hundred, the members of this group meet every two or three years to share their experience and deepen their understanding of issues—particularly from a feminist perspective. Unquestionably, the opening of the mission in Brazil affected all future decisions regarding IHM overseas missions.

In 1973 IHM missionaries went to Honduras. In contrast to the urban context of mission in Brazil, IHMs in Honduras lived and worked with poor peasants in isolated mountain areas. They were responsible for people in as many as forty to sixty villages, difficult to reach in dry weather, dangerous in the rainy season. The often desperate needs of the people called for a wide range of responses. IHMs have instructed catechists and Delegates of the Word (lay people who lead their communities in worship services), started youth groups, trained first-aid workers in isolated villages, encouraged the people to build schools and clinics, opened women's sewing and baking cooperatives, introduced solar ovens, and brought in medical and dental teams from the United States. In October 1998 Hurricane Mitch devastated Honduras—killing thousands of people, leaving a half-million homeless, and destroying an infrastructure that had taken fifty years to build. With donations from the IHM Congregation and from numerous friends and benefactors, Valerie Knoche and Barbara Zimmer provided emergency food and shelter and organized the people to begin replanting and rebuilding.

In 1995, while working in Minas de Oro, Comayagua, the IHMs joined in protests against a Canadian/Venezuelan mining company whose proposed open-pit mining and cyanide leaching processes threatened the environment. In a 1995 Christmas letter to family and friends, Valerie Knoche noted that they educated "the villages to speak up for this just cause, as many [were] already drinking water contaminated with the diesel, mud, and oil from the machines." This was not the IHMs' first involvement in justice issues. In 1975 the Olancho Massacre directly affected Anne Marie Hughes and Valerie Knoche. The public commitment of Bishop Nicholas D'Antonio to the rights of the poor in the Department (State) of Olancho placed all the Catholic missionaries in the diocese at risk of reprisals from wealthy landowners. In June, at Los Horcones, fourteen people—two priests, two lay women visitors, and ten peasants—were murdered, presumably by soldiers and agents of the landowners. The victims' bodies were dumped in a cistern that was then dynamited. From Tegucigalpa, leaders of Caritas (the Catholic international relief organization) sent personnel to Olancho to bring missionaries to the capital, where they remained under house arrest. After four months the Honduran government gave permission for the Catholic pastoral ministers to return to Olancho. Hughes and Knoche returned and were joined by two more IHMs. However, because of death threats, Bishop D'Antonio was not allowed to return to his diocese. A lack of leadership and continuous verbal threats resulted in a gradual withdrawal of all the Catholic missionaries from Olancho. In October 1980 the IHMs accepted an invitation from the bishop of Comayagua Diocese to open a mission in Esquías. From there, IHMs opened missions in Guajiquiro in 1988 and in Minas de Oro in 1990. Presently, the IHM missionaries are in San Ignacio (Archdiocese of Tegucigalpa).

Julie Slowik, the first IHM missionary to Mexico, arrived in Ciudad Juárez in 1985 and moved into a very poor neighborhood created by urban migration. Mexicans from rural areas were flocking to Juárez in hopes of finding work, better housing, schools, and health care services. They were bitterly disappointed. Inflation, unemployment, and a lack of adequate social services left them in poverty. The IHMs were soon engaged in visiting homes, taking the sick to doctors and hospitals, conducting religious services, counseling, finding and distributing food and clothing, helping the women start a food cooperative, forming catechists, and organizing adult Bible reflection groups. The latter effort was the first step toward the formation of base Christian communities—a priority to which the IHM missionaries devoted their energies at the local, diocesan, and national levels.

As in Puerto Rico, Brazil, and Honduras, IHMs in Mexico were keenly aware of the socioeconomic problems affecting the people. In her Christmas letter of 1985, Julie Slowik highlighted the problem of the *maquiladoras*—plants built by U.S. companies along the U.S.-Mexican border. She noted that Juárez alone had two hundred such plants but employed only a fraction of the number of people seeking work. "They hire youth, mostly women between the ages of 16 and 23. . . . With the devaluation of the *peso*, they receive the equivalent of U.S.$3.50 for a nine-hour day." Bill Moyers of CBS produced a documentary in 1986 entitled *One River, One Country*, giving a clear explanation of how U.S. companies were exploiting the poor of Mexico all along the border. Julie Slowik was his translator and appeared on the program. To raise the consciousness of North Americans, particularly those preparing to work among Hispanics in the United States, the IHMs invited individuals and groups to spend a day, a week, or even a month with them in Juárez.

In summary, the lifestyle and ministries of IHM missionaries in Latin America after the Second Vatican Council reflected a desire to be in solidarity with communities of poor people (simple houses, shortages of water and electricity, no telephone, and so on). They committed themselves to accompanying those communities in processes of empowerment through which the people themselves might transform their human situation. The missionaries did not go into a local community with a set of prepared programs. Rather, they first came to know the people, entered into their world, learned to respect their culture, and listened as the people expressed their needs. Although they sometimes had to provide food, clothing, and medical help, their principal objective was to foster initiative and skills in the people, with the intention of developing self-reliance rather than dependence on the "foreign" missionary.

AFRICA—THE CALL TO SERVE

In Africa, IHM missionaries had the same objectives, but their ministries were almost always a response to specific requests for help—particularly in education. Over the past thirty years they have helped to educate future teachers and priests, promoted education in very poor areas, and engaged in pastoral ministry. The first three IHM missionaries went to Uganda in September 1969 in response to a plea to help educate Catholic sisters who were preparing to be teachers. At the convent of the Daughters of Mary (known in Uganda as the Bannabikira), the oldest and largest congregation of African women religious, Anna Marie Grix taught religion, English, music, and typing. Ellen Balle taught mathematics, biology, and physical science—making use of ink bottles, folded strips of newspaper, foil from coffee tins, and bamboo pieces. Julia Seim, an experienced librarian, wrote in a September 28, 1969, letter to Margaret Brennan, of the collection of "new, old, clean, dirty, worm-eaten, ancient books" she transformed into a well-organized library of a thousand catalogued volumes. She then trained several Ugandan sisters to be librarians.

Living and teaching on the Bannabikira compound did not insulate the new missionaries from a deteriorating political situation. The years 1968 and 1969 were marked by labor unrest, student protests, rumors of an army plot to overthrow the government, the arrest and detention of some leading opponents of President Milton Obote, the attempted assassination of the president in December 1969, and the declaration of a state of emergency. In January 1971, Major General Idi Amin led a successful military coup, ousting Obote and inaugurating an eight-year reign of terror that nearly destroyed Uganda. Rather than withdraw personnel, as requested by the U.S. State Department, the IHMs sent six more missionaries to Uganda during that time. Two replaced those with the Bannabikira; four answered requests for teachers at seminaries or schools for Catholic sisters.

The IHM chronicles from Uganda from 1969 through 1981 record expulsions, disappearances, arrests, torture, murders, looting, and wanton destruction. Joan Mumaw, the only IHM in Uganda from 1976 through 1981, was also the only woman who remained with the international faculty at Katigondo Major Seminary near Masaka during the invasion by Tanzanian troops and the Ugandan exiles' army that drove Amin from the country. In January 1980 she wrote to friends, saying "every aspect of the structure of the society is in shambles." While Mumaw remained in Uganda until 1981, two of the IHM missionaries from Uganda went to Kenya in the late 1970s to teach at a seminary. Marie Miller, IHM, a Maryknoll Missioner Associate, worked in Mombasa with the Maryknoll Sisters in the formation of lay leaders from 1979 to 1983. In 1997 IHM missionaries returned to Uganda when Marie-Esther Haflett and Ann Aseltyne joined the faculty of the newly founded Uganda Martyrs University.

The IHM mission in Ghana, West Africa, which opened in 1976, was one of the poorest and physically most difficult of all the IHM missions. Marie Rebecca Vonderhaar and Agnes Anderson went to Navrongo in northeastern Ghana at the invitation of Bishop Rudolph Akanlu, who told the author in August 1974 that he wanted a "second mother" for the young boys at the high school seminary. Vonderhaar filled that role as the first and only woman on the faculty, while Anderson joined the faculty of St. John Bosco Teacher Training College. Although Susan Rakoczy spent five years at the Centre for Spiritual Renewal in Kumasi as a teacher of scripture and spiritual director, IHM missionaries who served in Ghana from 1976 through 1996 primarily concentrated on preparing teachers in the isolated and very poor northeastern part of the country. Marie Rebecca Vonderhaar, Rose Graham, and Ann Aseltyne were particularly challenged at Gbewaah Teacher Training College in Pusiga, a village close to the Burkina Faso and Togo borders. The college buildings were in disrepair, windows broken, benches and chairs scarce, library books old and unorganized. There was no electricity, and water had to be carried from boreholes (wells) and stored in barrels. Students rioted because of food shortages. Faculty and students lacked books, paper, and equipment—to the point where required exams could not be given. The conditions at the teacher-training college reflected those at the rural schools of northeastern Ghana. As Rose Graham reported to the IHM Missions Assembly at Monroe, Michigan, July 13-15, 1984, "We taught teachers how to teach in the bush when they had nothing—no classroom, no books, no paper or pencils—nothing!"

From 1976 to 1996 IHM missionaries in Ghana lived through severe shortages of food and fuel, impassable roads and collapsed bridges, military coups and border closings. But at the end of nearly twenty years, Marie Rebecca Vonderhaar reported that "for all the years the IHMs were in Ghana, at least one of our Sisters was always directly engaged in teacher training. By 1996, in every region of Ghana, you could find teachers who were formed by IHMs" (*Spinnaker* [April 1996], 9, 12).

The first invitation to send IHM missionaries to Zimbabwe came in 1976. At that time Zimbabwe was still known as Rhodesia, and the country was in the midst of a civil war in which the black African majority was fighting to take control from the minority white government. Because of a lack of personnel, the IHMs were unable to send anyone. However, in the early 1980s, after the war of liberation, the new Zimbabwe government appealed for teachers in rural areas in order to make education accessible to as many people as possible and to prevent a mass invasion of the cities. This effort was strongly supported by Catholic religious congregations, who pledged to recruit, place, and maintain committed religious and lay secondary school teachers for rural secondary schools. Genevieve Petrak, the first IHM to answer the call for rural secondary teachers, went to All Souls Mission in Mutoko, joining the Sisters of Notre Dame de Namur. In her 1986 report to the IHM Overseas Mission Province, she wrote: "[This] has been, without a doubt, the greatest teaching challenge I've ever had. . . . I continue to be amazed at our students—how much they put up with. . . . There is a great lack of furniture, books, proper bedding, balanced diet, and often we are without water and electricity."

In January 1988 Petrak, now joined by two more IHMs, responded to a call for rural secondary teachers at the isolated Embakwe Mission in Matebeleland. The mission had been abandoned during the war of liberation after the mission was attacked and two Mariannhill missionaries murdered. The Christian Brothers took over the abandoned mission school in 1981. The IHMs were qualified teachers with years of experience. They remained at Embakwe until the end of 1993. Marie-Esther Haflett joined the faculty of a teacher-training college in South Africa. Genevieve Petrak and Rose Graham moved into a poor township near Harare—Graham teaching in the public school, Petrak working in a Catholic parish. In 1997, because of a growing difficulty in getting their visas extended and a shortage of personnel, the IHMs left Zimbabwe.

The IHM mission in South Africa opened in October 1985. Despite nightly scenes on American television of violent civil unrest—riots, stonings, looting, necklacings, clubbings by police, bulldozing of township dwellings, and armored vehicles in the streets—the four IHM missionaries who had spent two years in preparation to go to South Africa never wavered in their commitment. At the invitation of Kevin Dowling, superior of the Redemptorists (now bishop of Rustenburg), the IHMs assumed major responsibility for pastoral ministry in two neighboring parishes in Natal Province. The pastors, Redemptorist priests, were full-time professors at the nearby seminary in Cedara. Eileen Karrer, who had extensive experience in parish ministry, became the administrator of St. Joseph Parish in Howick. Annette St. Amour worked with the people of St. Anne's in the Zulu Township of Mpophomeni. Annette Boyle, an experienced spiritual director, went on to Cape Town to assist a diocesan team. Judy Coyle worked with Eileen Karrer in the Howick parish and also began teaching courses in liturgy at the seminary.

From the opening of the IHM South African mission in 1985, Eileen Karrer put all of her energies into St. Joseph Parish, Howick. Although for forty-five years the parishioners in Howick had been predominantly black, at the time the IHMs arrived parishioners included Zulus, whites, coloureds (mixed race), and East Indians. The shift resulted from actions taken by the apartheid government, which rezoned Howick for whites in 1968 and relocated most of the large Zulu population to Mpophomeni Township in the early 1970s. Despite a storm of controversy with some of the white parishioners, Karrer set out to have the parish reflect its racial diversity in the parish council, liturgical leaders, choir, and catechumenate program. In addition, she initiated outreach to the people in the squatters' camps at the edge of Howick and in a very poor Zulu outstation where she arranged for teacher training, procured educational materials, initiated a feeding program, and organized Howick parishioners to build a small school. Today, Margaret O'Shea continues the work begun in Howick by Eileen Karrer and Judy Coyle, fostering religious education programs, preschools, outreach in squatters' camps, nutrition programs, and Guide/Scout groups that give destitute children a sense of belonging.

Annette St. Amour, immediately after her first visit to Mpophomeni Township in October 1985, began to study the Zulu language. For ten years, St. Amour and her pastoral teammate, Lawrence Dlungwane, worked together at St. Anne's and in six rural outstations. Eventually, St. Amour and other IHMs moved into a small house next to St. Anne Church. As tensions mounted in the country, living in the township gave St. Amour the opportunity to respond immediately to emergencies arising from violence. One of her last big contributions to Mpophomeni was establishing a preschool system by sending township women for training and having them use the church for classes. In 1996 St. Amour left Mpophomeni to assume responsibility for the catechetical program of the Archdiocese of Durban.

Because all the IHM missionaries were experienced teachers, it is not surprising that they responded to educational needs. Judy Coyle began teaching courses in liturgy at Cedara (now known as St. Joseph Theological Institute) in 1986, soon after arriving in South Africa. At the present time she and Susan Rakoczy are full-time faculty members, and Coyle is also a member of the administrative team. In addition to teaching seminarians, the two women have worked hard to initiate a program in theology for women. As Rakoczy pointed out in a written communication to the author, July 26, 1997, "[Our] work with the women at Cedara is extremely important since they are literally the future leaders of the church in their countries. . . . In teaching them [we] touch the future of Africa." A theological consultant to the Southern African Catholic Bishops' Conference, Rakoczy seized another opportunity to promote women's rights by editing a pamphlet decrying the evils of domestic violence. *Silent No Longer: The Church Responds to Sexual Violence*, an ecumenical project,[2] was published in English in June 2000 and is being translated into Zulu, Xhosa, and Afrikaans.

Mary Kinney and Joan Mumaw devoted themselves to promoting education for black students—discriminated against and neglected for decades. Under apartheid the greatest portion of funding for education went to schools for white students—ten times that for black students. Poverty-stricken and overcrowded areas restricted to black and coloured peoples received the lowest amount of educational funding, although they had the greatest number of students to educate and the least qualified teachers. These schools were housed in dilapidated buildings, very often without running water, toilets, or electricity—to say nothing of a

---

[2] *Silent No Longer: The Church Responds to Sexual Violence* was a joint publication of Lumko Institute, Pietermaritzburg Agency for Christian Social Awareness, National Justice and Peace Commission of Southern African Catholic Bishops' Conference (SACBC), and the Theological Advisory Commission of SACBC.

lack of books, paper, and other basic educational materials. In 1985, in an effort to address the inequities, the Southern African Catholic Bishops' Conference founded the Catholic Institute of Education (CIE). CIE was already making progress when the new multiracial South African government was elected in 1994. In 1995 Mary Kinney, an experienced teacher and educational adminis-trator, took charge of the CIE program in the Eastern Cape—one of the poorest areas in South Africa, with nine school districts and an enrollment of 500,000 students, many in extremely remote mountain areas.

Joan Mumaw joined the staff of the national office of CIE in 1996; her prin-cipal responsibility is the formidable task of raising funds through grants. By visiting CIE regional offices around the country, working with their teams, get-ting out to the rural schools, and talking with teachers eager for training, Mumaw keeps in touch with the overwhelming educational needs of the country. Pres-ently, Mumaw also represents CIE in the collaborative efforts of many organi-zations to deal with the pandemic of AIDS in South Africa.

The IHM missionaries in South Africa supported the struggle for racial jus-tice in that country and played an active role in the national election of 1994—the first time in 350 years that persons of every race were allowed to vote. IHM missionaries assisted in the electoral process by obtaining identity documents for people, providing voter education, and acting as official election monitors or observers. In an April 29, 1994, letter to friends, Eileen Karrer (an election monitor) described how, at 9:00 P.M. on the last day of voting in Howick, she found herself squashed in the front seat of a car between the presiding election officer and a South African policeman. As they traveled in a police-escorted con-voy to Pietermaritzburg to deliver the sealed ballot boxes, Karrer mused: "Here I am in South Africa, delivering ballots for the first democratic election in their history! How did a little girl from Roseville [Michigan] ever end up here?"

As in Latin America, IHM missionaries in Africa were willing and able to move and adapt in response to new needs. The fact that the IHM missions did not own institutions such as schools or clinics gave the missionaries the free-dom to move when they felt it was time to accept new invitations for service.

My own conclusion after many conversations with IHM missionaries from 1972 to 2000 is that they attribute their willingness and ability to adapt to new situations and new challenges to their personal integration of five elements—fidelity to prayer, a liberal arts education, multiple skills acquired as teachers, the discipline they internalized during their formation in religious life, and the experience of living together in community.

IHM RESPONSES TO GLOBAL NEEDS

The sending of IHM Sisters as overseas missionaries has not been the sole response of the IHM Congregation to global needs. Both individual IHMs and the IHM Congregation through its elected leaders have, over the years, demon-strated astute global consciousness and a willingness to share generously with people in other countries. The following are a few examples.

In 1972 Margaret Brennan, the IHM general superior, asked Mary Lou Theisen (missionary in Puerto Rico, 1954-57) to go to India for several months so that Mother Teresa of Calcutta could send members of her own community to Bangladesh to assist victims of a severe famine. In May 1974 Margaret Brennan herself visited Vietnam to find out how IHM Sisters might help with the thousands of orphans, many of whom had been fathered by American soldiers. Three IHMs were able to do so. In November 1974 Anne Wisda spent a month in Saigon with Friends of All the Children, helping to care for approximately five hundred infants and toddlers. Therese LeBlanc (missionary in Puerto Rico, 1973-75) and Nancy Ayotte arrived in Saigon on March 11, 1975, and were soon caught up in the frantic and chaotic evacuation of hundreds of orphans known as the baby-lift. With the staff of Friends of the Children of Vietnam, LeBlanc and Ayotte each made two trips from Saigon to San Francisco. LeBlanc was on the last baby-lift out of Saigon on April 27. The following day, Tan Son Nhut Airport was bombed. Saigon fell to the North Vietnamese on April 30.

By the summer of 1975 Therese LeBlanc was coordinating IHM volunteers at Fort Indiantown Gap, Pennsylvania, where the IHMs taught English and helped care for the fifteen thousand Vietnamese and Cambodian refugees awaiting resettlement in the United States. By the fall of 1975, IHM Sisters, particularly in the Archdiocese of Detroit (southeastern Michigan), were active in encouraging parish communities to adopt refugee families. Some IHMs worked full-time in refugee resettlement. The IHM Congregation at its motherhouse in Monroe, Michigan, sponsored and housed a Laotian family. Between 1976 and 1983 Anne Wisda found homes in southwestern Oklahoma for over eight thousand refugees from twenty-five ethnic groups. Wisda also went to refugee camps in Thailand, Korea, and the Philippines to create files for orphans and unaccompanied minors and to process individuals and families hoping to be admitted to the United States.

In the 1980s, as hundreds of Central American refugees fleeing El Salvador and Guatemala began arriving in Detroit with the hope of admission into Canada, the refugee shelter in Detroit requested help with housing. The IHM Congregation brought a Guatemalan family of eight into its motherhouse in April 1988. This was the first of fifty-two families (235 adults, teenagers, and children) from Latin America, Africa, the Middle East, Asia, and Eastern Europe who from 1988 to 2000 temporarily made their home with the IHM community. Muslims, Buddhists, Christians, and those of no religious affiliation felt welcomed, accepted, and loved by the more than one hundred "grandmother sisters" in the motherhouse community who taught them English, listened to their stories, prayed for them, and applauded the first steps of their little ones.

These and other responses to global needs, while not directly the work of the IHM Overseas Missions Province (the group of overseas missionaries within the IHM Congregation), illustrate the global consciousness and social commitment of the IHM Congregation as a whole and express the spirit out of which IHM sisters volunteered for overseas mission work over the past fifty years. Beginning with the opening of the mission in Brazil in 1965, all IHM overseas missionaries have been volunteers. This was generally true, also, from 1948 to 1965.

IHM OVERSEAS MISSION—A CORPORATE MINISTRY

From 1948 until 1969 the IHM central government coordinated overseas mission work. When, in the late 1960s, the IHM Congregation was reorganized into governmental subgroups called provinces, the overseas missionaries gradually formed a special group that, by 1976, was known as the Overseas Missions Province. Unlike most non-mission-sending religious congregations whose few overseas missionaries belong to different provinces, Monroe IHM overseas missionaries had the advantage of being united in one governmental unit. Mary Jo Maher, who talked with many women missionaries from 1972 to 2000, found that among those who were members of U.S. non-mission-sending religious congregations, those who were the only overseas missionary or among the few missionaries of their congregation generally experienced a sense of isolation and a lack of understanding and support for what they were doing.

The missionaries elected their own leaders, held their own assemblies, and had their own fund-raising program. The small number of missionaries helped to foster understanding and mutual trust between elected leaders and missionaries in the field. Small numbers also contributed to the active involvement of all members in major decisions (for example, establishing priorities, determining major policies, taking on new responsibilities, and so on). The best time and place to interact and to make these kinds of decisions was at the mission assembly held every two or three years.

One of the most important actions of the mission assemblies was to formulate or reaffirm the mission vision of the province. The introductory paragraph to the 1984 vision statement is quoted at the beginning of this article. The statement, which the missionaries continued to reaffirm, continues:

Called to participate in the Redeeming Mission of Jesus Christ and sustained by faith, prayer, and community life, we make a commitment
  • to insert ourselves into the life of the local people, the local culture, the local church;
  • to respond to the needs of the people in the light of mission priorities discerned with the local church and province leadership;
  • to build basic faith communities and the human community to work for a just world order and to foster recognition of our global interdependence;
  • to collaborate with individuals and groups who share our values of human dignity, justice, and peace;
  • to participate in a process of continual conversion in and through the Spirit of God;
in order that
  • people can assume power over their own lives and direct their own destiny;

- individuals and communities may grow in wholeness, integrity, and truth; and
- the Reign of God—a Reign of Liberation—may come more fully in our world.

The mission vision was a strong unifying element for the small number of missionaries dispersed across Africa and Latin America. Not only the vision statement but also the collaborative process of drafting the mission vision united and energized the group. The most important role of the province leadership was to keep that clear and compelling vision before the members and to relate everything to that vision. Isolated by distance, cultural milieu, and the poverty in which most of the IHM missionaries lived, it was essential to keep before them the *why* of what each mission community and each member was doing. From the mission vision, the province established mission priorities and drafted policies for the screening of volunteers, preparation for cross-cultural overseas ministry (for example, language study, acculturation, orientation), and accountability in establishing and implementing goals and objectives at the local level.

Leadership kept abreast of mission trends, searched out new needs, recruited new missionaries, provided personal support for the missionaries, and challenged them to evaluate their life and ministry in the light of the mission vision. But the leadership style was definitely collaborative. The provincial superior respected the experience and judgment of the missionaries at the local level. In the various countries it was usually the missionaries who decided when it was time to "move on," what new ministries ought to be undertaken, and which missionaries should form a mission community. Collaborative decisions were particularly evident at times of crisis (for example, Uganda in 1972-81, Honduras in 1975, Zimbabwe in 1988). The 1975 Honduras crisis and the crisis in Uganda in the 1970s are explained in this article. In Zimbabwe, on April 19, 1988, the neighboring mission to Embakwe was attacked. A brother was killed, a priest badly beaten, and the mission looted. The identities of the attackers were never verified, but after the government granted amnesty to all the rebels in Matabeleland, no other attacks occurred. In each instance, leadership and the local community, after careful assessment of the situation, made a collaborative decision in regard to remaining or withdrawing from a country. In each instance, IHM missionaries took extra precautions for safety, but they never withdrew from a country because of violence and attacks on other missionaries.

IHM missionaries were very aware of current social, economic, and political developments in their respective countries. Social analysis and theological reflection were part of the preparation for their mission assemblies. In the 1980s, when the IHM Congregation adopted a process authorizing elected leaders to speak publicly on behalf of the members regarding justice and human rights issues, the Overseas Missions Province unanimously passed four corporate stances (1) criticizing the U.S. militarization of Puerto Rico, (2) denouncing U.S. policies and actions in Central America, (3) supporting the sanctuary movement that gave asylum to Central American refugees, and (4) pledging to work for racial justice in South Africa. Beginning in 1984 the Province had a full-time coordinator of global/mission awareness. In this role Anne Wisda gave hundreds of presentations on justice issues, became an active member of justice/human rights/ solidarity organizations, and was an official observer of the 1990 Nicaraguan election and, with Joan Mumaw, an official observer in the 1995 Haiti elections.

IHM overseas missionaries were not individuals "doing their own thing." Each missionary was respected as a gifted, educated, prepared, and committed member of a group united in faith, motivation, and purpose. This explains to a great degree why they were able to accomplish so much in such a variety of cultures, conditions, and circumstances. It may also explain why two IHM missionaries were able to play such an active role in the preparation of others for overseas mission life and in the reintegration of missionaries to their own country/culture in a way that made their experience a positive influence on the U.S. church. Kathryn Pierce (missionary in Puerto Rico, 1963-76) has been director of the Maryknoll Cross-Cultural Training Center since 1979. Patricia McCluskey (missionary in Puerto Rico, 1968-71, and in Brazil, 1971-83) was national coordinator of the Federation of Returned Overseas Missioners (FROM) from 1985 to 1995. FROM's overarching goal is to help permanently returning missionaries integrate their experience, adjust to life in their own country, and share the richness of their cross-cultural experience through ministry in North America.

On July 19, 1998, at a special eucharistic celebration, the Monroe IHM Sisters gave thanks for fifty years in overseas missions. As the long line of missionaries and former missionaries—five of them in wheelchairs—came down the middle aisle of the motherhouse chapel, the congregation was swept by a wave of enthusiasm. The joyful singing of the processional hymn concluded with thunderous applause. In turn, the missionaries expressed their own deep gratitude for the privilege and gift of being in the overseas missions. The transforming experience of mission was captured by Ann Aseltyne (missionary in Ghana, South Africa, and Uganda): "From the extreme heat and desert-like land of Ghana with its hungry poor sheltered in straw-roofed huts to the beautiful hills, valleys, trees, and biting cold of South Africa that eats into the very bones of those huddled in cardboard boxes, my view of life has been flung upside down in terms of what the world and its people are really like."

11

"On Planting Dates"

The Consequences of Missionary Activity
on U.S.-Based Franciscan Sisterhoods (1960-2000)

Margaret Eletta Guider, OSF

It is time to stop planting pumpkins.
Let us plant dates,
even though those who plant them will never eat them ...
We must live by the love of what we will never see.
This is the secret discipline.
—Rubem A. Alves, Tomorrow's Child

    Since the early thirteenth century the missionary charism of Francis of Assisi (1182-1226) and the "date seeds" of his original inspiration have germinated throughout the world. Although some of his followers are known to have planted pumpkins along the way, the witness of those responsible for planting and cultivating date trees, the fruits of which they would never see, remains a constant source of inspiration. Their example is an enduring testimony to Francis's exhortation *to live the gospel life, to preach the good news of Jesus Christ by example, and, if necessary, to use words.* This essay is about some contemporary Franciscan women who continue to carry on this evangelical tradition and the historical circumstances that enabled them to better understand the *secret discipline* of living by the love of what they might never live to see.

    In 1959 the Vatican made an appeal to religious congregations in Europe and North America. The appeal came in the form of a request to send missionaries to serve the church in Latin America (Costello 1979; Dries 1998, 179-246). Many Franciscan sisterhoods based in the United States responded to this call to mission. Some of these congregations began new missionary ventures in Brazil, while others intensified their commitment of personnel and resources to Brazilian missions that had been established in previous decades. These congregations fall into three categories, those of United States origin, those of European origin, and one of Brazilian origin. The listing includes the name of the congregation, the year of its foundation in the United States and if relevant the year of its original foundation in Europe or Brazil (see Slowick 1999). For most of these congregations, the desire and decision to "plant dates" in Brazil proved to be a defining moment that would shape and in many cases change the course of their respective histories and legacies. The following study is an analysis of the evolution of this missionary venture and its consequences.

ON CHARTING THE GROWTH OF THE DATE TREES

In an effort to gain insight into the missionary activity of the Franciscan sisterhoods identified in this study, I propose an evolutionary approach to analysis that focuses on events, trends, and developments while attending to the interactive dynamics of social relationships, adapting the methodology of Hilgartner and Bosk (1988, 53-78). Although technically speaking, this method is taken from the field of social psychology, it is useful in studying social history as well. The process of analysis involves the identification and examination of six stages of development, while acknowledging that, though all stage theories have inherent limitations, they also have advantages and benefits. When it comes to tracing the ebb and flow of interests, concerns, and commitments, such theories make it possible to conceptualize and categorize a great deal of material in a clear, concise, and coherent manner. The stages and periodization are outlined in Table 1.

Table 1
Staging Trends and Developments in Missionary Activity and Missionary Identity among U.S.-based Franciscan Congregations

Stage 0	Baseline	Prior to 1960
Stage 1	Incipiency	1960-1974
Stage 2	Coalescence	1975-1984
Stage 3	Institutionalization	1985-1994
Stage 4	Fragmentation	1995-
Stage 5	Demise	????

STAGE ZERO: BASELINE
The Delineation of Identities and the Reality
of Franciscan Sisterhoods before 1960

Prior to 1960 involvement in foreign missionary activity and an explicit missionary identity were generally speaking the reserve of missionary-sending societies as well as some international religious orders and congregations. To the extent that a number of Franciscan sisterhoods based in the United States were usually not identified as missionary or international, they tended not to have a highly developed missionary identity or international profile. In effect, most national Franciscan sisterhoods reflected the assumptions and attitudes of a pre–Vatican II ecclesiology, missiology, and spirituality. The missionary vocation was understood to be a special vocation. Though it was grounded in the general baptismal call to Christian witness and service, it was given added value. The missionary vocation was usually lived out within the context of a missionary congregation or a mission society committed to spreading the gospel message to non-Christians and nonbelievers. For the most part the needs of overseas missions, especially with regard to personnel, made few direct claims on national congregations or their members. Neither the call nor a commitment to foreign missionary service disturbed the equilibrium of these congregations. Generally speaking, a Franciscan *missionary* identity was rarely acknowledged, appropriated, or advanced.

In the years immediately preceding the Second Vatican Council (1962-65), Franciscan congregations of women were national, international, or missionary. In terms of lifestyle and orientation, congregations were either active and apostolic *or* contemplative and monastic. Vocational discernment was linked to sources of inspiration, experiences of call, spiritual inclinations, and ministerial interests. Among the active congregations, most were associated with specific apostolates such as teaching, nursing, or social work *in the world*. Lives of enclosure, prayer, and penance set contemplative congregations *apart from the world*.

International identity or *internationality* consisted in belonging to a congregation made up of women from various cultures in various regions of the world, without the expectation of necessarily having to leave one's own country except for reasons of education and/or religious formation. Most international congregations were based in Europe. Ordinarily, a particular cultural ethos and a normative language pervaded the social and religious customs of these congregations.

For many congregations internationality was the twentieth-century consequence of nineteenth-century missionary outreach, much of which was linked to the accompaniment of European emigrants or a religious extension of colonial expansion. The determining factor that distinguished international congregations was the tendency to reproduce and generalize their particular apostolates in different cultural contexts. The crucial task entrusted to them was keeping Roman Catholics faithful to the church and its teachings, especially in circumstances where faith, morals, and Roman Catholic identity were subjected to scrutiny, attack, and ridicule. Although participation in cross-cultural mission to non-Christians was seen as a value, and visibly upheld by the occasional assignment of specially selected sisters to non-Christian areas, such activity was not perceived to be *the* primary calling of the congregation.

Missionary identity, on the other hand, was founded upon a well-defined commitment to convert non-Christians to Christianity, to actively accompany non-Westerners who were new in the faith, and/or to be an active Christian presence in contexts hostile to Christian proselytizing. Some missionary congregations were international. Their members included sisters from several nations. Others were national in the sense that their members were from one country alone.

U.S.-based congregations with *national identities* emerged as committed Roman Catholic women endeavored to respond to the pastoral, educational, and social welfare needs of people throughout the United States, and frequently in designated regions or states. Sometimes identified by their immigrant roots or ethnic descent, national congregations took pride in their independence and self-governance without foreign intervention. Their apostolic commitment to serve the church locally, regionally, and nationally was intentional and meaningful. Some national congregations began as offshoots or splinter groups from international, missionary, or other national congregations. Some came into existence with the assistance of a few sisters from other congregations who agreed to help form a new congregation until such time as their assistance was no longer needed. Other congregations came into existence through the charismatic leadership of one or more committed women who had the moral support of a priest or bishop and the resources to finance their vision.

Historically speaking, a number of Franciscan sisterhoods were truly *national* congregations, while others simply functioned as such given their relative lack of connectedness with their sisters in Europe, Asia, Oceania, or the Caribbean. In the light of this study, however, the potential problem of coupling a *national* identity with a *congregational* identity should not be overlooked or underestimated.

STAGE ONE: INCIPIENCY (1960-1974)
U.S. Sisters from National Congregations
and the Unsettling Search for a Missionary Identity

This period was marked by the presence of an *emergent missionary identity* among national and international Franciscan sisterhoods, which carried with it a heightened awareness of missionary identity as a potentially positive yet destabilizing force in terms of congregational equilibrium. Religious congregations and their leaders were invited, coerced, or persuaded by individuals, groups, or institutions from within the church or the broader society to recognize that congregations had something to lose if they failed to acknowledge the ways in which the emergence of a missionary identity could alter the status quo. Congregations began to experiment with some aspects of missionary identity in limited and informal ways, ordinarily in the sphere of private negotiations or individual actions.

The 1959 Vatican request to women's congregations in the United States to send personnel to Latin America was a major turning point for religious sisters in general and Franciscan sisters in particular. Inasmuch as this invitation was issued prior to the Second Vatican Council, narrow understandings of Christian mission and missionary activity were informed by an *ad gentes* model of mission, which focused on outreach to people to who knew little or nothing about the gospel of Jesus Christ. Although Franciscan sisters from international and missionary congregations often had more experience dealing with the practical challenges and physical rigors of cross-cultural encounters than sisters from national congregations, there are some ways in which the sisters overall tended to be more like each other than different. As citizens of the United States, American cultural values and national ideals had shaped them. Yet, as Roman Catholic missionary sisters, their engagement with a larger world caused them to perceive and interpret reality somewhat differently from other Americans as well as other Roman Catholics.

Regardless of their respective Franciscan congregations of origin, United States sisters venturing into Brazil on their first missionary experience were often inspired by images from works such as *A Day in the Life of Sister Bernie,* the story of a Maryknoll missionary sister. Heroine of many Catholic schoolgirls, the *ideal* American missionary sister possessed the courage of an Amelia Earhart, the natural beauty of a Katharine Hepburn, the leadership abilities of an Eleanor Roosevelt, and the spiritual convictions of a Dorothy Day. She put her hand to the plow and never looked back.

As might be expected, sisters from national congregations were unaccustomed to the glory and the burden of such characterizations, having come into their missionary identities as much by chance as by grace. Unlike their counterparts from international or missionary congregations, Franciscan sisters from national congregations experienced the limitations of having a religious formation that was neither missionary nor international in orientation. Awareness of such limitations was unsettling at many levels: political, cultural, ecclesial, congregational, and personal.

For a number of sisters the initial experience of being forced to come to terms with the inadequacies of their preparation for missionary activity took place at the Center for Intercultural Formation (CENFI). During the 1960s through the mid-1970s, CENFI was the Brazilian point of entry for many Franciscan sisters from the United States. It was the Brazilian equivalent to the better-known center for Latin American missionary formation in Cuernavaca, Mexico, associated and identified with the work of Ivan Illich (see Illich 1970). Initially located in the city of Petrópolis, the center moved to Rio de Janeiro and eventually relocated to Brasília. The purpose of the institute was to prepare foreign missionaries culturally and linguistically for ministry in Brazil. Instructors included socially conscious and politically active Brazilians, a number of whom were university students. Committed to the struggle for democracy and social justice, these teachers were adept at raising the consciousness of foreign missionaries, especially those from the United States. The experience at CENFI, in addition to providing sisters with the language skills necessary for mission, served as a catalyst for critical thinking about the socio-political and economic underpinnings of their missionary activity, the Brazilian reality, U.S. foreign policy in Brazil, and its support for the right-wing military forces. Predating the clear articulation of liberation theology and the anti-imperialist, anti-colonialist critique of Christian missionary activity, CENFI laid the foundation in the hearts and minds of many for what would later emerge as a "preferential option for the poor" and a faith that does justice.

For many sisters, especially those from national congregations, the process of acquiring a new kind of ecclesial and political consciousness was not an easy one. No sooner had they taken on a missionary identity than the very identity itself was called into question! No sooner had they left the United States, many

162   *Margaret Eletta Guider, OSF*

for the first time, than they discovered the degree to which their own government was implicated in the military coup of 1964, the establishment of a national security state, and the torturous years of repression that followed. Sisters were ill prepared to recognize the shadow side of the United States' involvement in the socio-political and economic affairs of the Brazilian military dictatorship. The few who dared to confront this reality frequently paid a high price for their *conscientizicão*, often among their own sisters.

As efforts intensified to implement the documents of Vatican II, particularly *Lumen Gentium* (*Dogmatic Constitution on the Church*, 1964), *Gaudium et Spes* (*Pastoral Constitution on the Church in the Modern World,* 1965), *Ad Gentes* (*Decree on the Church's Missionary Activity,* 1965) and *Perfectae Caritatis* (*Decree on the Renewal of Religious Life*, 1965) as well as the 1968 CELAM documents of Medellín, the sisters found themselves not only in a world reality they did not understand but in an ecclesial reality where expectations and orientations changed radically and rapidly. Suddenly, everyone was called to be missionary, religious were no longer special, and solidarity with the poor emerged as a constitutive part of evangelization. These dramatic shifts in consciousness demanded a radicality and a resiliency that left many sisters divided among themselves and within themselves.

Endeavoring to establish themselves in mission or expand already existing commitments in rural and urban areas throughout Brazil, many U.S. sisters from Franciscan congregations were taken by surprise as young Brazilian women readily presented themselves, not only as eager collaborators in ministry, but as aspirants and candidates for religious life. Although the formation of young Brazilian women for religious life was part of the raison d'être for U.S. sisters going to Brazil, few congregations anticipated that they would be facing the challenges that this proposal posed so soon after arriving in the country. Many U.S. sisters from national congregations were at a loss for knowing exactly where and how to begin the process of religious formation in a culture other than their own *and* at a period when religious life itself was undergoing an unprecedented renewal. Having limited points of reference in terms of the policies and procedures used by international or missionary congregations, sisters from national congregations often found themselves with no alternative other than that of attuning themselves to the wisdom of a familiar Brazilian proverb: They had to make the road by walking.

Negotiating the personal changes brought about by political consciousness, cultural adaptation, and the renewal of religious life was more than a rocky road for U.S. sisters and the young Brazilian women who desired to join them. For some, it proved to be a labyrinth of dead ends, which involved a constant retracing of steps and backtracking in order to find the unobstructed road to their destination. Deciding whether or not to establish new Brazilian congregations or to incorporate Brazilian women into already existing U.S. congregations was only the beginning of a much larger discernment. Although most congregations sought out the counsel and advice of more experienced missionary and international congregations, some U.S. sisters found the suggested criteria and discernment practices to be at odds with their own intuitions, contrary to the spirit of the times, and out of step with their respective congregational charisms. In a number of cases these U.S. sisters in Brazil became advocates, sponsors, and risk-takers on behalf of the young Brazilian women who appeared rather spontaneously and often without recruitment. The decision to receive young Brazilians into U.S.-based congregations was the first step in practicing the *secret discipline* and coming to terms with the process of being transformed *by* mission and *for* mission.

STAGE TWO: COALESCENCE (1975-1984)
Creating the Conditions for New Ways of Being in Mission

This period was characterized by the presence of an emerging missionary identity and the presence of organized congregational efforts to contain the challenges and problems associated with missionary activity. Indeed, the emergence of a more prominent missionary identity succeeded in upsetting the equilibrium of U.S.-based congregations. Many congregations found it necessary to suppress, contain, regulate, or redirect the dynamics of the missionary impulse. Attempts to influence or restrict the actions of those entrusted with the responsibility of carrying out, promoting, or facilitating missionary ventures were in evidence. Congregations admonished those who seemed to go too far and called for obedience from those acting outside the acceptable limits set by a congregation that was experiencing the growth pains of being transformed by mission.

Beginning the Transition from Being a Missionary Community in Brazil to an Intercultural Community in Mission

In U.S.-based congregations of Franciscan sisters with so-called missions in Brazil, growing concerns about the missionary commitments of expatriate sisters as well as the full incorporation of Brazilian sisters led to intense questioning about the advisability of assigning new North American sisters to Brazil and the criteria for accepting young Brazilian women as new members. At issue were heightened uncertainties about the feasibility and probability of long-term commitments, candidate suitability, and ultimately, congregational unity in terms of identity, vision, and mission.

The desire for a permanent core community of U.S. sisters was an appeal expressed by U.S. and Brazilian sisters in Brazil. Though not a preoccupation of all congregations, this initiative was directly related to another critical concern, namely, hesitation about receiving any more sisters from the United States given the long-term effects of affective exhaustion on the part of the local communities and individual sisters who regularly received newly arrived U.S. missionaries. Cultural adaptation, language acquisition, ongoing formation, and building bonds of interpersonal confidence were continuous challenges. Constant change, frequent transitions, and the predictable return of many missionary sisters to the United States took a toll on the well-being of all involved.

In line with standard missionary practice during the mid 1970s through the early 1980s, a relative moratorium was placed on encouraging, recruiting, or supporting U.S. sisters interested in going to Brazil. Inasmuch as this decision coincided with a generalized decline in vocations to Franciscan sisterhoods within the United States, it was largely uncontested. For the most part the era of the *missionary sister* from national Franciscan congregations came to a rather swift and definitive conclusion. Those U.S. sisters living in Brazil, including many of the first missionaries, were asked to declare where they stood on the subject of making a permanent commitment in Brazil. Unlike sisters from missionary congregations, whose aim was to make themselves obsolete, or sisters from international congregations who moved in and out of countries as a matter of practice, the future of U.S. sisters in Brazilian foundations established by U.S. national congregations took a different turn. The missionary sisters of U.S. origin who remained in Brazil intensified their commitment to their Brazilian sisters and the Brazilian people. They became more identified with the Brazilian reality than that of the United States, a few to the point of becoming Brazilian citizens. As for the Brazilian sisters who were formed in the respective charisms of these U.S.-based congregations, it was not yet clear what such incorporation would or could mean over time. It was evident, however, that more awaited them in the future than anyone in 1960 could have asked for or imagined.

Paradoxically, the missionary endeavor that began as a consequence of the Vatican's appeal to strengthen the church in Latin America underwent an unanticipated metamorphosis that forty years later began to disclose its potential for strengthening the church in North America and elsewhere in the world. Though foundations in Brazil became more consciously Brazilian, they remained completely *identified with* and *connected to* their respective congregations in the United States. Secessions or break-offs were few and far between. Though issues regarding autonomy, subsidiarity, and inculturation would require ongoing reflection, discernment, and deliberation, that which began as a unilateral missionary venture evolved into an intercultural commitment to embrace the challenge of the Franciscan missionary charism in the twenty-first century.

Rethinking the Meaning of Mission in Brazil

From the mid-1970s through the early 1980s the Brazilian Centro de Estudos Franciscanos e Pastorais de America Latina, more commonly known as CEFEPAL, proved to be an organizing principle around which Franciscans throughout Brazil were introduced to the Franciscan sources as well as liberating ways of doing theology and being present in ministry. Among the most widely known members of the permanent faculty was Leonardo Boff. The interactive forces of the Franciscan tradition, its various forms, and Brazilian liberation theology proved to be dynamic sources of inspiration for uniting and animating Franciscans in general and Franciscan sisters in particular. Although the importance of regional differences, national identities, and cultural particularities was never minimized, there was a way in which Franciscans from Brazil and Franciscan missionaries from around the world serving in Brazil were united in the process of being and becoming Franciscans in mission. Formed in the

Franciscan spiritual tradition and oriented by a preferential option for the poor, generations of Franciscans were touched directly and indirectly by CEFEPAL's transformative ethos, the global significance of which has yet to be fully assessed in terms of scope and influence.

For Franciscan sisters in Brazil, identification with and participation in the larger Franciscan family dissolved the categories that once served to differentiate national, international, and missionary congregations. In terms of Franciscan life and practice, such categories ceased to be of any real significance as interest in discovering and recovering the Franciscan missionary charism was shared by all.

In addition to the broad influence of CEFEPAL, which eventually began to touch U.S-based congregations of Franciscan sisters through the contributions of their sisters in Brazil, the Franciscan Federation of the United States, like CEFEPAL in Brazil, engaged Franciscan sisters in the United States in a series of reflections on the Third Order Rule (1982) and its significance for Franciscan sisterhoods throughout the world. Enthusiasm and interest in Franciscan identity and mission were further galvanized by international celebrations of the eight-hundredth anniversary of the birth of Francis of Assisi in 1982. This enthusiasm was most clearly manifested at the Inter-Franciscan Congress held in Mattli, Switzerland, an event that proved to be a genuine catalyst for the Franciscan missionary charism for and from the entire world (see Boff and Bühlmann 1984, 215-24).

All of this served to reinforce the encouragement given to religious congregations in the wake of Vatican II to return to their roots and recover the original inspiration of their respective founders and foundresses. Congregations of women were invited by the church to reinvest in their futures on the basis of the legacy entrusted to them by previous generations of sisters. In the process, most of the Franciscan congregations considered in this study rediscovered that many of their respective foundresses were nineteenth-century and early twentieth-century missionaries and immigrants to the United States. Although most of these women were not members of missionary congregations per se, they were heirs of the nineteenth-century missionary impulse. Often collaborating with friars, priests, and bishops who were missionaries, they left their own lands to become agents of evangelization in North America. Identifying with the missionary zeal of nineteenth-century foremothers, congregations began to look at their histories and legacies through the lens of mission. Grafted on to the tree of the Franciscan family, they tapped into a common root that grounded them all in the evangelical vision of Francis and Clare.

STAGE THREE: INSTITUTIONALIZATION (1985-1994)
Embracing the Franciscan Missionary Charism

This stage was marked by the presence of a missionary identity, the actual upset of congregational equilibrium, and organized congregational efforts to deal with the challenges posed by mission. There was a heightened realization on the part of some members that these challenges were not only congregational

concerns with internal ramifications but social and ecclesial concerns with global implications. The Franciscan missionary identity was not a random ecclesial
or social phenomenon. It had a rationalization that found grounding and support
in identification with Franciscans internationally.

Franciscan Sisterhoods and the Challenges of the Correspondence Course on the Franciscan Missionary Charism

Shortly following the Mattli Congress in 1982 a German Franciscan friar,
Andreas Mueller, in the company of internationally recognized Franciscan theologians and missiologists from around the world, became a leading proponent
of a vision for an international program for Franciscan missionary formation.
Mueller was conscious of the many challenges that the world and the world
church placed before the Franciscan family. Under his direction Missionszentrale
der Franziskaner in Bonn, Germany, an entity with longstanding connections to
CEFEPAL/Brasil, set the idea of a correspondence course in motion. Building
on the Franciscan momentum of previous years, along with a growing interest
in deepening an understanding of Franciscan approaches to Christian mission
on the part of Franciscans, especially in Asia, Africa, and Latin America, a plan
of action was put in place. This plan involved the design and development of a
twenty-six chapter correspondence course on the Franciscan missionary charism,
translated into more than eleven languages, covering every theme in contemporary world mission studies (see *Build with Living Stones* 1989). Twenty-six
international contributors wrote chapters focused on their respective areas of
expertise. An editorial committee revised the chapters to achieve a certain balance, consistency, and clarity. Each continent and specific country had representatives training and debriefing mentors for the course. Enthusiasm for the
course was broad-based. It gradually became a formative piece of common instruction and reflection in the lives of Franciscan sisters regardless of age, education, or location.

As a consequence, Franciscan sisterhoods in Brazil and the United States
entered into a collective and shared process of intensifying their Franciscan
missionary identity and their commitment to the promotion of peace, justice,
and reconciliation. Since the self-regulated moratorium on mission that had taken
place during the late 1970s and early 1980s, little reflection had been devoted to
the subjects of missionary activity or missionary consciousness in the United
States. Participation in the Correspondence Course on the Franciscan Missionary Charism (CCFMC) changed perceptions and called into question prevalent
assumptions about mission. The convergence of a deeper understanding of their
Franciscan identity along with a genuine willingness to probe a new and renewed understanding of Christian mission resulted in an unprecedented dialogue within and across cultural contexts. The questions raised through the course
were critical ones. No one walked away from the course unchanged, and there
was some aspect of the course that managed to unsettle everyone in some way.

More than anything else, the CCFMC opened up discussions in Brazil as well as in the United States about patterns of human interaction that were undermining the effective preaching and proclamation of the gospel message. Embracing a Franciscan missionary identity uncritically was not possible. Facing the legacy of oppression based on race, ethnicity, class, gender, age, ability, and religion was no easier in Brazil than it was in the United States. Working within the structures of the institutional church was no less a source of anxiety, anger, frustration, and disillusionment in the United States than in Brazil. Although the Brazilian reality was significantly different from that of the United States, there were common themes that proved to be a common ground for dialogue despite obvious and subtle differences.

The ongoing process of being transformed for mission revealed new challenges to Franciscan congregations with sisters in Brazil and the United States. One of the most important was that of beginning to negotiate authentic relationships of interdependency, a challenge that was predicated on recognizing, valuing, and assuming an intercultural identity. While membership in the larger Franciscan family had served as an arena for mutual sharing and coming together in surprising and unexpected ways, the challenges of creating congregational bonds among and between sisters in Brazil and sisters in the United States were key to ensuring a common future. Generally speaking, there was no lack of good will or desire on the part of sisters to face these challenges, but they involved overcoming both anticipated and unforeseen obstacles in terms of communication, location, and viability.

Unlike European-based sisterhoods, which required competence in their home language, the U.S.-based sisterhoods tended to refrain from demanding competency in English as part of the formation of Brazilian sisters. This decision, while made with the best of intentions in the 1960s and 1970s, had its eventual downside in the 1980s and 1990s. U.S. sisters who had been in Brazil and Brazilian sisters who had lived for a time in the United States could serve as interlocutors, but not to the extent that the exigencies of intercultural communication demanded. They were simply too few in numbers, and under the best of circumstances communicating through a translator is less than ideal.

Among other important opportunities for encounter, such as short-term immersion experiences and longer-term visitations, the broad-based participation of Brazilian and U.S. sisters at general chapters, provincial chapters, and congregational assemblies held in the United States and Brazil provided countless possibilities and challenges for those responsible for moving intercultural communication out of the realm of theory and into the realm of genuine relationships. The election of Brazilian sisters to positions of congregational leadership at the level of general and regional administration signaled a coming of age marked by reciprocity, mutuality, and interdependence. Ultimately, all of these experiences created and contributed to a desire on the part of sisters throughout these congregations to know more about another culture, to learn another language, and to sustain relationships over time. As efforts to enhance

communication through translations and technology began to bridge the existing gaps in language and long-distance communication, access and availability
of transportation facilitated more frequent personal encounters.

As a consequence of collective reflection on Franciscan sisterhood and the
Franciscan missionary charism, the emergence of an intercultural identity enabled sisters from the contexts of Brazil and the United States to participate in
one another's lives and ministry in ways that would have been unimaginable in
previous years. All of this was the good news, but it was not the only news.

STAGE FOUR: FRAGMENTATION (1995-)
A Certain Hope, an Uncertain Future

This stage continues to be marked by the presence of a *Franciscan* missionary identity, the accommodation or resistance on the part of a congregation to
ongoing upsets to its equilibrium, contradictory or disorganized congregational
efforts to cope with the demands of its missionary charism, and the identification of the congregation as complicit in the weakening of or indifference toward
missionary identity. In this stage there is recognition that the weakening of or
indifference toward missionary identity may be symptomatic of a far larger
congregational problem. Admission of this awareness causes a shift in consciousness that directs or diverts the attention of the congregation from *mission*
to *viability*.

During the 1990s the demographics of Franciscan sisterhoods in the United
States proved to be cause for concern. A sense of insecurity about the future
arose. Preoccupation with viability consumed inordinate amounts of energy.
Strategic planning dealt more with issues of survival than mission. The decline
in numbers and, in some congregations, the absence of younger U.S. members
was disheartening and unsettling for many. A bird's-eye view of reality across
congregations revealed that the majority of sisters living in the United States
were over sixty-five; most, in some cases all, sisters under forty-five lived in
Brazil. Although numbers are never the whole story, demographic realities cannot be dismissed or ignored altogether.

In addition to concerns related to membership, one of the most serious issues
facing Franciscan congregations with sisters in the United States and Brazil
relates to the need for leaders who are good stewards and good animators, and
individuals capable of embodying and fostering intercultural consciousness and
relationships of interdependency. Until recent years Brazilian sisters primarily
served in congregational leadership positions in Brazil. By the mid-1990s the
possibility of Brazilian sisters being called forth to serve the leadership needs of
the entire congregation was no longer a theoretical proposition but a real development in the central administrations of U.S.-based congregations. By the late
1990s the possibility of Brazilian sisters leaving Brazil to serve the pastoral
needs of Brazilian immigrants in various regions of the world, including the
United States, as well as undertaking missionary commitments in Africa, Eastern Europe, and the Caribbean was a reality.

On the one hand, these facts are a cause for celebration, gratitude, and wonder. On the other hand, one cannot lose sight of another fact: at the same time that U.S.-based congregations are most dependent on their own members to meet internal and institutional needs, the postmodern world and the world church are making unprecedented claims on those who have embraced the Franciscan missionary charism. And so the unavoidable question must be raised: For what end do we plant date trees? Negotiating the criteria for discerning participation in the *missio Dei* is a complex and often controversial undertaking. It requires courage and creativity as well as a tenacity and tenderness that is undaunted by the fragmenting power of despair and fear.

As leaders and as members of congregations that are currently U.S.-based, Brazilian sisters have and are discovering their own answers to the question: To what end? Eager to follow the example of their pioneering nineteenth-century foundresses and their twentieth-century missionary sisters, there is a sense that one of their answers is *to give others a reason for daring to plant again.* For at least a few Brazilian sisters, the missionary impulse is alive and well and residing in their hearts. They are eager to respond to an altogether new call to mission in Asia, Eastern Europe, the Caribbean, Africa, the United States, or other regions of Latin America. Although some sisters in Brazil as well as the United States hesitate to support initiatives, ostensibly because there are so many needs in Brazil, Brazilian sisters are quick to underscore the fact that there were plenty of needs in the United States in 1962, but that did not prevent U.S. sisters from responding to the call to mission in Brazil.

Among the choices facing Franciscan congregations discussed in this study, the decision to find ways of providing the infrastructure needed to create a future for mission in the twenty-first century is a compelling one and may be the measure of their hope. I would argue further that viability in the twenty-first century is dependent upon the flourishing of interdependent and intercultural relationships expressed in and through mission. If there is one insight in this study worth remembering, it is this: viability is a consequence of mission, not a criterion.

For congregations willing and capable of holding fast to a certain hope despite an uncertain future, the question of what will happen to sisters in Brazil should the congregations in the United States undergo an irreversible diminishment and decline is all too real. However, among those sisters invested in creating a sustainable future for mission, it is reasonable to anticipate that once again this is a way that can only be made by walking.

STAGE FIVE: DEMISE?

This stage is marked by a diminishment in missionary identity, a concentrated congregational effort to regain equilibrium through strategies of maintenance, and the collapse of congregational efforts to support missionary efforts. In effect, missionary identity and activity fall out of congregational consciousness. The Franciscan missionary charism becomes invisible once again.

In studying the future of religious life some analysts suggest that the large number of vocations in other regions of the world is a recapitulation of what happened in the United States and Europe in previous decades of the nineteenth and twentieth centuries. They predict that in the near future numbers will decline in places like Brazil and that these trends are already in evidence. Noting changes in women's status in society as one possible reason for such decline, other reasons also are proposed, such as the breakdown in community life, a diminished or diffuse sense of mission, and a diluted spirituality. If these theories prove to be true, it seems reasonable to conclude that congregations made up of U.S. and Brazilian sisters who are unable to extend themselves in mission will cease to grow and ultimately to exist. This is no congregation's preferred scenario, yet it may be the inevitable end for some.

CONCLUSION

The main objective of this essay has been to identify some of the ways in which the *missionary activity* of a few sisters contributed to the emergence, development, and reappropriation of a Franciscan *missionary identity* among many sisters, thereby laying the groundwork for the transformation of a number of U.S.-based Franciscan sisterhoods *by* mission, *in* mission, and *for* mission. Admittedly, the observations made in this essay are tentative and, at best, an initial attempt to trace some important aspects and consequences of a significant though little known chapter in the twentieth-century history of women and mission.

To the best of my knowledge a study of the consequences and implications of U.S. missionary activity in Brazil has not been done in any systematic way within or among Franciscan congregations of women identified in this study. I believe that until now the failure to do so has resulted in three lost opportunities for critical reflection. The first has to do with understanding the centrality, indispensability, and exigencies of intercultural relationships for mission in the twenty-first century. The second has to do with acknowledging that participation in the *missio Dei* is an enduring evangelical imperative for Franciscan sisterhoods. The third has to do with rediscovering the *secret discipline* of planting dates and daring to live by the love of what one might never see.

12

From the Inside Out

Gender Ideologies and Christian Mission in Indonesia

Frances S. Adeney

In 1991, when I went to Indonesia to work with a graduate program in religion and society at a Christian university, I believed that practicing and teaching gender equality were part of my task, both as a university professor and as a Presbyterian Mission Co-worker. That conviction was supported by the university, which encouraged women students in its graduate program. It was also supported, albeit ambivalently, by a government that had declared women's political and economic equality in 1948 when the nation began.

I included in my courses a study of women and gender issues, the social contexts affecting those issues, and the interaction of religious ethics and gender. I saw Indonesia as a society in the midst of a transition from traditional gender ideologies to a society of gender equality. That transition affects the Christian church as well as indigenous cultures and people of other religions, particularly Islam, the predominant religion of Indonesia. A decade later I have not lost the excitement engendered by those ideas, but my method of going about the practice and teaching of gender equality while working in another culture has changed.

To the Western mind, Indonesia is a many-layered puzzle. Addressing Christian mission and women in Indonesia begins, first, with attempting to understand that puzzle. Only when traditional approaches to gender and their influence on modern Indonesian women are understood can one begin to see how progress toward gender equality can be fostered by persons like myself, who come into Indonesian society to participate in university and church communities.

Indonesia presents many faces to the world. Westerners know it as a tropical paradise of exotic cultures. At the same time, Indonesia shows the world the face of economic instability. Political turmoil and change in government also color the economic decline of the country. Indonesia has other faces that Westerners rarely see. It is a society that prizes equilibrium of mind, loyalty in the family, and harmony in society. Values like the importance of appearances in the struggle for inner and outer calm, the centrality of gift giving and receiving to maintain social relations, and the role of the community in life passage events are often hidden from foreign eyes. Conflicts among those values, and between those and more individualistic Western ones, produce both art and protest as Indonesians struggle with ambivalence toward the West. Indonesia can seem at once tranquil and violent, progressive and anti-modern, at once accepting and rejecting of gender equality.

METHOD: INSIDE-OUT APPROACH

An analysis of women and mission in Indonesia must concern itself with all of the faces of Indonesia—the ones more apparent to the West and the less clear visages known to Indonesian Christian women—and with their struggles, values, and mission.

As a Western woman working as a professor in Indonesia, I could not escape the all-pervasive influence of gendered opinions. Through observing and seeking out opinions of church leaders in Indonesia, I began to understand how deeply gender ideologies in Indonesian cultures affect every area of life. I became convinced that an approach to women and mission that begins with Indonesian ideas and actions regarding gender can foster an understanding that leads to successful mission interactions with Western Christians.

In setting a context for missions in Indonesia, this essay attempts to look from the inside out. It includes viewpoints of Indonesian Christian women: their context in the nation and in the church, how they interact with gender ideologies and Western Christian theologies, and what their future role in Indonesia and the international church can become. This approach to the dynamics of Christian mission and women in Indonesia brings together the historical effects of Western missions and the resulting actions of Indonesians. More important, it highlights the roles and future of women in the Indonesian church. Besides seeking to understand Christian mission from the point of view of the insiders, the inside-out approach emphasizes the importance of national churches in the development of contemporary approaches to mission studies and to Christian mission in a new era.

CULTURAL DIVERSITY AND CHRISTIAN INFLUENCES
ON WOMEN'S ROLES

Indonesia contains many distinct culture groups, each with its own ethnicity, language, traditions, religious beliefs, and mores. There are at least thirty-four major culture groups in Indonesia and over 450 distinct languages (Cohen 1997). Muslims, Hindus, Buddhists, Christians, and practitioners of indigenous religions perform colorful rituals in villages across the archipelago. Sumatra, Flores,

Irian Jaya, Kalimantan, Timor, and the well-known island of Bali display in-credible diversity, their indigenous and modern blendings forming an ever-chang-ing cultural-religious scene.

As Christianity spread its influence, slowly at first but gaining momentum in the early part of the twentieth century, different forms of Christianity were es-tablished. Portuguese Catholics established churches in Flores and East Timor. Dutch Reformed Calvinism flourished in the Moluccas and later reached as far as Java and Northern Sulawesi. American Presbyterians, Catholics, Baptists, Lutherans, and Assemblies of God churches joined Dutch Reformed Churches in Java during the twentieth century.

Various theologies of women's status and roles were brought to Indonesia by those Christian denominations. Some culture groups expanded opportunities and roles for women based on Christian interpretations. Others used church influence to curtail women's roles, silencing or subordinating them.

By studying the indigenous cultures, contradictory accounts of the influence of the Christian church on women's roles can be understood. The authority of the father was a prominent feature of the unwritten mores of indigenous groups in Irian Jaya. Women's subordination was clearly delineated in the society. Contemporary women pastors and leaders from Irian understandably see Chris-tianity as a liberating influence in their society. By contrast, women from Manado in North Sulawesi claim that the coming of Christianity curtailed women's op-portunities. Before Westerners brought Christianity to North Sulawesi, women were strong leaders in the religious and public life of the Manado people. Today they struggle for leadership roles in the church. In Java, another indigenous culture described a wife as "the one at the back of the house." The kitchen was at the back of the house, and the wife was expected to be in it. Javanese women were trained to be soft-spoken and deferential to men. Churches in Java still reflect those cultural mores. In Sumatra, the Batak women were strong and central to traditional family life. Today, a strong stream of patriarchy in Batak society keeps even hardworking, assertive women in positions of economic dep-rivation and low status. Christian women in Sumatra, while recognizing the force women have had in spreading Christianity, still struggle under an oppres-sive patriarchy.

Economic and political factors influenced changes in gender ideology as colonization and later nationalization made their way across the archipelago. However, a pattern that is related to Christian teachings and indigenous cultures can be seen in Christian areas. Cultures in which women traditionally held power, particularly in the religious sphere, experienced new limitations for women. In cultures where patriarchal hierarchies thrived, women found Christianity to be a liberalizing influence.

PLURALISM AND MAJOR RELIGIONS

Christianity, however, was only the latest in a series of foreign religious influences adding to an already complex amalgamation of cultures. Before Christianity came to Indonesia, waves of Hinduism, Buddhism, and Islam swept through the islands. Each was incorporated into the society, overlaid upon the indigenous religions already present. Animistic beliefs and rituals of sacrifice combine with Hindu, Christian, and Islamic formal religions. (For an intriguing and brief historical account, see Oey 1989, parts I and II.)

Hinduism, over centuries of influence, established a deep cultural base— providing myths, affecting attitudes, and establishing mores that are still very much present in Indonesian society today. The first signs of both Hindu and Buddhist influence in Indonesia date back to the early fifth century c.e. Borobudur and Prambanan, the Buddhist and Hindu temple complexes in Central Java, were erected in the eighth and ninth centuries respectively (Oey 1989, 21-23). Other religious traditions join Hinduism in their acquiescence to fate and traditional attitudes of tolerance.

Chinese Buddhism, with its Confucian influences, supports an ethic of hard work and the importance of family ties that carries over into the work of Christian Chinese women. Active at every level of church life, Chinese women will take on multiple tasks, supporting the church as an extended family network.

Islam is the major religion in Indonesia today, with nearly 170 million adherents. Statistics vary. The *Index on Censorship* (1997) puts the population of Indonesia at 197.6 million, with 85 percent Muslims. Islamic social customs require women to dress modestly, covering their bodies from shoulder to knee or ankle. School uniforms and Western clothes have become acceptable for young people, but tight-fitting blouses and short skirts are still considered immodest. One is less likely to notice modesty in women's apparel when visiting Jakarta, a city of over eleven million inhabitants. A few Indonesians told me with embarrassed smiles that "Jakarta is not really Indonesia." This was their way of apologizing for dress that they considered unacceptable by Indonesian standards of etiquette. A quiet decorum in women's behavior is also evident. Although there is not a separation of women from men in public places, women are expected to be unassuming, accommodating to men, hardworking, and dedicated to their families.

In accordance with the Indonesian value of harmony, efforts are made to honor all religions. Holidays of each major religion are observed. Intermarriage between followers of different religions is tolerated. Extended families often meet for both Christian and Muslim holidays when followers of both religions are family members. The Muslim husband of a Christian woman who worked in my home described with some pride the family's peaceful participation in both Islamic holidays and Christian celebrations (interview with Bapak and Ibu Ismina, April 1994). Good will characterizes these celebrations in Java, where religious pluralism is most evident and accepted.

These cultural influences shape the ways that Indonesian Christian women understand mission. The strong emphasis on integrating varying points of view, for example, leads to a focus on the partnership of men and women in developing church leadership. Gender differences are seen as complementary, and competition is studiously avoided. In the interests of harmony, women leaders will honor men rather than put themselves forward. If a woman taking action would embarrass a man, usually the woman leader will defer to him. Practicing these values, while producing harmony, sometimes curtails the mission work of Christian women.

SOCIETAL TRANSITION AND ROLE CONFLICTS

Besides social and cultural attempts to unify this diverse society, some groups order and dominate social structures as well as economic and political life. Although for many years national life in Indonesia appeared unified under Suharto, the widely reported movement for independence in East Timor was not the only example of a group trying to break away. Centralization of power and wealth in Java bred dissatisfaction in poorer, less economically developed areas throughout the archipelago. In Irian Jaya, for example, profits from the rich gold resources were used to build golf courses and high-rise hotels for international corporate executives and wealthy Javanese partners in the industry, while poverty and malnutrition among poorer classes remained basically unchanged. Since political pressure forced President Suharto to step down from power, other unhappy groups have made their voices heard. Conflicts have erupted in Ambon, Irian Jaya, Halmahera, and other eastern islands. Recent political unrest and conflicts between Muslims and Christians in those areas show the difficulty of maintaining the ideal of unity in diversity upon which Indonesia was founded. These conflicts deeply affect women in Indonesia.

The conflicts occurring during this time of societal transition include not only political, ethnic, and religious conflicts, but dissension among those who are in the midst of the transition from a traditional to a more egalitarian understanding of gender—a transition acute in the Republic of Indonesia today. Women's equal status, equal opportunity, and equal responsibility for national development have been part of the political platform of the Indonesian government since independence from Dutch colonial rule and Japanese occupation was declared on August 18, 1945. The Indonesian resistance movement took the opportunity to declare independence when the Allied troops declared the end of World War II. The constitution was developed during the first year (1945-46), while the revolution was actually being fought. Strong women involved in the liberation movement contributed to the constitutional rights achieved by women citizens of the new republic. Indonesian women are enjoined to work at all levels of economic and social life to build the nation. That new ideology has enabled dynamic changes in women's status and self-perception. Better-educated, more assertive women are finding their way into leadership in businesses, educational institutions, and religious organizations.

At the same time, traditional gender ideology clearly delineates separate social roles. The belief that women and men differ markedly in "innate" abilities and psychological traits leads to a strict division of roles. Since men and women are thought to have complementary traits, it is commonly held that only in marriage can both men and women achieve their full potential as human beings.

Because gender role division is based on naturalistic explanations of abilities and understandings of marriage, these beliefs are very deeply rooted in the various societies that make up the Republic of Indonesia.

Economic factors add to social constraints to keep traditional roles for women intact in Indonesian society. Financial needs keep village women working in the fields and the markets. Lack of accessibility or use of birth-control methods keep them bearing children and caring for the home. Child-care demands and other responsibilities tie them to their homes and villages, keeping them from better paying jobs. The income women do earn as petty traders at village markets is routinely spent on household necessities, children's school fees, and social contributions to neighbors and relatives.

The same is true of middle-class women, whose social networks demand both time and financial contributions. Social obligations within extended family and neighborhood networks include frequent visits to neighbors, regular gift-giving, Selamatans (life-passage celebrations), and organizing neighborhood meetings and work parties. Often young people from the extended family come to live with relatives who live in a university town. The economic burden this presents can be heavy, because university lecturers, their wives, and other urban workers usually do not earn large salaries.

Patriarchy in cultural forms also supports women's traditional roles. *Adat* customs among indigenous religions support the same view. It is also common for small shopkeepers or market women to extend credit to villagers even when they are not financially able to do so (see Krisnawati and Utrecht 1992). *Adat* systems of informal rules define relative positions of women and men in family and social life in indigenous cultures. Even in matrifocal societies such as the Minangkabau and Javanese, women's role as childbearer and homemaker is clear (for Java, see Sullivan 1994 and Brenner 1995; for Minangkabau, see Krier 1995b and Blackwood 1995). Islam's traditional view of women places them firmly in the private realm. Even attendance at the mosque is dominated by men, since women's attendance is not required. Views of the other major world religions present in Indonesia are also used to argue that women's "place" is subordinate to men and must be exercised in the private sphere of the household. Rita Gross argues that each of the major world religions supports patriarchy, although their rituals and texts can be reinterpreted to support equality between women and men (Gross 1995).

The social roles that spring from traditional gender ideology in Indonesia are at odds with the roles demarcated by the gender ideology of equality purported by the Republic of Indonesia. While equality of opportunity and ability is the official state ideology, traditional gender ideologies understand women to be less intelligent than men, more emotional, and more suited for nurturing roles in the private sphere.

As women attempt to act out of conflicting ideologies with competing value systems, ideological confusion occurs. Choosing among the responsibilities of home, neighborhood, job, and religious life when one is expected to fulfill duties in all of them exacts a price. Feelings of inadequacy arise as a woman cannot fulfill all of her social obligations. Some values must be underplayed in order to act on others. A research scientist for Pertamina, Indonesia's state-owned oil company, for example, turned down a scholarship to the United States, saying, "I really wanted to go so that I could realize my potential. But I felt my first responsibility was to my family. I had to decide in favor of my husband and my son" (*AsiaWeek* [May 30-June 5, 1993], 22). As roles conflict, often it is personal and professional goals that give way to serving needs of family and neighborhood.

The government also displays ideological confusion as it attempts to implement its gender ideology of equality. According to government statements, women's primary role as "partners in national development" is to support men in their work and public roles and to raise future economic contributors through good parenting. While ostensibly supporting equality of women and men, the government has established formal women's groups to develop programs to facilitate these domestic roles (see Murdiati and Sabarish 1985).

Despite government pressure for women to express their "partnership in development" through a homemaker's role, and the social consensus regarding traditional home and family roles for women, income-producing work among village women and work outside the home among middle-class women are common occurrences. The double burden that this creates for women increases in agricultural settings as factory jobs take men to the cities for a large part of the year. In middle-class families, increasing work pressures keep men out of the home for most of the week. Working women, subjected to the same pressures, must also manage the household. These ideological confusions and pressures and the behaviors that result from them may seem strange or nonproductive to Western Christians interacting with Indonesian women leaders. The church in Indonesia will find a path through the societal transition on gender roles more easily if Western Christians understand the deep roots in cultures and political ideologies and the powerful effects of traditional views of gender on Indonesian Christian women leaders.

GENDER IDEOLOGY IN THE CHURCH

Finding time for church activities and leadership roles proves difficult for women in the Indonesian social milieu. Time is not the only issue, however. The situation of the Christian church in Indonesia increases the pressure that women encounter as they find their way into leadership roles in the church. As members of a minority religion in a time of unrest, male church leaders already feel besieged and discriminated against. Although freedom of religion is the official government policy, "Islamization of culture" spreads Muslim ideas and practices throughout Indonesia. Competition from women for leadership positions is often resisted by male leaders as one more attack on their authority.

Contemporary Christian women also encounter particular resistance from Christian gender ideologies that utilize theological arguments. The husband as head of the household, requiring submission from his wife, is one such interpretation from the letters of the apostle Paul in the New Testament (see 1 Cor 11:3, Eph 5:22-24, 1 Tm 2:11-14). A related view that hinders women's advancement is an order-of-creation argument that relegates women to secondary and dependent status because Eve was said to have been created from Adam's rib. The first creation story in Genesis 1 includes both man and woman, created together as equal caretakers of the earth. The order-of-creation argument is based on the second creation account in Genesis 2. Adam, after naming the animals, could find no counterpart to himself. According to this account, God then put Adam to sleep and, taking out one of his ribs, created a woman. An aside on the Pauline texts cited when women's roles in the church are discussed may be useful. The emphases of her likeness to Adam, her sameness, and her ability to be an equal partner with him are lost in the interpretation that Adam had authority over her because he was created first and woman was made from him. The apostle Paul partly supports this traditional interpretation in 1 Corinthians 11, with some qualifications. Unfortunately, in his first letter to Timothy he ignores those qualifications (1 Tm 2:8-15). They have generally been ignored in the church since, and women's subordination has been a standard part of Christian theologies for many centuries.

These religious ideas augment and reinforce traditional Indonesian gender ideologies that describe woman's central life tasks as childbearing and devoting herself to her husband and family. The force of religious authority is here added to arguments from nature, custom, and tradition. The theological dictums that arise from interpretations of the Bible that relegate women to secondary status demand that women ignore the call to religious leadership. The situation is similar to the one faced by nineteenth-century American women in Protestant churches who felt called to preach or enter seminary. In Indonesia today, if Christian women do listen to and follow the call to leadership, they encounter resistance from church authorities and their theological interpretations of women's role in the church. This resistance is allegedly backed up by "the voice of God." But if women resist their sense of calling to a religious vocation, they encounter resistance from their inner spirit that calls them with "the voice of God."

Indonesian theologian Stephen Suleeman argues that the church should take responsibility for this state of affairs:

> In practice we have seen how much churches have put a limit on women so that they only occupy the private or domestic realm. It is true that we see a growing number of women students and faculty members in our theological education, as well as women pastors in the churches. Nevertheless their positions are often very much limited and do not have much influence. . . . Churches tend to ignore the presence of women. . . . Churches should be more active in their struggle for women, and pro-actively take the initiative to fight against patriarchy even within its structures. (Suleeman, n.d.)

STRUCTURAL RESISTANCE
AND SOCIAL DIMENSIONS OF SELF-IDENTITY

What happens when societal or church structures prevent a woman from fulfilling a call that she senses has come to her from God? One can fulfill a life task only if one's community affirms that task and allows one to practice it. In part the meaning of a statement or an act is determined by the response that the act elicits (see Mead 1934). If women try to act as leaders but are responded to as dependent followers, they cannot become leaders. Community feedback and affirmation are integral to leadership development. A professor is dependent on the affirmation of her intellectual ideas in the community. A church leader is dependent on the recognition of her calling by the community. A woman with a call to church leadership may be thwarted if she cannot find that assent in her community. The social expectation in Indonesian society that a leader calls forth salutations of honor from others illustrates this point. If a woman pastor, for example, cannot elicit respectful salutations and acts that honor her from the congregation, she is considered unworthy of the post of leadership. If the community, on its part, refuses to give these honorary tokens of respect because it does not truly accept leadership from a woman, the woman will not be honored no matter how much respect her personal achievements deserve.

To lead women's ministries in the local churches is more acceptable in Indonesia than to lead women and men together at the regional or national levels. Becoming a theologian is even more difficult because of the authority theologians receive to shape the life and doctrines of the church. Church leaders of every type are chosen by the community and are supported by them. Without that support women cannot reach positions of leadership, or if they do, they are subtly discounted and marginalized as leaders.

Recognition by accepted authorities is extremely important in Indonesia. Because of the tradition of *bapakism*, in which the father figure seeks consensus and expresses that consensus to the group, little advancement can be made without the affirmation of male leaders. In addition, a woman who establishes herself as a leader more powerful than most men around her is in a very tenuous position. Men receive the honored positions, particularly older men. If a woman for some reason is advanced above the majority of men in a particular group, reasons for lowering her status easily can be found.

A recent example of this reality was the appointment of Sukarnoputri as leader of the opposition political party in Indonesia. While she was officially appointed, some leaders in her party opposed her, stating that she was chosen not for her qualifications but because she was the eldest daughter of the first president of Indonesia. When political issues with the party became tense, the Suharto government removed Sukarnoputri from her post as party leader. Party criticism and government action combined to strip Sukarnoputri of her position and her power. It wasn't until after Suharto's power was broken and his image as the father figure of the nation removed that Sukarnoputri rose to a leadership role as vice-president of the new government.

Women can go only so far in establishing new paths and gaining recognition. Gender equality cannot become a reality without changes in customs and social structures that keep women from positions of leadership in church and society.

POSITIVE STEREOTYPES

Social controls take effect not only through an unwillingness to affirm women as leaders on the part of recognized authorities. Women are also kept from advancement by seemingly positive attitudes toward them.

One common stereotype in Indonesia is that women need protection. I encountered male church leaders in Ambon who expressed this attitude during a discussion of women's roles in the church on December 5, 1992. "Our women are strong and feisty, but they still need us men to protect them," stated one. A result of such paternalism is that women are considered unable to supervise work in the church in outlying island areas. Travel to remote islands during the monsoon season was considered too dangerous for a woman to undertake alone. Social custom frowned upon a single woman traveling with men. Since visiting the churches regularly was part of the job of the regional director, these attitudes kept women from becoming regional leaders in the outer islands. "A woman traveling in a small boat alone during the monsoon season? How could a woman do that?" asked one male regional leader.

While in Sangir Terlaud for a Protestant Church of Indonesia Regional Women's Meeting in May 1993, I met one woman who managed to circumvent the protective customs. She was the first woman regional leader of those northern islands, a robust woman in her late thirties. I asked her if it was difficult for her to travel to churches during the stormy season. "It's my job. I do it," she replied matter-of-factly. This kind of quiet self-confidence is a boon to women breaking into new roles of leadership in Indonesian society. The example both empowers other women and corrects the reified attitudes of society that insist that women are weak and need male protection.

The notion of gender partnership itself can hamper women in developing as leaders. "Partnership" in church work, as "partnership in development," can be construed as women supporting men in their public roles as leaders—the model of partnership most evident in Indonesian society. "Women hold up the world" remarked a male church leader in Ambon. This remark, made during the same conversation in Ambon with church leaders in December 1992, showed a respect for women's strength but gave no assent to women's ability as church leaders. Yes, it seems that Indonesian women hold up the world—while men govern its affairs.

Because of the role differences that are implied by this view of partnership, a few women at the national conference in Tomohon voiced dissatisfaction with that theme. One suggested that partnership had been a common theme for years but not much seemed to be changing in the church organizational structures to mirror the egalitarian notion of partnership that women in the church were advocating.

Recognizing the hidden agenda of apparently positive attitudes of men toward women is the first step in establishing that more egalitarian partnership. Jennifer Krier's study of "disruptive discourses" reveals that positive attitudes toward "strong women" may encourage outspoken behavior that ultimately undermines their power and demonstrates their marginalization (Krier 1995a). In a research study of the financial arrangements between spouses in Java, Norma Sullivan found that the purported equality of spouses exhibited by the woman's role as "manager" of family finances masked a deeper reality of men as "masters" over women (Sullivan 1994).

Such studies signal the necessity of applying a hermeneutic of suspicion to attitudes and customs that appear to affirm women in situations where women do not seem to be experiencing the affirmation or equality that would result from those attitudes. Elisabeth Schüssler Fiorenza suggests that women ask who benefits from particular customs or power arrangements rather than accepting without question that the reasons given for these arrangements are the true reasons. This "hermeneutic of suspicion" can unmask hidden agendas and deceptive power arrangements that oppress women through seemingly acceptable attitudes and social structures (Schüssler Fiorenza 1983).

INTERNAL BARRIERS

Sometimes women cannot meet the demands of leadership, not because of external social pressures or stereotypes, but because of internal barriers. Those barriers result, in part, from societal dictums or stereotypes of women's abilities. No longer recognized as merely human constructions, restrictive attitudes have been internalized and accepted as a part of reality. Peter Berger (1969) outlines a theory of the social construction of reality. First, human societies create social structures—they make a social world. Then that world takes on an objectivity of its own, appearing stable and real and affecting human actions and attitudes. Finally, that construction of how the world really is becomes internalized, influencing the limits and possibilities that humans understand themselves to have. Women's attitudes then reflect the oppressive social arrangements that accompany the traditional ideology.

The idea of *kodrat* in Indonesian society carries with it connotations of both fate and God's will. It is considered an unalterable yet good fate for a woman to have children and supply devoted care to them, to her husband, to aging parents, and to members of the extended family. A full and well-ordered home, good food, disciplined and well-attired children, and a strong and happy husband show that a woman has fulfilled her reason for living.

Whatever else a modern woman may achieve, the family role remains primary and central. As this religious conception of the meaning of life for women, brought to Indonesia by Islam and supported by some of the indigenous cultures, becomes internalized in the psyches of women, doing anything else with their lives seems impossible. Fulfilling one's *kodrat* by becoming a fertile, good, and care-giving woman is not a concept that is, or should be, easily laid aside for Indonesian women. But it can unconsciously direct a woman away from using her more public talents by filling her days with the ordinary and useful activities of family life.

Women in Indonesia also struggle against the stereotype, reinforced in church, that they are inferior to men. Continuously referred to as the weaker sex—physically, mentally, and emotionally—women sometimes lack confidence in their intellectual skills or do not appreciate their own emotional strengths. They often feel unable to protect themselves against emotional or physical victimization. It would be strange if women did not internalize these negative attitudes about themselves.

What is amazing is the indomitable spirit of women who, in addition to raising their families, supporting their husbands and extended families, working in their neighborhoods, and earning income, still find the time and inner strength to pursue graduate studies and become leaders in the church.

LEARNING THROUGH LISTENING AND RESPONSE

A greater tolerance toward different ways of acting and different habits of living is necessary before an ideology of gender equality can be integrated into Indonesian society. The Javanese and other sophisticated Indonesian cultures see their ways as the best ways. Contact with other indigenous cultures and Western civilizations fosters a recognition of the acceptability and richness of other ways of life. That recognition allows notions of gender equality to be implemented increasingly in Indonesia.

At the same time, Western understandings need to be broadened so that our mission interaction with churches in Indonesia and elsewhere can be wisdom-filled rather than culturally imperialistic. As I interacted with Indonesians during five years as a professor, I learned that I needed to listen long and well before proposing any course of action to foster gender equality. Learning cultural traditions, listening to women's dilemmas with men in the church and university, and hearing the men talk of their tensions and pressures to conform to traditional patterns of behavior provided a beginning for dialogues about gender equality. I would like to suggest six benefits of this inside-out approach for mission.

Cross-Cultural Understanding

The work of Christian mission puts us in daily contact with those of other ethnic and social groups. Understanding how Indonesians perceive the world, arrange social structures and mores, and create religious ideals enables us to communicate more effectively and develop mutual understanding.

Rather than perpetuate misunderstandings or reinforce theologically constricting viewpoints on gender, we can encourage, empower, and enable Indonesian women leaders to flourish. Educating Westerners about Indonesian institutions and the roles of women in their complex cultures and social settings can make dialogue about views of equality and human rights for women more relevant to actual situations of Indonesian church women.

Our Historical Situatedness Becomes Clear

Western churches will benefit greatly as we more deeply understand our differences from the church in Indonesia. As understanding of difference grows, the distinctiveness of our own views and ways of doing things becomes clearer. What once seemed natural and universal is now seen as culturally and historically situated. We can evaluate our own mores and cultural ideas from a broader horizon of meanings. Christian women from West and East can learn to see our differences, both theological and practice-oriented, as contributions to the richness of the church itself.

Greater Acceptance of Others and Their Ways

Seeing that there are other ways of constructing gender, mores, and institutions by studying cultural norms and attitudes of Indonesians shows us that goodness can be packaged in many ways. The beauty of a Muslim friend's hospitality as she brings food to my apartment, while clothed in gendered habits, is not less gracious for the form it takes. As we see that our own socially constructed reality does not present the only way of doing things, we become less quick to rule different cultural forms or social mores as inferior or wrong and become more willing to accept them as simply different.

I experienced this move toward greater acceptance while in Indonesia. I was anxious for women in Indonesia to succeed as academic leaders. I saw my own Western, efficient, outspoken style as the way to gain that success. But after working for three years as a professor in Indonesia, I became less critical of the soft-spoken, polite ways of some of my Indonesian women colleagues. Recognizing the history and values that lay behind certain forms of dress in Java also helped me to understand why some women preferred what I saw to be constrictive clothing. As my understanding of Indonesian values grew, I began to listen more, facilitating rather than directing change in social and cultural styles that seemed to inhibit women in leadership roles.

As men and women see others negotiating gender ideologies in transition, empathy can grow among peoples across the world. It was my students at the Graduate Theological Union, where I spent a semester in 1994, who pointed out to me that I was perhaps over-directive in my approach to necessary changes for women aspiring to leadership in Indonesia. They encouraged me to listen more deeply, allowing Indonesian women to devise their own emancipatory actions. Our ways may be different, but our struggles are shared. This sense of commonality is important for women who are breaking out of old patterns and seeking support for risky choices and different lifestyles.

Value of Gender Equality

Cross-cultural interaction shows the value of gender equality itself. Despite differences in cultural forms, social mores, lifestyle choices, and practices, women I met in several countries held equal dignity, recognition, and opportunity as core values. It appears that a more universally understood value lies beneath differing social mores and customs. Finding that universal value beneath the varying cultural forms in Indonesia and the West strengthens our conviction and motivates women to struggle for equality.

Contribution to Christian Theology

Studying other cultures also makes a contribution to theology. Study done by outsiders enhances discussion of theological issues within a specific context. Offering new perspectives from another cultural viewpoint and discussing theologies of gender in both cultures generate ideas for alternative ways of looking at issues. Theologies of gender will benefit greatly from this cross-fertilization with Indonesian views. Networking with the Ecumenical Association of Third World Theologians (EATWOT) and PERWATI, two national organizations for Christian theologians in Indonesia, can empower Indonesian women in their callings to Christian leadership and societal change.

Developing Partnerships

Christian mission is no longer a West to East project. By working with the Indonesian church to discover the potential and possibilities for women in leadership, Western mission efforts will develop true partnerships with Indonesian churches. Working alongside Indonesian Christians in the struggle for economic development, against the threat of AIDS, and for women's education and equality can display the unity of the church in its worldwide diversity. Listening and learning from Indonesian theological insights and cultural styles can broaden Western understandings.

As we take an inside-out approach toward understanding each other, not only will gender equality free up the potential of Indonesian women leaders, but a deeper and broader egalitarianism in the universal body of Christ can become a major direction for Christian mission in the twenty-first century.

13

Without a Face

The Nineteenth-Century Bible Woman
and Twentieth-Century Female *Jeondosa*

Young Lee Hertig

INTRODUCTION

History is often written for, by, and about the people at the center. Those who are on the margins, no matter how much they contribute to society, are excluded from the historical records. Korean church history is not exempt from the above statement, with its exclusion of women's contribution. Furthermore, many contemporary Christian women, unordained and ordained, are still confined by the image of the nineteenth-century Bible woman. Paradoxically, women leaders play the internal patriarchal tapes on the one hand, while feeling abused by the system on the other hand. Both patriarchal male pastors and congregations, indoctrinated by patriarchal messages, project the Bible woman image as the only female leadership model.

The questions raised in this study are twofold. What kind of reality does the image of Bible women in the nineteenth century create for female church leaders in the twentieth century? How does the image influence the Korean churchwomen's sense of who we are and our relations with one another? I seek to answer the above questions through in-depth case studies of two contemporary Bible women—Korean female *jeondosa* (evangelist). By documenting two women *jeondosa*'s experiences, this study first intends to empower the unmarked, undefined, invisible, and faceless. Second, it seeks to offer an alternative image of contemporary female leadership by deconstructing Confucian hierarchy and reconstructing Taoism, utilizing a *Yinist* alternative. The term *Yinist,* the female energy of Taoism, is comprehensive because it encompasses gender, ecology, nature, health, and God. The *yin* is holistic, dynamic, synthesizing, and complementary with *yang*, the male energy. *Yinist* feminism, therefore, diffuses false dichotomies deriving from the dualistic paradigm: male against female, human being against nature, God apart from human being, this world apart from that world (Hertig 1998, 16).

The *Yinist* image for contemporary Korean women's leadership is also found in Jesus' modeling of leadership. Jesus restored the broken image of God in humanity when he treated women with dignity.

THE NINETEENTH- AND TWENTIETH-CENTURY BIBLE WOMEN

The Korean Christian women's leadership journey is rooted in the Bible women of the nineteenth century. Western missionaries offered Korean women an informal and yet very effective leadership role in spreading the gospel in Korea. In fact, the first Methodist woman missionary to Korea, Mary F. Scranton, an American Methodist, viewed Korean women as cultural, linguistic, and social "brokers" in evangelism. Because women readily had access to the private sphere, the home, the Bible women became the pioneers of door-to-door evangelism. They carried the gospel from house to house and were sacrificially devoted to their labor of love. Informal women's time and space gave birth to the fast-paced spread of the gospel like yeast in Korea in the early twentieth century.

As in the case of the early church, the beginning of Christianity in Korea also started out as *oikos,* or household. Therefore, women's leadership was very effective. Once Christianity grew in numbers, it grew out of the house church to the public arenas of the church building. The institutionalization of the church structures created a lag between women's participation and equal opportunity. In other words, what was initially a liberating role for Korean women became stilted and confining once the patriarchal system reasserted itself in the church. We can see parallels with church women in other cultures as well—an initial period of creativity that encourages women followed by routinization under male authority (see Robert 1997). As in the case of the adoption of Christianity by the Roman Empire, sharp gender role boundaries evolved and shattered the *oikos* concept. In Karen Tørjeson's words:

> For more than two hundred years Christianity was essentially a religion of the private sphere, practiced in the private space of the household rather than the public space of a temple. . . . But during the third century Christianity began evolving toward its eventual form as a public religion. . . . As Christianity entered the public sphere, male leaders began to demand the same subjugation of women in the churches as prevailed in Greco-Roman society at large. (Tørjeson 1993, 37-38)

Likewise, masculinization of the Korean church took place, and the hard labor of the Bible women remained invisible and faceless. Patriarchal leadership took over and continued to harvest the Bible women's work with women's labor credited to the male leadership.

This essay contends that the image of the faceless, nameless Bible woman is firmly grounded in the minds of both Korean patriarchal church leaders and congregations today. While women find Christianity liberating personally, a huge discrepancy exists between the personal liberation and the message preached in the androcentric homily. Instead of the gospel transforming patriarchal culture, cultural values dominate the interpretation of the gospel. Projecting the crucified Christ on the one hand, and Confucian patriarchalism on the other, women's leadership qualities in the church are defined by sacrifice, dedication, and obedience. Due to the lack of any other images of women's leadership, contemporary female church leaders, whether ordained or unordained, are confined by the frozen image of the nineteenth-century Bible woman.

The thesis of this study is that the strong image of Korean Bible women is still pervasive at the beginning of the twenty-first century and that the modern-day Bible women in the church are those women referred to as *jeondosa*. However, depending on gender, the position means either an ordination track or a trap. For male *jeondosa*, it is an ordination-track internship; in the case of the female *jeondosa,* in denominations that exclude ordination of women, it involves home visitation and chores for lower salaries, as did the Bible woman role in the nineteenth century. It is a position of permanence without opportunity for upward mobility. Therefore, this study, at the turn of a new century, focuses on how such a strong image of Bible woman affects the Korean women's leadership role and congregations' expectations.

THE GENERAL CONTEXT OF GENDERED LEADERSHIP

In comparison to the Korean church in Korea, the Korean immigrant church, with its island mentality, lags even further behind in social change. In fact, what the Korean church imported from the American church was tested in Korea and then is exported back to the Korean immigrant churches by the megachurch leaders who are invited by the immigrant churches in the United States. A quantitative survey conducted in Korea provides background to the gendered pastoral leadership of the twentieth-century Korean church. Considering that mainstream Korean culture changes more quickly than immigrant minority culture, the survey titled "Is the Korean Church a Community of Equals?" shows significant implications for the Korean American churches as well (Kang 1995).

Exactly 877 women from nine major denominations responded to a survey that depicted gender hierarchy in the Korean church. The data was interpreted by Nam Soon Kang, a woman systematic theologian. The alarming survey results pointed to an extremely patriarchal church structure. Women make up at least 70 percent of the churches and yet only 11 percent participate in the decision-making body (Kang 1995, 68). In other words, a 30 percent male minority exercises decision-making power over the female majority within the church.

In response to the question as to why they were not participating in the decision-making, 40.7 percent of the women replied that they lacked consciousness, and 16.9 percent indicated that women do not elect women representatives.

While 57.6 percent of the women attributed the lack to women themselves, 13 percent also responded that for the sake of women's active representation in the decision-making processes, male pastors' consciousness ought to be shifted. Furthermore, 18.7 percent of the women attributed the lack of women's participation in decision-making to the male-dominated society and Confucian influence. Only 0.6 percent of the women attributed it to the pastor's sermon, and 12.7 percent brought up the denomination's policy of not ordaining women as clergy (Kang 1995).

Kang sharply points out the absence of churchwomen's consciousness regarding structural, ideological power. In fact, women are quick to blame themselves for lack of motivation and consciousness in decision-making and are blinded about the core of the problems. In response to the question of female pastoral leaders, only 51.1 percent of churchwomen thought female pastoral leaders would be helpful for improving women's leadership qualities (Kang 1995, 68-70). Contrary to the perceived ideal of representing women's leadership, in reality, only 2.5 percent of the women responded positively to women preaching and leading worship.

When asked about their own responsibility in the church, 51 percent of 877 churchwomen replied that their responsibility in the church involved cleaning and cooking. However, only 0.3 percent of them indicated these chores are what they desire to do. Governed by traditional patriarchal values, the majority of the Korean women manifest incongruence between their value and desire in perceiving their own role and women's pastoral roles. According to the data, Korean churchwomen find it difficult to accept ordained women because their role deviates from their own role as women centered in patriarchal values. Consequently, the majority of the women are occupied with cleaning and cooking in the church, while in decision-making bodies only 2.3 percent participate on committees, and 2.1 percent in the session (the governing body of a local Presbyterian church). The data reveal that Christian Korean women today simply repeat household work in the church. They lack meaningful participation and decision-making in the church and thus feel insignificant (Kang 1995).

Why do Korean female Christians lack consciousness when Christianity at the beginning served to elevate women's status? Female missiologist Kwang-Soon Lee indicates that despite being the numerical majority in the church, women's status has been locked in a standstill position. Lee explains that women's status was frozen through a longstanding anti-ordination policy against women that two years ago was finally reversed by the Tonghap Presbyterian denomination. Lee also differentiates female laity's status from that of clergy. While laity might gain upward mobility within the church hierarchy, female clergy do not have access to upward mobility (Lee 1995, 131).

Women's consciousness raising is a threat to the status quo of the male-dominated church structure and thus has been discouraged from the pulpit through the use of the Bible as a weapon. Churchwomen do not have any opportunities to see beyond their own patriarchal contexts within the church. Internalized sexism among the churchwomen is also evident. A change in women's status within the church will take a major shift in Korean patriarchal theology and praxis. The male-to-female ratio in the Protestant churches in Korea was one to four in 1990 (Lee 1995, 133-34). While the enrollment of female students in theological institutions has been increasing, actual representation of females on the church staff in major Korean churches has been reduced sharply. Most megachurches in Korea today have broken away from the tradition of having a female *jeondosa* who does home visitation as the Bible women did. Professionalization of the church further masculinized the church structure while key leaders boast that they are feminists by having a token female elder in the session. Women's leadership on staff has taken a step backward in Korea. Under the self-proclaimed feminist patriarchal leaders, gender disparity is sharpened in contradiction to the historical fact that originally Christianity counterculturally advocated women's education and leadership when Korean society did not allow these.

In this milieu the gospel and Christianity continue to be masculine in image and practice, lacking the holistic theological anthropology of Genesis 1:28, where both male and female represent the image of God. Against androcentric and patriarchal church structures, female Korean church leaders seek to swim against the current amid huge ocean waves.

THE IMAGE OF BIBLE WOMEN IN THE TWENTIETH CENTURY

In this study two women *jeondosa*, one single and the other married, are key informants. The married *jeondosa* is Esther (a pseudonym) and the single *jeondosa* is named Sunjoo (also a pseudonym). Esther *jeondosa* is in her mid-thirties and has two little children. Sunjoo *jeondosa* is in her mid-forties and is a single mother of two teenagers. They were chosen because both have ministered in Korean immigrant churches that prohibit woman's ordination. Their church leadership experience as Korean women in America depicts the excruciating pain of exclusion, which is commonly shared by many other women in ministry in Korean-American churches. Furthermore, these women leaders' suffering is silenced and denied. In fact, their suffering is spiritually and theologically justified through the emphasis of Jesus on the cross without the balance of the resurrected Christ. The goal of this study is to break the silence and honor their marginalized pain and to enter into their struggling leadership journey as they are bombarded with the frozen image of faceless women from the nineteenth century. They tell their stories so that the Korean church may restore the broken image of God (Gn 1:26-27).

These two Korean women leaders are alienated because of the male-oriented interpretation of the Godhead. The separation of femaleness from the Godhead either alienates or excludes womanhood in ministry. Both *jeondosa*, Esther and Sunjoo, feel blatant discrimination in three major areas: (1) salary gap and workload; (2) exclusion from any public role such as preaching or public prayer; and (3) internalized sexism from women.

Married Jeondosa?

I interviewed Esther in July, August, and September 2000. An educated, married woman with multiple roles, she shared her experience in the church:

> My multifaceted background, *jeondosa*, a mother of two little children, doctoral candidate, is perceived as a liability rather than an asset in the Korean immigrant church simply because I am a woman. I do not even fit into the church's Bible woman image of female leadership. My background deviates from the "Bible woman" image and becomes a topic for a discussion among church leaders and laity in general. They do not have any category to place me in. In the case of male leaders, married status is preferred.

Projecting the nineteenth-century image of Bible women upon a twentieth-century leader like Esther elucidates the manipulative use of imagery by the androcentric church structure. Patristic theological anthropology exempts females from the *imago Dei* and interprets the Godhead exclusively from the male image. Considering this traditional androcentric notion of theological anthropology, it is not a coincidence that nineteenth-century Bible women were mostly widows who dedicated all of their time and energy to evangelism and Bible sales. Consequently, Esther faces multiple strikes against her as a woman called to ministry. As a married woman she deviates from the prescribed sexless image of Bible women and its modern-day parallel, the female *jeondosa*. As an associate pastor's wife, she also deviates from the image of the backseat pastor's wife. As a doctoral candidate, Esther deviates from the role expectation of "hands" and "feet." As a mother, she deviates from the Bible woman's total devotion of all of her time and energy to the church. With all of these strikes against her, Esther as a *jeondosa* tried to overcompensate until her body was stretched beyond exhaustion.

> In the church where I served, the female staff consisted of two-thirds of the leadership. In the case of married women, the husbands were usually involved with different vocations. However, my co-partnership in marriage does not translate into the church structure. The church takes the two leaders under one person's salary while demanding two full workloads.

It is a taboo in the Korean church for Esther, a staff member, to bring up the salary issue. She has to take whatever the church decides to give. Otherwise, her leadership credibility would be at stake, and her already quadruple marginal status would be worsened.

Trapped in a Jeondosa's *Position*

Esther *jeondosa* connects economic exploitation with the exclusion of women's ordination:

The fact that the denomination of this church prohibits women's ordination binds female leaders forever in the *jeondosa* position, no matter how long one has worked for the church. Compared to even the brand-new associate male pastor, the female *jeondosa* dedicates most of her time for a longer period of time yet is compensated financially far less. Many female church staff members consider the earning gap as legitimate simply because Korean churches unanimously treat women staff with disparity. The patriarchal leadership justifies the disparity by viewing the male as the head of the household. In the case of women leaders, the church sees them as either single or the wife of the patriarch whose earning power excels women's. A strong view of a male-dominant financial picture is in operation here.

Esther's keen consciousness of the majority female *jeondosa*'s acceptance of discrimination as a norm also makes her into an "other." Esther's experience reflects the injustice of excluding women from ordination and thus binding them to second-class salary and leadership roles. The Korean women *jeondosa* have to accept ministry opportunities whenever they can, regardless of ordination limitations. Therefore, the *jeondosa* is equivalent to the Bible woman in the nineteenth century. The struggles of Esther typify many other evangelical church women *jeondosa* who are grossly under-represented, considering the 70 percent women membership in the church.

More Work, Less Pay

Sunjoo *jeondosa*, also interviewed in July, August, and September 2000, describes her ministry in the Korean immigrant church as "hitting a rock with an egg." Sunjoo has been in a full-time position for four years. Prior to her ministry in the church Sunjoo had worked in the business world where she found more gender equality. She had to go through a severe culture shock with the church culture during her first two years of service. Sensitized to the women's leadership issue, Sunjoo could not bear blatant discrimination and shocking comments against woman's leadership in the church. Sunjoo *jeondosa* addresses the injustice of a salary gap based on gender:

> During the annual planning and report meeting at the church, one of the young deacons raised a question about the salary gap between male and female staff. The senior pastor, who was presiding, chose not to comment on that particular issue and asked one of the elders to answer on the spot. He rambled and did not answer the question raised. After the meeting all the male pastors were upset by the fact that the salary inequality between male and female staff was raised as an issue during the public meeting. The general attitude of the congregation was negative about it becoming an issue itself. I was blamed as the one who stirred up the deacon to turn the salary disparity into an issue. During the staff meeting the senior pastor

scolded me, saying, "In the future do not try to control church members."
I had to remain silent because I could not provide any evidence to prove
him wrong.

Those who set the agenda are the ones with power. The ways in which a power
holder exploits power include avoidance, silence, deviation, and scapegoating.
Through the eyes of the senior staff, the question by a lay person on the salary
gap between the male and female staff was not supposed to be raised and thus it
was delegated to an elder on the spot. The senior staff did not even have to
acknowledge it in public. In private, Sunjoo *jeondosa* received the brunt of the
criticism. The above vignette describes the power dynamics around gender,
money, and social ranking. As long as Korean churches maintain that women
should be silent in the church as an unchanging rule for women, the witness and
integrity of the church will be jeopardized.

Another factor here lies in the triple marginalization of women staff around
economics, gender, and silencing. It is the senior staff and the session, an all-
male governing body of the church, that unfairly decides the female staff members' salaries. Esther *jeondosa* serves in a Presbyterian church and Sunjoo
jeondosa serves in a Holiness church. Both churches utilize sessions as their
mode of governance. By turning the money matter into an issue of faithfulness,
the staff traps women without a medium to address oppression. Any attempt to
bring up economic injustice would label women such as Sunjoo *jeondosa* as
"ungrateful" and "spiritually bankrupt." Her only option at the moment is to
suffer silently from the church's unfaithfulness to the witness of Jesus Christ.

Excluded from Preaching

What seems to keep the church fixed in the nineteenth century is the fusion
of the Korean Confucian hierarchy and patristic theological anthropology (Gn
1—3). Lacking a holistic interpretation of the *imago Dei,* discrimination against
women leaders in the church is legitimized. In addition to the culturally defined
gender hierarchy, patriarchal theology explained gender discrimination as ordained by God. Sadly, both *jeondosa* can find strength through the journey within
only by reminding themselves of Jesus' liberation of women like themselves.
However, the constant reminder of being second class because of gender differences is a difficult burden to bear. Esther feels violated by the church's exclusion of her gifts and qualifications:

I have been a part-time *jeondosa* for the preschoolers for five years. Although this church is a flagship mega church among Korean immigrant
churches with its innovative programs, female leadership lags behind by
one century. I have not been allowed to preach in this church. All the
worship services are conducted by males. Early morning services offered
opportunity for the part-time male *jeondosa* but not for me, simply because I am a woman. My age, theological training, and Ph.D. did not

matter, while the brand-new seminary student intern preached during the early morning service.

The polarization of the public and private sphere around gender lines restricts women's leadership role. Male leaders exclusively occupy the pulpit because it is a powerful public setting. The androcentric pulpit and homily send the message to both female *jeondosa* and the congregation that the proclamation of the word and sacrament belong to males only, contrary to the gospel message.

Anthropologist Edward Hall, in *The Dance of Life,* discusses two different kinds of time: monochronic and polychronic (Hall 1983, 52-53). Hall identifies males within the monochronic sphere of time and females in the polychronic sphere. He points out that the American public square is dominated by monochronic time, with its task-oriented bureaucracies and schedules. Conversely, private space, such as in the traditional home, revolves around polychronic time, as indicated by Esther's multiple roles as mother, wife, associate pastor's wife, doctoral student, and *jeondosa.*

Time differentiation along gender lines also concurs with spatial differences between gender. By confining women *jeondosa*'s ministry to the private sphere, behind the scenes, women's workload multiplies; yet this workload is not publicly recognized or rewarded financially. Thus the injustice of overwork in the private space of polychronic time continues to plague women pastoral leaders emotionally, physically, and financially.

The androcentric interpretation of the *imago Dei* leaves women without direct access to preaching responsibilities. Male preachers, regardless of their qualifications or gifts, are given opportunities solely because they are males. For the same reason—gender—a woman *jeondosa* like Esther is excluded from preaching of any kind, regardless of her educational background. In fact, she is not only excluded but is also invisible. It does not even occur in the mind of the senior pastor that he has excluded her. Two-thirds of the women on staff do not even feel the injustice; they accept exclusive male preaching as biblical. Ironically, Esther's Ph.D. is considered a liability rather than an asset, simply because she is a woman.

Regrettably, a woman's gift as a preacher finds no access to the pulpit, only to the polychronic sphere of private home visitation. Discrimination based on ascribed status such as gender and race is most oppressive because the victim has played no role in earning such mistreatment. Neither does the oppressor deserve his privilege, because he did not earn the position of power. Gender as a primary social construct within the Korean church dismisses women and their educational background in serving God and the church.

Sunjoo shares Esther's pain of being excluded in the lineup of preaching in the various services. According to the Korean immigrant church culture, the exclusion and absence of women's voice in the pulpit is normative. Some of the Korean immigrant churches will occasionally permit women leaders to preach in one of the numerous worship services other than Sunday morning—for example, Sunday afternoon, Wednesday evening, or during early morning services.

Discriminatory Preaching against Women

Male-dominated preaching not only causes gender discrimination in terms of "messenger" but also in the "message" itself. According to Sunjoo, the senior pastor "puts down" women during his sermon, an idea that trickles down to the associate pastors and to the laity. Those who address injustice are viewed as abnormal. The blaming-the-victim theory dominates and keeps the patriarchal system intact. Sunjoo shares intolerable gender discrimination preached from the pulpit:

> When the senior pastor preaches that women should lower themselves and be humble, all the associate pastors tell me to go down and be humble. I respond to them, "How low is low?" In the name of God's grace, male pastors justify oppressing women *jeondosa*.

While the indoctrination of the androcentric homily still occupies the pulpits, the representation and status of women in political and social arenas are slowly rising. This improvement in women's status makes Korean males feel that the world has turned upside down and that the whole society has changed into a woman's world. As long as women's ordination is blocked, male pastors feel they can preserve patriarchal and androcentric messages from the pulpit and control the congregation.

In an Asian North American conference, male-centered interpretation of the Bible was exposed. This vignette illustrates how the Bible was used as a justification for oppressing women's leadership:

> There was a forum on Asian North American Ministry at a local church. The panelists were Asian North American males. When the subject turned to the issue of female leadership, typical Christian jargon was expressed by a male professional. "Women should be silent in the church. This applies today because biblical truth does not change with time." At this, an Asian North American female professional disagreed. The male erupted at the female's disagreement. (Ng 1996, 118)

Scriptures are often proof-texted and repetitiously quoted without balancing them with other scriptures that approve of women leading and prophesying. A traditional, static, literal understanding of the Bible still represents the majority of Asian North American patriarchs. Feeling powerless in America, Asian Christian males project a Confucian image of God. The Korean parallel to the verse "Women should be silent in the church" (1 Tm 2:12) can be found in the proverb "If a female chicken cries, the whole household will be bankrupt." The Confucian gender hierarchy upholds silent, obedient women as ideal. Therefore, verses such as 1 Timothy 2:12 seem self-evident to many Asian male Christians.

Exclusion from Public Prayer

Both Confucianism and Christianity reinforce the patriarchalism of the Korean church, and thus women are invisible. Pioneer women leaders like Esther suffer the pain of exclusion to which the church is oblivious. She lamented that when the laity came forward for intercessory prayers, because it was during the public community gathering, only male staff members were invited to the pulpit to pray for those who came forward. She was not allowed. Esther recalls:

> This church has several annual revival meetings and prayer meetings. The congregation offers prayer requests to the senior pastors and takes all the prayer requests to the pulpit. Then he lays hands over people and prays for people who come up to the front. The senior pastor announces, "All the associate staff, please come up to the pulpit and join me in praying for the people." All the female staff remain in their seats, knowing the unwritten rule of excluding women staff from the public role of leadership. No matter how much I was compelled to pray for the people who came forward, I had to abstain from walking to them in the front and praying. Eventually my desire for intercessory prayer subsided.

The hierarchy of priesthood tainted Esther's experience of intercessory prayer. The exclusiveness of how prayer was structured contradicted the inclusive power of prayer that transcends human boundaries of time, space, and gender hierarchy. The church as a body of Christ is yet to democratize compassion, love, and gifts as highlighted in 1 Corinthians 12:12-31. In a sense it is more painful for Esther to experience exclusion from praying for the people than from preaching. Compared to logocentric preaching, prayer ministry historically was exercised by women leaders. What was traditionally women's domain even among Bible women of the nineteenth century is also blocked by clerical hierarchy, against the leading of the Holy Spirit. Intercessory prayer has been many suffering women's outlet while preaching has been practiced exclusively by males and thus claimed as masculine.

Female Leader, a Maid?

Sunjoo *jeondosa* depicts blatant gender discrimination around cooking:

> During the staff meeting, the senior pastor allocates various jobs. When he assigns workload which falls onto me, he deliberately tells one of the male associate pastors. Then the associate pastor comes to me after the meeting and tells me to do the job.
> Another humiliating issue was cooking in the church. At the very beginning of my work in this church, I cooked lunch for the staff several times. One day the senior pastor's secretary told me to cook lunch for the

staff. I replied, "No." She said, "Isn't cooking part of your job description?"

Cooking and feeding represent women's household work. By keeping women's leadership role in the church in private time and space, the leadership role of women *jeondosa* becomes a mere extension of household chores. In this case, gender exploitation portrays Sunjoo's image as a maid, not the mother who has authority. The outright injustice is in the patriarch's unspoken assumption that part of the female leader's unwritten job description automatically includes cooking for the entire staff.

Internalized Sexism among Women

The patriarchal pastor sees female leaders' roles in service of his interests so that he may serve God more effectively. In a projection of Confucian and paternalistic values, the clear message here is that male leaders have direct access to God. When God is seen as responsible for gender hierarchy, although it is human culture projected onto God, women leaders are left with having to hit the rock with an egg. The privatized roles of women leaders are justified, and thus the nineteenth-century's Bible woman's image of the "rag" (signifying cleaning and dirty work) stands strong in the twentieth century. Women leaders like Sunjoo *jeondosa* are expected to perform maid-like responsibilities in contrast to the elevated status of women in the public arena. Sunjoo shares her shocking experience with women in the church:

> Pastors' wives and another female *jeondosa* were sitting around and talking about the taboo of female preaching. All of them were in agreement when one of the pastor's wives stressed, "Who would sit in the pew to listen to female clergy's preaching? Can anyone of you stand it?" A woman *jeondosa*, nodding her head, agreed with the pastor's wife.

One of the most difficult barriers women *jeondosa* face is from women in the congregation who have internalized sexism. They simply cannot become accustomed to women clergy's preaching because they have not been exposed to it. This reaction of the women members in the church against women's preaching provides male pastors with ample justification for their androcentric patriarchal preaching. A typical comment made by Korean male pastors is, "I cannot invite female clergy to preach at my church because women in the church protest."

By scapegoating women for the patriarchal problems of preaching, male pastors readily exempt themselves from their responsibility as leaders. Then the issue of the male-centered pulpit becomes women's problem, not the patriarchs' problem. The male-only pulpit is justified by turning women against women. Using women laity to justify male exclusion of women preachers involves a double dimension of injustice—the commission and omission of action. Regrettably, the male pastors' response to the internalized sexism of women in the church manifests a blaming-the-victim dynamic in the church. The powers of denial, abdicating responsibility, and blaming the victim further marginalize women.

A very intricate gender dynamic plays out in the leadership roles between the male pastors and the congregation in excluding women's leadership role in preaching. In addition to internalized sexism, women members see a woman *jeondosa* or clergy as one of them, and yet different, rather than set apart as male pastors are. Drawing a certain professional distance with fellow women becomes challenging while they are still embedded in a patriarchal, androcentric leadership image. The difficulty presented by women against women's leadership roles is that they provide more room for preaching on such Bible verses as, "Women should be silent in the church" (1 Tm 2:12).

Against such a church culture, women *jeondosa* like Sunjoo persevere. But many prominent, competent women leaders find no place in the church. One of the rare strengths Sunjoo *jeondosa* has is her endurance based on her work experiences in society. She has overcome many obstacles to be where she is; her perseverance helps her remain centered during trial and persecution. Gender bias as a primary social construct in the Korean immigrant church cancels out other positive qualities of women leaders: competence, hard work, creativity, educational background, and experiences. Sunjoo says, "I have lasted in this position for four years while the male pastor's position in this department has had four different ones in the last four years."

Staff Development

As Sunjoo *jeondosa* has persevered through the oppressive culture in the church, she has earned informal relational power with key laity in the session and the congregation. Her access to congregational matters in the private sphere strengthens her power as a leader, although she still remains faceless and nameless in a public setting. She struggles with male pastors taking credit for all her work in public meetings. Sunjoo depicts her role in the church as "hands" and "feet," while male counterparts are "heads." In hiring a female leader, the qualifications are set for someone who is willing to do the work of "hands" and "feet" rather than the decision-making of the "head." Women leaders' other qualifications such as competence, knowledge, and degrees do not matter in church hiring criteria, while they matter for male staff. According to Sunjoo in a document I received in September 2000:

Even though the female staff amounts to one-third of all staff, only male staff were encouraged to pursue higher education—M.Div., Th.M., D.Min. In fact the church discouraged female staff from further education. The unwritten criterion of selecting female staff was to hire women

who attended second-class theological institutions such as non-accred-
ited informal institutions, while they required higher education for male
staff. Women with higher education such as a doctoral degree are viewed
as potential problem makers. Ironically women's higher educational background in the leadership in this church was perceived as a liability not an
asset. There is an expectation gap from the church toward women's leadership depending on generations. In other words, the first-generation
woman leader is not expected to have higher education, while English-
speaking first-generation-and-a-half and second-generation female leaders are expected to have higher education even if they are women.

In 1922 three hundred Southern Methodist women *jeondosa* came together and
protested against salary disparities between male and female *jeondosa*. Core
issues raised by the two women *jeondosa* today in Korean immigrant churches
parallel the earlier Bible women's struggle. Three issues raised in 1922 about
gender discrimination were (1) salary gap and parsonage; (2) an androcentric
church structure with a male-only ordination policy; and (3) low social rank,
exemplified by referring to women *jeondosa* as "rag." Most Bible women were
either single or widowed, which meant they had no status in a strong patriarchal
society.

The women united and demanded a raise in salary, addressing themselves to
the newly appointed bishop of the Southern Methodist Church. This was one of
the earliest instances of churchwomen seeking equal rights with men. The pay
for men preachers was from seventy-eight *won* to 100 *won*; the women's pay
was around twenty *won*. Bible women's pay was 20 to 30 percent of male
jeondosa pay in the early 1900s. Furthermore, the male *jeondosa* was offered a
parsonage, while the female *jeondosa* was not. The demand for equal rights for
women in church matters continued to be a serious issue from the 1920s through
the early 1930s.

In the nineteenth century women's voice in the society was not represented.
However, Christianity began elevating Korean women's status by building educational facilities for women. Korean women's consciousness rose. In fact, during the Japanese occupation, Christian women educated in mission schools led
the independence movement, thus crossing from private into the public realm.
During the national crisis, women's leadership was allowed. However, once the
Japanese occupation and Korean War ceased, traditional power took over in
seeking stability and joined the forces of American fundamentalism.

At the beginning of the twenty-first century the Korean female *jeondosa* still
struggles with discrimination. Women leaders in various evangelical denominations suffer silently and thus their pain is hidden. Unlike in the nineteenth
century, when Korean women's status in society was low, today society permits
leadership and representation to women, while church culture lags behind. Bible
women today, therefore, face more difficulties with the church's position on
female leadership than did Bible women a century ago. In Esther *jeondosa*'s
case, she married into a denomination that does not see women's ordination as

biblical. In Sunjoo *jeondosa*'s case, she does not see any solution but persists in the struggle, knowing that no other position is available if she wants to continue her ministry and follow her calling. The female *jeondosa*'s leadership is undefined, unmarked, and invisible, and therefore exploited.

RE-CREATING THE IMAGE OF WOMEN'S LEADERSHIP

Some missiological questions arise concerning the problem of restoring holistic theological anthropology and its practices. How can we recover the ideals of humanity, created according to the image of God? What interplay takes place between the biblical texts and culture? Are Christian churches made up of broken people striving toward biblical ideals in a vacuum—or within the provisions of love, which fulfills all commandments? Concerning the gendered image of God, Kari Elisabeth Børresen stresses: "When both women and men are understood to be theomorphic, God can be described by both male and female metaphors. Only when verbalized in terms of both women's and men's equivalent gendered experience does theology become a fully human discourse" (Børresen 1995, 4).

A *Yinist* feminist epistemology allows interconnectedness between the paradox of order and chaos. It attempts to connect reality through the lens of integrated wholes whose properties cannot be reduced to those of smaller units. Thus this essay argues for a *Yinist* alternative to the Confucianized notion of Bible women for Korean churchwomen in the twenty-first century. *Yinist* epistemology also reconciles the paternalistic, androcentric interpretation of incompatibility between femaleness and the Godhead.

As long as sexism, machismo, and domination replace aspects of human relationships, the authentic image of God in humanity is destroyed. Because the values of conquest and autonomy directly challenge gender relationships, they need to be confronted and transformed into the greater values of interdependency, mutuality, and respect that builds the loving community in which human relationships can be nourished. Our broken world is in need of many bridges of love.

14

Mission as Witness to African-American Muslims

A Womanist Approach

Marsha Snulligan Haney

The conceptual framework for this essay emerged while I was serving as a mission worker with the Sudan Council of Churches (Juba) from 1979 to 1981. While living in a country torn by a long history of Muslim and Christian conflict and destruction, I became aware of the growth of Islam worldwide and various responses to religious pluralism. Since then, I have served the church in mission in the Cameroon (Kumba), where relationships between Muslims and Christians were marked by religious cooperation, as well as in various contexts in the United States where Muslims and Christians struggled to respond to each other with a sense of integrity. At the beginning of a new century, Islam is a rapidly growing faith community in the United States. The African-American Protestant community has an unprecedented opportunity to use its unique history, gifts, experiences, spirituality, faith, and social relevance to assist North American churches in understanding the significance of Islam in the context of religious diversity.

Moreover, women in both Islam and African-American Protestantism have demonstrated that they can seize opportunities as well as confront obstacles. Through a womanist missiological understanding of Islamic faith and practices, African-American Protestant churches will become conscious of and empowered to respond with contextual models of the Christian faith. With the word *womanist* I refer to theological discourse that takes the interconnected, three-dimensional experience of racism, sexism, and classism as a source of God's revelation. It emerges from the context of theology in the lives of African-American women in the United States. The hermeneutical, multidialogical, liturgical, and ethical analysis that is embedded in womanist discourse has significantly broadened Christian understandings of how God's power is at work in human experience by articulating important, illuminating, and fresh insights.

The central thesis of this essay, therefore, is that it will be primarily through the development of a womanist approach to religious diversity that the Black Church, and hopefully the North Atlantic Church as a whole, will become empowered to respond faithfully to the challenge of religious plurality, especially from the perspective of Islam as both a religion of the individual and the community. Confidence in this approach as described by womanist ethicists and scholars in other academic fields is based on the fact that womanist theologians, unlike others committed to traditional theological paradigms, have already demonstrated their ability and willingness to allow space for the discussion of plurality as pluralism.

The task of this essay, therefore is threefold. First I will support my claim that while Muslims have actively engaged in a unique process of Islamic contextualization (or Islamicization) with emphasis on a Qur'anic paradigm, a lack of awareness created by Christian hegemony has allowed the Black Church and western scholars to ignore the presence and vitality of non-Christian religious communities. Second, I will provide a praxiological model suggesting how womanist scholars, theologians, and mission activists may engage in mission as witness to people of other living faiths in an effort to comprehend and respond authentically, and with integrity, as Christians within the current religious landscape. Finally, I will conclude by identifying some of the key missiological concerns related to the analysis of mission as witness to people of other living faiths.

ISLAM AND AFRICAN AMERICANS

Because of the broad diversity of religious beliefs among African Americans and the crucial intersection of the religious and social aspects of life in the African-American community, we can no longer ignore, silence, or oppress the "religious other" with whom we share common social and geographical space. Today, Christianity is being challenged by orthodox Islamic practice, particularly by its contrasting ideological and theological worldview.

Since 1975 the leadership of Imam W. D. Mohammad, known as the Mujjaddid (meaning "renewer" in Arabic) has been a primary factor in leading 1.5 to 2 million African Americans to embrace Islam, making Islam, early in the new millennium, the second largest religion in the United States. In 1989 C. Eric Lincoln recognized W. D. Mohammad for making Islam "in a relatively short period of time, the major religion in America after Christianity" (Lincoln 1989). A year later, Lincoln and Lawrence Mamiya observed:

> The Black Church . . . must not underestimate the Islamic challenge on the horizon. Islam is a proven universal religion that is undergoing a worldwide fundamental resurgence and the Muslims in the Black communities have proven themselves to be highly motivated evangelists. (Lincoln and Mamiya 1990)

The overwhelming majority of mainstream Muslims (excluding the members of the Nation of Islam) in the United States are African Americans, estimated at 65 to 85 percent of all Muslims in America. According to Earl Waugh, "Probably the most spectacular phase in the history of Islam in the U.S. was the conversion of Black Muslims to true Islam after pilgrimages to Mecca and visits to other Muslim countries by such leaders as Malcolm X" (Waugh 1983). In addition, one must acknowledge historic Islamic movements with a long history of interaction within African-American communities. They include the Ahmadiyyah's, the Islamic Mission (Sheikh Dauod Fasil), the Hanafis, the Shiites (especially the Islamic Societies of Georgia and Virginia), the Muslim World League, and other proto-Islamic organizations. It is also important to remember that due to the influence of persons such as Imam Abdallah Yasin (1996) and Steven Barboza (1994), W. D. Mohammad's agenda of contextualization is not embraced by all African-American Muslims despite his influential leadership.

By the intentional and strategic use of a vast array of both international and national missional resources, W. D. Mohammad has led Sunni Islamic leadership in the United States to nurture an Islamic identity based on a synthetic model of contextualization centered on the following four influential factors:

1. A focus on the religious believer (and inquirer) as a self-defining process;

2. The tenet that religion must challenge culture, thus shaping the way Islam is articulated;

3. An insistence on the divine message of the Qur'an as an unchanging and unchangeable message; and

4. Unique belief in the Qur'an's special revelation and infallible authority in such a way that all inquirers into the faith must themselves become contextualizers (see also Haney 1999).

Perhaps Christian educator Colleen Birchett best articulated how Islamic values have affected the local African-American community: "While Islam has offered many positive benefits to its converts, such as discipline, business sense, and a commitment to the Black community, the main danger that it poses in the Black community is that it has been drawing people away from a commitment to Jesus Christ as their personal Saviour" (Birchett 1992, 34). Dr. Lawrence N. Jones, the former dean of the Howard University School of Divinity, has made a similar observation: "The past quarter-century has witnessed revolutionary social change, teaching us that today's realities may be tomorrow's curiosities. These changes have altered the world in which African-American Protestant churches exist. Their position of authority has been challenged, and to some degree, diminished by the Muslim community and other non-Protestant organizations of believers" (Jones 1992, 21).

On the international level there has been a growing, conscious effort for Africans and African Americans to develop cross-cultural faith linkages. Partnerships often involve Christians with Christians, and Muslims with Muslims, and the content is missiological—that is, with strategic missions and evangelism and their global impact. These linkages were confirmed in 1999 at a consultation of

Christian and Muslim theologians and religious leaders, organized in part by Muslim woman scholar Rabiatu Ammah, at the University of Ghana (Legon). Present was Imam Elijah Suleman who stated: "We [African Muslims] say they [African Americans] left Africa with the Qur'an, endured with the Qur'an, persevered with the Qur'an, and are now returning with the Qur'an." This observation speaks not only to the spirituality of African peoples but also to the missiological perspective attributed to and presented through a Qur'anic paradigm of great interest to both Muslims and Christians around the world.

A WOMANIST APPROACH TO MISSION AS WITNESS AMONG THOSE OF ANOTHER LIVING FAITH

With a concern and respect for human spirituality, common life in local communities, and the need for transformation (individual and communal), women from varied religious communities, sometimes in conflict, can form a basis for mutual, shared theological reflection across the boundary of differences. There are four fundamental concerns that serve as basic beliefs in my assertion. First is an "ethic of risk" (see Welch 1990). At this juncture in the history of religious plurality it is critical to be willing to risk entering unfamiliar religious landscapes and to risk the possibility of criticism. "To fail to risk moving beyond religious difference is to continue to live and move into the same terrain that has fostered racism, sexism, ethnic oppression, and cross-cultural misunderstanding" (ibid.). Second is an ethic of responsibility, growing out of a sense of both personal religious commitment and communal responsibility. Third is an affirmation of religious pluralism as an opportunity for creative conflict. This is the view of Hassan Askari, who believes that Islam and Christianity stand in need of each other. I too am among those who believe that dialogue and witness cannot be separate. Dialogue, to the extent that it involves referring to one's own beliefs, inevitably includes an element of witness; mission in the broadest sense must necessarily encompass the dialogue process (see Zebiri 1997, 38-39). Muslim Khurram Murad expresses this same view when he says, "There is no point in entering into dialogue unless it is *Da'wah*" (ibid., 43). And fourth is a comprehension of the importance of interreligious or interfaith dialogue as integral to both Christian mission and Islamic *da'wah*.

While the womanist approach contains elements of comparative religious methodology, it shifts focus from stagnant traits to human activity. Unlike academic models that focus primarily on commonalities in an all-encompassing hegemonic discourse, we start from the margins of the debate where analysis of who we are helps us understand the differences and concerns among dominant discourse, individual perceptions, and self representation (see Ask and Tjornstand 1998). Adapting the womanist notion that religion is both personal and political invites reflections on the relationship between resistance and complicity in ways that emphasize women's experience as a historical process (see Cannon 1988; Grant 1989; and Williams 1999).

FIRST PHASE OF THE WOMANIST APPROACH

The first phase, based on the notions of personal virtues and social values, and motivated by a clear sense of religious responsibility and accountability, is perhaps the most important. In this place Christians and Muslims agree to create space—social as well as religious and physical—where conversations can take place. These dialogues, specifically as Christians engage in dialogue with Muslims, tend to center on three areas of concern: personal experience, cultural information, and religious truth. Research data support the significance of these categories as foundational for theological and religious comprehension, as Christians on every part of the theological continuum (evangelical as well as liberational) seek to understand current trends of faith, especially that of movement from Christianity to Islam. Christian mission as witness to people of other living faiths must first seek understanding, utilizing a narrative theological approach consisting of these categories:

1. *Personal information:* "How did you become a Muslim? What has been your religious journey?" This component of the theological examination process refers to an individual's personal and collective religious experiences of a particular religious body and its adherents. Individuals reflect on their own religious experience, including memories, convictions, feelings, ideas, and biases.

2. *Cultural information:* "What is the meaning of your body coverings?" At this stage the dialogue is open to receiving cultural information. Here I have adapted the Whiteheads' mono-theological model to accommodate religious pluralism (see Whitehead and Whitehead 1980). The cultural information exchange stage refers to the willingness of Muslims and Christians to engage in an exchange of information about one another. The information presents an opportunity for furthering the dialogue at a level built on the respect that was planted through the sharing of personal stories as narrative theology. One can, for example ask, "If Muslim women have no authority over men, why did Minister Louis Farrakhan appoint Minister Ava Muhammad?" Gaining greater recognition of beliefs and practices that influence the movement away from Christianity facilitates a keener awareness of the social and religious factors that mark the presence of not one but many branches or streams within Islam.

3. *Source of religious truth:* "What is important to you, a Muslim, as a person of faith?" By viewing religion as a process that relates to a goal or purpose, attention is drawn to the primary sources (scripture, tradition, history, and experience) and the various roles and significance each plays in the lives of women. By focusing on women as symbols of the authentic and sacred community of believers, we are better able to recognize the work of the mosque in both personal and community development based on the distinct "felt needs" of women.

In that context, Muslim women manifest a wide range of involvement in religious activity and in the process of Islamicization. The process of ensuring that the Islamic faith is embraced, nurtured, and practiced correctly occurs on several levels. Women activists engaged as leaders of women's religious associations help to create a new model of Muslim womanhood within American society. For them, the emphasis is on the role of women from a Qur'anic paradigm, that stresses the role of woman as mother and wife in a divinely ordered society. Another group consists of women involved in support groups for Islamic movements dominated by men. Finally there are women involved in the maintenance and creation of orthopraxy in the home, work, and community.

By engaging in dialogue, Christians and Muslims remain faithful to their beliefs, convictions, and journeys, while at the same time they understand how women engage in reshaping theological and religious reflections, especially as they are centered on the "felt needs" of identity, belonging, and leadership.

SECOND PHASE OF THE WOMANIST APPROACH

The second phase of the model involves Christians and Muslims engaging separately in dialogues within their own distinct faith communions. As a dynamic and continuous process of theological reflection, the goal is to lead toward the development of a theology of religious pluralism. This area represents the greatest struggle for Christians, especially those with a high Christology.

As a post-Christian religion, Islamic reflections on Christianity are incorporated into the Qur'anic framework. Although interpretations may vary, some guides exist that provide Muslims with parameters for shaping their relationships with Christians and other religious persons. The same is true of Catholic Christians. Unlike in Protestantism, papal directives have provided guidance to Catholics as they confront the questions of whether Christianity is essentially unique and how Christianity relates to other religions.

Among Protestants, with the exception of a few black churches and church leaders like Marcus Garvey and the Black Manifest Destiny movements, the majority of African-American Christians held attitudes toward Muslims and other non-Christian believers that paralleled those of mainstream Christianity. Today, belief in the necessity of Christ for salvation still tends to be the mark of the contemporary evangelical theological position, which represents many black churches. Given this reality, how does the church move in the direction of developing a theology of religion "characterized by creative tension, which reaches beyond the sterile alternative between a comfortable claim to absoluteness and arbitrary pluralism"? (Bosch 1991, 483).

The discipline of theology of religions, according to David Bosch, raises one of the largest unsolved problems for the Christian church, namely, whether the Christian church and mission are equipped to respond to the challenge emanating from other living religions in a common cultural context. If this question is to be addressed faithfully and responsibly, it must be raised and responded to in local communities by women and men of Christian faith as they seek to live in various contexts of religious pluralism—in the work place, in local community interactions, and within interreligious households. It is crucial to recognize that there are within each religion mutually exclusive claims to universality and finality. It is also important to develop a perspective identified as "accompaniment" that emphasizes behavior which acknowledges the value of religious belief and convictions in a manner that respects the needs and convictions of those who are seeking truth and life through faith. The apostle Paul frequently demonstrated this missional posture of "accompaniment"; for example, he appealed to both Judaism and other belief systems on Mars Hill.

Finally, there is "advocacy." Advocacy is best represented in John's gospel as Jesus converses with the Samaritan woman. It represents putting forward one's own specific beliefs and practices, with which one engages persons and communities from a different religious worldview. Christians witness from within their Christian identity.

THIRD PHASE OF THE WOMANIST APPROACH

This final phase is based on the assumption that Muslims and Christians have engaged one another with integrity in the dialogue of life, as described in the first and second phases. Within a common context of community there may now exist a willingness to demonstrate in local communities the uniqueness of the faith claims in ways that allow cooperation without compromise. With an emphasis on what has been termed *diapraxis,* several forms of ministry indicate the need for interreligious cooperation—an interreligious method of active reflection on the practice of theology that takes place in discerning the meaning of life present in common human existence. While diapraxis is committed to the dialogue of life, it presupposes praxis based on a progressive spiritual dialogue that is nourished by engagement of both the external critique of the sociocultural context, as well as the internal dialectic of actions in faith. For instance, the intersection of mission and dialogue between Christians and Muslims may be seen in areas of community health care, a concern for children and community safety, and in issues of social service among the poor.

What will be interesting to discover is whether the current expressed need among some women in the Womanist Group of the American Academy of Religion and evangelical African-American women to engage in diapraxis with Muslim women is able to move beyond academic rhetoric. Can African-American women obtain the next level of religious interchange where women, Muslim and Christian, can discover a common womanist hermeneutic? Can they develop the hermeneutic by using the sacred texts of the Bible and Qur'an to recover liberating texts, silenced texts, and offer alternative perspectives on texts that have been interpreted in ways harmful to women? Discourse on issues such as these will allow Muslims and Christians to appreciate how both the Bible and the Qur'an have functioned in the construction of worldviews, not only against women, but also against one another.

MISSIOLOGICAL IMPLICATIONS

It is important to recognize not only Islam and Muslims as part of a growing and dynamic movement related to the quest for holistic spiritual fulfillment in the postmodern era, but also movements toward other faiths (including the Christian faith) as well. We must acknowledge that we find ourselves in a climate of spiritual crisis of which Cornel West has observed:

> The spiritual crisis in Afro-America results principally from new class and strata divisions, the impact of mass culture, and the invasion of drugs in the black community. The slow but sure polarization among the growing middle class, the working poor, and the underclass creates immense problems of black communication and organization. These problems have spiritual consequences in that distrust and disrespect for one another are rising among blacks, producing widespread frustration and cynicism. (West 1988, 36)

It is only through shared dialogue (dialogue as diapraxis) with Muslims that Christians can grow in a holistic understanding of how often churches, and Christian leaders, are unaware of where the Christian faith is socially located in the contemporary religious marketplace and the implications for faithful Christian missions. In utilizing the recommended three-pronged womanist approach as a means of addressing the challenge of religious pluralism, as evidenced in Islamic and Christian relationship through the experiences of women, three major concerns emerge: The first is the determination of the "dialogue of life," which many believe is the most appropriate form of interfaith dialogue among women. Second is the need for efforts toward an alliance of Muslim and Christian scholars and mission activists who engage in direct action/reflection/research/advocacy models of relevant and interrelated issues. We would benefit from the learning and experience of scholars from various parts of the world, who have longer histories of wrestling theologically with such issues, especially those from Africa and Asia. Third is the need to contextualize and restructure current theological education regarding how the study of world religions is approached. The majority of our theological education curricula were designed when it was assumed that Christianity was the only viable religious faith accepted and practiced among African Americans. Regarding the development of a Christian theology of religious pluralism, the approach suggested in this essay argues for a more inclusive approach to the questions raised by Muslims and other people of faith, without undermining either the reality of the nature of religious pluralism or the religious requirement for missional engagement. Rather than focusing narrowly upon the issues of the salvation of non-Christians, the primary question to ask instead is, What is the Christian message to a society where there is religious diversity, and Islam is perceived as a nurturing faith?

From the perspective of Christian faith, five crucial concerns emerge for further theological investigation: (1) the development of a biblical perspective by which to regard Hagar and Ishmael (representative of Muslims) as members of the Abrahamic (Judeo-Christian-Islamic) tradition; (2) a concern for how the Black Church can develop a theology of Islam that not only accepts Islam as part of God's plan for salvation, but also allows Christians freedom to struggle theologically with issues such as the prophethood of Muhammad and the Qur'anic revelation after the gospels; (3) a concern for raising local Christian congregational awareness of the church's communal role in the faithful communication of the Christian witness, in word, deed and lifestyle; (4) the development of resources to help Christians and congregations respond with a variety of contextually appropriate models of community ministries based on the "felt needs" of communal caring, economic empowerment, and religious identity; and (5) the development of Christian scholars and community leaders who are well-versed in the Qur'an and Islamic traditions.

Such a multifaceted approach has the potential of helping Christian mission and evangelism become a process of strengthening spiritual awareness, Christ-centered faith, and incarnational praxis. An important outcome of engaging in such an approach is that we will discover that people of faith have always been called upon to wrestle with the matter of religious diversity, and the way they finally succeed is by interaction, not isolation.

Academic as well as applied theology and ministry in local urban contexts have helped to identify other emerging issues critical for engaging in interfaith dialogue and diapraxis with African-American Muslims. Specific attention should be given to the following contemporary concerns: the biblical and Christian theology that identifies sin as originating with a woman, which is absent in the Qur'anic paradigm; the concept of the personhood (that is, the Trinity) of God, which Muslims consider idolatry; the notion of a black Christ/Godhead; the need for humanity not to be transformed (as viewed by Christian doctrine) but rather to be guided (according to Islamic tradition); and the nature of the divisions within Christianity, which according to Muslim intellectuals have led not only to the corruption of Allah's revealed message but also to the exaggerations of the teachings of Christ and his divinity.

CONCLUSION

In closing, given the African-American community's strong need for solidarity, there is no great desire to explore any forces that may work against solidarity in the African-American community. Given this reality, the tradition of religious pluralism inherent within local communities has not been, but must be, fully explored and appreciated as "one of the creation of life-sustaining traditions that has re/membered what hostile sociohistorical forces tried to dis/member" (Williams 1999). In other words, religious diversity must be viewed as a community resource, and our neighborhoods and communities require the participation of all faith-based communities to develop new paradigms for a renewed sense of personal and communal hope. Women in both Christian and Muslim faith traditions have demonstrated their power to embrace religious, social, and personal change. If they choose, they can continue to seize opportunities as well as confront obstacles that must be faced related to religious choice and missional responsibility. Only through the contributions of womanist thought and womanist perspectives on religious pluralism—especially those that relate to Muslim faith and practice—will the Black Church be able to respond appropriately and with authenticity to issues of faith and culture, mission and evangelism (and *da'wah*), and the struggle for life, hope, and wholeness within a common public life.

15

Do Missions Raise or Lower the Status of Women?

Conflicting Reports from Africa

Miriam Adeney

"God and nature intended you for a missionary wife."

In this quotation from one of the most famous novels in the English language, St. John Rivers proposes marriage to Jane Eyre. But he wants more. He presses her to join him not only in marriage but also in mission.

Jane considers it. All things being equal, she would like to please God. She would like to alleviate suffering, which is in part how Rivers envisions missionary work.

Yet she herself does not feel free in relation to Rivers.

"He has told me that I am formed for labour," she confides to her friend Diane. "Would it not be strange, Di, to be chained for life to a man who regarded one but as a useful tool?" (Bronte 1963, 369, 381).

Eventually Jane rejects Rivers. Why? Partly because she does not love him. She loves Rochester. But also Jane rejects Rivers because she cannot see herself an unliberated liberator.

In this dialogue we glimpse the germ of a more general issue: Do Christian missionaries liberate women? Do they raise women's status? Especially in Africa, where many of Jane Eyre's contemporaries set the standards, there is an ongoing dichotomy in the literature on this question. Two bodies of data-rich material exist: missionary reports and anthropological studies. On this issue they often differ sharply. Whereas missionary literature credits missions with increasing opportunities for women, much recent anthropological literature speaks of colonial and missionary programs' adverse effects on women's status. Each body throbs with anecdotal evidence. Neither offers more than cursory acknowledgment of the other (see Van der Geest and Kirby 1992). Both continue on their courses, passing silently like ships in the night.

211

Is one of these traditions based on faulty selection of data? Quite the contrary, I would argue. Rather, the two literatures may be viewed as complementary, focused on different domains. Economically, politically, and religiously, there is evidence that missions sometimes have marginalized women's roles, contributing to the lowering of their status. Ideologically, however, missions have affirmed women's essential nature as persons. This affirmation has buttressed women's dignity and engendered seeds of liberation, even in economic, political, and religious arenas.

The concept of women's status itself is problematic. How do we rank conflicting definitions? Human rights discussions have called attention to this issue. In Africa, in particular, debate has raged over whether human rights are individual or collective. The Banjul Charter on Human Rights asserts that in African societies "peoples," not individuals, have rights, and individual freedoms may have to be sacrificed for the good of the group (Messer 1993, 227). In practical terms, does this mean that—for the good of the group—in times of scarcity women and girls should be fed less than men and boys? (Kilbride 1990). Clitoridectomy, bride price, and the international export economy are other areas where women's status and rights are issues.

ECONOMY OR EMBROIDERY

Increasingly in the literature on underdevelopment, there is recognition of colonialism's "pernicious effects on women's status in Africa" (Barthel 1975, 1). These lines open an *African Studies Review* issue focused on women, part of the research generated during the first United Nations Year for Women. While this quotation refers to the colonial period, other studies connect recent Western-dominated international trade and aid programs with continued marginalization of African women. Since the United Nations Year for Women brought this data to public awareness, some programs have attempted to redress the imbalance.

It is argued that European colonial governors, educators, and missionaries of that era were not accustomed to women's political or economic leadership in their home countries. Therefore they overlooked women leaders in traditional institutions in Africa. They ignored, for example, the market traders in Nigeria and Ghana, who were strong local leaders. Accordingly, when they replaced traditional institutions with modern ones, they did not offer positions to women. In the post-independence period, those structures continue to constrain women.

When the colonial governments administered modern land titles, for example, they tended to do it in men's names, and women's traditional rights to land were lost. Consider the Tonga Valley in Zimbabwe, a matrilineal region. Prior to the construction of the Kariba Dam, both women and men inherited titles to land—some through their lineages and some through their fathers. Building the dam required relocating the population. In the subsequent land distribution, titles were allocated exclusively to men. The continuing breakup and allocation of "free" land furthered "the progressive discontinuation of the habit of diverting land to women" (Cutrufelli 1983, 69).

When Europeans encouraged cash crops, women's traditional subsistence gardens, or gathering grounds—which continued to keep the family fed—were shoved to the margins. When public and private powers—including missions— offered business connections and loans, women often were bypassed. When, in more recent years, Western development agencies offered agricultural extension training course, women gardeners again were ignored. "African women perform most of the agricultural labor, but one of the most salient aspects of women's education in Africa is their exclusion from agricultural education, which has been well documented for a number of countries" (Robertson and Berger 1986, 109).

On one hand, women's already exhausting jobs in agricultural production often increase with the introduction of cash-crop farming, education for children, wage employment for men in the towns, and so forth, but their access to incomes which would alleviate their situation changes only slightly or not at all. On the other hand, mechanization of agriculture can drive women out of economic productivity, with no substitutes offered. Also, women are being pushed out of traditional marketing. But relatively little compensation is made for uneducated women through employment in the modern sector. It is mostly educated women who participate in the progressive specialization of work. (Women's Research and Training Centre, U.N.E.C. for Africa 1975, 55)

Of Nigeria, anthropologist Audrey Smock observed, "Economic development may adversely affect the position of women in Third World countries by offering men disproportionately greater opportunities in the modern sector of society" (Smock 1977, 192). Similarly of Senegal, Barthel contended that under Western rule

women's economic roles were stripped from them, they were increasingly restricted to the home, and found sooner or later that the delicate balance of sex roles had been upset through colonialism's differential treatment of men and women. (Barthel 1975, 17)

Missions are implicated strongly in the field of education. Education for domesticity rather than for income generation sticks in the craw of many anthropologists. Although missions founded girls' schools—far fewer than boys' schools—the girls' curricula often emphasized domestic and consumer skills rather than preparation for higher education, business, or leadership (Bowie 1993, 13; Hansen 1992b).[1] When Queens College was founded in Lagos for the

---

[1] The "civilizing" power of femininity, and the domestic ideal, shaped the lives of many European and American women missionaries in the colonial period. On the relationship among domestic ideals, missions, gender, and colonialism, see Beaver 1980; Biedelman 1982; Birkett 1992; Bowers 1984; Burton 1992; Calloway 1987; Chaudhuri and Strobel 1992; Christensen and Hutchison 1982; Flemming 1992; Garrett 1982; Jacobs 1992; Robert 1993, 1997, 1998; Swaisland 1992; and Tucker 1990.

secondary education of girls in 1927, the curriculum consisted of needlework, domestic science, and singing. Even when parents requested more academic training for their girls, the Queens College principal vigorously defended a domestic curriculum (Johnson 1986, 240; Hansen 1992b, 172-76). One reason explicitly stated elsewhere for giving girls domestic education was so they would not compete with men for jobs (Bowie 1993, 13). Governor Lugard of Nigeria wrote in 1922 that the purpose of female education was to make better wives and mothers, "showing little understanding that women of some ethnic groups in Nigeria were actively engaged in economic production and marketing and held public roles in political and religious spheres" (in Calloway 1987, 111).

Adult education for women also emphasized home arts. In *African Encounters with Domesticity* Hansen comments on a Rhodesian project observed in the mid-twentieth century:

> Women's Institute activities glorified a domestic ideal that introduced a gender dichotomy between public and private that was foreign to rural African lives and applied poorly to the changing livelihood of urban African households. . . . African women's lack of enthusiasm for WI activities might be due to the fact that they had enough to do already, and that most saw little use in learning skills without being consulted about their needs and desires. The abridged version of the "European way of life" they were imparted in WI classes did not lessen but accentuated their dependence on men. (Hansen 1992b, 260)

When certificates were distributed at a graduation from a similar project in 1954, class participants' friends commented, "Look at our friends. . . . The winners are given only pieces of paper which have no use at all. . . . If they were not given money, it would have been nicer if they would have been given needles and cotton. These women are no better than we, who do not go to classes" (in Powdermaker 1962, 109).

In an unpublished paper in 1996 Kila Reimer, a Christian development worker in Eritrea (now director of World Concern in Cambodia), observed that "the only Christian efforts for women concentrate on traditional home economic type programmes such as sewing classes, training in handicraft production, and education in childcare and cooking." Yet the National Union of Eritrean Women wanted training for income-generating jobs, thoroughly integrated into the national economy. One Eritrean woman told Reimer the existing curriculum was "constrained by ascribed notions of women's place, which are counterproductive. This concentrates on the old colonial 'home economics model,' rather than equipping women with the skills and scientific and technical expertise that is required for them to participate more equitably in the production and development of their societies."

"When a Ghanaian woman is educated, she is expected to *do* something with her education," a West African woman says (Pellow 1977, 116). She had seen daughters of independent Ghanaian traders sent to school who ended up less employable than their mothers. They simply became part of the *lumpen-bourgeoisie* oozing across Africa. In a similar vein a contemporary researcher in rural Liberia suggests that "*not* sending girls to school is a rational choice" (Robertson and Berger 1986, 109).

In sum, it has been argued that Christian missionaries sometimes have contributed to the marginalization of African women economically, politically, and educationally, because they were not equipped to see African women's strong roles in traditional society. For example, according to Carol Johnson,

> Yoruba women held certain rights in the public domain: to participate in discussions of public policy; to be represented on governmental decision-making bodies; to own and inherit property; and the freedom to pursue, control, and defend their own economic interests. . . . These rights did not make women equal partners in society with men. . . . But women's prominence in the public economy and their legitimacy as public actors in the political arena were well established, as was their collective mode of protecting their interests and advancing their aims. . . .
>
> It was women's political and economic roles that were most devastated during the colonial period. Colonial administrations refused to recognize that women's organizations and roles were more than social in nature. . . . By refusing women the vote until 1950, not appointing them to any important governmental bodies, and neglecting their education and employment, the British in Nigeria pursued a policy of alienation and exclusion of Yoruba women from the economic and political arenas. (Johnson 1986, 239)

PROPHETESS OR DEVIL'S GATE

As in the political and economic spheres, so in the religious: most early foreign missionaries in Africa were not accustomed to women's leadership back home. Thus they did not recognize it in Africa. They overlooked—or considered unimportant—female prophets, diviners, and curers; women's religious gatherings and ceremonies; and the rich application of religion to areas of life with which women particularly were concerned, such as fertility, barrenness, blessing for illegitimate as well as legitimate children, blessing for polygamous as well as monogamous marriages, co-wife conflict mediation, and resources for coping with the demands of a multigenerational extended family. Whatever the reason, they sometimes neglected cultivating women's leadership in the churches. The resulting frustration with peripheral roles on the part of African churchwomen has been an important stimulus to the development of the thousands of African Instituted Churches all across the continent. According to David Barrett:

> The assault which the missions were seen to be mounting against African traditional family structure was felt primarily by women. . . . Disillusionment with missions spread until renewal movements leading to

independence began, under which new regime the status of women altered radically for the better. (Barrett 1968, 150)

In many of the non-Western indigenous movements, a woman can lead. She may be a prophetess-founder; a prophetess-pastor-healer-counselor; the leader of a powerful women's fellowship group; or a member of a pastoral team headed by a male pastor. Describing a prophetess/founder, Lehmann explicitly contrasted this woman's opportunities for leadership inside and outside of mission churches:

> Lenchina is nowadays much like a mature and successful chieftainess, hearing her people's cases, engaging in profitable business, ordering her communities. But (when) she started . . . she rebelled against the elders' verdict that her visions were not genuine, and that as a woman of the catechumen class she could not be allowed to preach. . . . It is a great loss to the church in her home district that it could not retain in its service so strong a personality, who has manifested great pastoral gifts in inspiring trust in Christ's power over all kinds of evil and adversity in the hearts of thousands of people who have brought their magic articles to her to be destroyed. We lost a great potential woman leader because an African minister applied what he thought was a Christian principle but was in reality a prejudice of Western history. The nineteenth century pattern of man-woman relationships was taught by some missions as the Christian one—a great mistake. (Lehmann 1963, 68)

Bowie commented similarly about the sister of a Nigerian Anglican bishop who was the lead prophetess in the Cherubim and Seraphim Society, "a role she could not have achieved in a mainstream church" (Bowie 1993, 16; cf. Brandel-Syrier 1984).

In his ground-breaking study of thousands of African Instituted Churches, Barrett formulated eighteen indicators by which to measure the likelihood that a breakaway religious movement would occur in a given ethnic group. Barrett argued that if six of the indicators were present, a breakaway was likely; if twelve were present, a breakaway was certain. Among these indicators were several that concerned women. If, for example, women had active religious leadership roles in the pre-contact religion, a breakaway was likely. If an earth goddess was prominent, a breakaway was likely. Women from such backgrounds often felt stifled in mission churches. They experienced a "discrepancy between missions and scriptures" in the churches which "failed to offer them the full status accorded in the Bible" (Barrett 1968, 146).

Listening to the Old Testament, African women heard about political leaders like Deborah, and godly polygamous wives like Sarah. In the New Testament they found strong women like Mary, Anna, Priscilla, Lydia, and the sisters Mary and Martha. In the Lord Jesus they saw a religious leader who treated women with respect, a man who worked with women without demeaning them and who listened seriously to their theological views.

What a contrast with those church fathers who disparaged women! Tertullian called Eve "the Devil's gateway" and blamed her for making it necessary for Jesus to die (see Tucker and Liefeld 1987). Augustine counseled, "A good Christian is found to love in one woman the creature of God . . . but to hate in her what pertains to a wife" (*On the Sermon on the Mount* 1.15.41). Aquinas, according to historian Will Durant, held that "a woman is something defective and accidental . . . dominated by her sexual appetite, whereas a man is ruled by reason" (in Durant 1950, 973). Examples could be multiplied. According to historian Adrian Hastings, women were often the first to convert to Christianity in a given community because they perceived its potential to liberate them from traditional narrow social roles. Yet, "as the church became more socially central [in African communities] . . . women's role within it appeared to grow far more marginal: the basic requirements of patriarchy were reasserted" by the African male leadership (Hastings 1993, 121). However, Hastings adds, while this was true during the first half of the twentieth century, in the 1950s many churches experienced new vitality. As a result, new opportunities for women appeared.

WHEN PIONEERS TURN BUREAUCRATS

There is an intriguing second component to mission marginalization of women suggested in the anthropological literature. This is a social process not specific to missions but applicable to missions. In many societies, when organization intensifies—in established churches, for example—women get sidelined. From being partners and producers, women are relegated to being decorative assistants. In horticultural societies, for example, women generally control some important resources and decisions. When people live off the land, women's productivity matters and is valued. But as people become richer, women may be valued more as decoration, property, or lineage connectors than as producers. Also, when an economic system becomes complex, creating surpluses, as with the development of grain agriculture or as in the Industrial Revolution of the nineteenth century, men tend to take control of the system. Women's freedom, leadership, and even economic compensation decline relatively. Increased wealth also requires increased upkeep at home, and women may be allocated to that (Mukhopadhyay and Higgins 1988, 477, 478).

Why women are marginalized continues to be debated. In Naomi Quinn's overview of research on women's status, she suggested five "universal determinants of women's status" (Quinn 1977). These are women's role in childbearing and child-rearing, men's greater physical strength, men's greater aggressiveness, women's compliance, and children's socialization to behave as male and female. Quinn also pinpointed three "cross-cultural variables" that affect women's status: social structure, economy, and ideologies of opposition. A decade later a major review article suggested that the issue is more complex and confusing (Mukhopadhyay and Higgins 1988, 477-78; see also Silverblatt 1988). Still, the preponderance of findings suggests that in classless societies, where surplus wealth is minimal, women experience opportunities to lead in important domains. Yet when classes develop, women's leadership opportunities diminish relative to the men in their class, at least initially.

A parallel to the economic situation may exist in the sphere of religion. The bureaucratization of a religious movement seems to consolidate and quantitatively reduce numbers of opportunities for leaders. When a movement is pioneering and stretching, every worker counts. But when an organization is consolidating, women become decorative assistants. When this process occurs in the context of "ideologies of opposition" regarding women, such as those adopted by many church fathers, women are doubly bound.

Among both African churchmen and American churchwomen there are parallel examples of bureaucratization resulting in disempowerment. Concerning the former, native clergy in West Africa were more numerous *before* the period of "high empire" than during it (1880-1920). After 1880, the "dismantling of indigenous Christian structures, and the supplanting of indigenous Christian leaders, paralleled developments in the colonial administration" (Walls 1982, 163). Similarly, American churchwomen have experienced disempowerment resulting from bureaucratic concentration (Robert 1993, 109, 112).

Such an experience—which we sometimes interpret as a tension between gospel and tradition—may in fact be common in religions. Like Christian feminists who want to get beyond the church fathers to Jesus, so some Muslim fundamentalist feminists advise, "Go back to the Prophet Muhammad for true freedom." Similarly, some devout Hindu feminists hark back to a more emancipated period before the Code of Manu. According to N. E. A. Falk, male and female often symbolize complementary modes of creative power. Yet, Falk continues:

> Here we come to a puzzling problem. Many tribal religions, and apparently also many of ancient times, have drawn upon women's sacred and symbolic values to weave rich fabrics of cosmic and ritual balance. In such traditions women often assume roles as significant ritual functionaries, shamans, and seers. The world's largest and most successful religions, however, have often used the same values to exclude women from many important arenas of religious life and to justify their practical subordination to men. The reasons for this apparent reversal are complex, but the facts are indisputable. As a normal rule, in the great religious traditions of the world, women have been expected to play a role, religious and social, second to that of men. (Falk 1981, 806)

Nevertheless, Falk's observation is not the last word.

PERSONS OF ETERNAL VALUE

Ideal Christian status is rooted in the teaching that women and men are made equally in the image of God, equally sinners, yet equally objects of God's grace and the Holy Spirit's empowering. Hence, women are to be respected not abused. In spite of constricting structures, this ideology has empowered women. Indeed, both missionary women like Mary Slessor (Bonk 1980; Buchan 1981), and African women such as those in the Nigerian Women's Party (Johnson 1986, 246-48) have been propelled by their Christian ideology to confront unjust structures.

Among three powerful Nigerian women's political movements during the colonial period, two were led by women rooted in the church. The Nigerian Women's Party was founded by Lady Oyinkan Abayomi in 1944. Among the objectives of educational, agricultural, and industrial development of Nigeria was the aim "to work for the amelioration of the condition of the women of Nigeria, not merely by sympathy for their aspirations but by recognition of their equal status with men" (Johnson 1986, 246).

Sometimes the gospel empowers women for confrontation, and at other times it empowers them for *compliance*. However, simple *coping* is the challenge facing many African women. While some enjoy stable, progressive lives, millions of others have been disrupted by economic, political, and health (AIDS) crises. Religion, according to the anthropologist Clifford Geertz, helps people rise above their limits in three areas: limits of analysis, limits of endurance, and limits of moral insight (Geertz 1973, 100). Many African women have hit their limits on all fronts. How do they find meaning and motivation to cope? For some, it is their Christian faith and fellowship that carries them. In the words of Kenyatta University professor Anne Nasimiyu-Wasike:

> Most African women spend sixteen to eighteen hours daily working to provide their families with food, shelter, water, clothing, medicine, and education. They have very little time to seriously reflect on their relationship with other people and with God. Nevertheless, these women believe that their lives are lived in union with God; their theology is not one which is written and articulated but one which is lived and practised in everyday activities and experiences. . . .
>
> In his own lifetime, Jesus rejected the androcentric culture of the Jewish people. He gave special attention to the marginalized. . . . And most of these people were women. . . . There are several christological models that emerge. . . . In the eschatological model, Christ is sent by God to an alienated world where the presence of God takes the shape of the Crucified One. Why? . . . In his suffering Christ took on the conditions of the African woman and conditions of the whole of humanity, and in his resurrection the African woman is called to participate in the restoration of harmony. (Nasimiyu-Wasike 1991, 76-77)

In *Faces of Jesus in Africa*, Robert J. Schreiter suggests several African understandings of Christ: Jesus the master of initiation, Jesus the chief, Jesus the elder brother, and Jesus the healer. While these models speak to women, others that may touch women more are Jesus the life-giver, Jesus the sufferer, and Jesus the nurturer (Schreiter 1991, vii-viii). Women immersed in such paradigms may find their hope renewed. Communing with the God who took on human form to visit this planet, who entered into our pain to the point of death, and who generated the energy to start over, women may find the power to transcend the ordinary limits of their endurance.

Such vibrant resilience nurtured by Christian faith flows through the twenty life histories of African women published in *Surviving without Romance: African Women Tell Their Stories* (Cummings 1991). Set in East Africa, these narratives of childless women, wives in polygamous families, and women in other roles illustrate how mission churches have enabled women to cope.

It would appear that while missions sometimes have marginalized African women economically and religiously, simultaneously missions have affirmed them as persons of eternal value. On the one hand, missionaries in this region actively favored a patrilineal system over the existing matrilineal one, because the former was closer to a European model of marriage and inheritance. The resulting erosion of their matrilineages caused women to lose mobility and independence. On the other hand, Anaguta women had not held important religious roles until the mission came. Christianity opened these to them. Historian Elizabeth Isichei observes:

> The suggestion that Christianity can empower women seems implausible to many Western feminists. Some have concluded that Christianity is irredeemably patriarchal. . . . Feminists who remain Christians have tended to stress the silencing, marginalization and oppression of women in earlier and contemporary churches. In the Nigerian context, a colonial official's report on an Igbo community in the 1930s made the interesting point that Christianity reinforced traditional patriarchal values (Vaux 1936, paras. 62-66). But it seems to be much more generally true in Africa that women experienced Christianity as empowering. It gave them a place on which to stand, from which they could bypass or challenge male-dominated sacred worlds. Truth is always complex, however, and sometimes Christianity paved the way to new forms of marginalization. (Isichei 1993, 209)

Although in this essay I have accented differences between mission and African Instituted Churches, in practice the streams merge. Anglican bishops speak in tongues and dance in the aisles, and indigenous leaders take management seminars and M.Div. degrees. This happy marriage is illustrated by research reported in a dissertation entitled *Conversion to Greater Freedom?: Women, Church and Social Change in Northwest Tanzania under Colonial Rule* (Larsson 1991).

Here the early Lutheran mission in the 1930s was traditional: "The main aim of girls' education . . . was apparently to make them suitable for assisting their husbands" (Larsson 1991, 215). Today, however, women speak and even preach in Christian meetings. A major influence has been the East African revival that blew through the region from the 1940s through the 1960s. Now, in fellowship groups and teaching teams, Christians make decisions by consensus. Equality of believers is practiced. Women speak and preach. Sermon texts have a modernizing flavor: how to improve marriage, build a better house, take care of property, or divide labor. At first the historic local denomination, the Evangelical Lutheran Church, resisted the revival, fearing doctrinal deviation, legalism, and a creeping Anglican influence. By 1948, however, "there was a meeting between the pastors, the leaders of the revival and the missionaries, where the revival was discussed from all angles. It was agreed that the Church needed the revival and the revival needed the Church" (ibid., 147). Many pastors have identified with the movement, and synod meetings have been affected significantly. Thus, while local Christians' enthusiastic egalitarian behavior may be similar to that in indigenous movements, these believers remain rooted in their historic denomination. Such continuity between a mission and an independent movement may be more widespread throughout African Christianity than academic categories would suggest.

Even in the beginning of the mission work in Tanzania described by Larsson, benefits for women were notable. Childless women were not sent away anymore. Drunkenness ended, and with it the abuse of women and children that had accompanied it. "Conversion implied both religious and social improvement, and women utilized that for greater dignity and freedom" (Larsson 1991, 216). The newfound freedoms included the freedom not to be married to a rich old polygamist, the freedom not to have to abandon twin babies, the freedom to be valued sufficiently to be taught in school, and the freedom not to marry at all but to be independent, especially as a religious worker. These freedoms were exercised gratefully. The revival movement took freedom a step further, "bringing drastic change through the ideas and practice of greater equality and dignity" (ibid., 207).

SIN AND GRACE

Do missions raise or lower the status of women? A paradox appears. On the one hand, there has been "a logical flaw and serious moral contradiction in Christian endeavor that would seek to elevate, educate, and emancipate Eastern women but saw no need to challenge the kinds of subordination required of the very European women who were invited to become . . . agents of that liberation" (Cunningham 1992, 98). Jane Eyre rightly was bothered by this. Second, there has been a sin of omission in missionaries' blindness to African women's traditional opportunities and powers. Third, there has been a sin of conformity to the idols of the time, the bureaucratic processes that marginalize women.

At the same time, a pulse of freedom flows from the gospel: women and men are equally made in the image of God, equally objects of God's grace, and equally empowered by the Holy Spirit. Once this liberating word is let loose, it cannot be completely shoved back in the box. Nor can women. In sum, Christian mission's empowerment of African women has been real, yet rife with contradictions, some of them costly.

Contributors

Christina Tellechea Accornero is the Executive Director of Community Management Partners in Anderson, Indiana. She has served as a short-term missionary in the Philippines and as an urban missionary in Los Angeles. Her publications include "A Common Ministry, a Common Vocation," in *God So Loves The City*, edited by Charles Van Engen and Jude Tiersma (MARC Publications, 1994.) Ordained in the Church of God (Anderson, Indiana), she holds the Ph.D. in Intercultural Studies from Fuller School of World Mission.

Frances S. Adeney is William A. Benfield Jr. Associate Professor of Evangelism and Global Mission at Louisville Presbyterian Seminary. She has teaching and missionary experience in Singapore, the Philippines, England, Switzerland, and most recently five years in Indonesia. Her publications include "Feet First: How Practices Have Shaped My Theology of Evangelism and Mission," in *Teaching Mission in a Global Context*, edited by Patricia Lloyd-Sadle and Bonnie Sue Lewis (Geneva Press, 2001). Her book *Making Oneself Strange: Gender Ideology, Moral Agency and Social Change*, is forthcoming from Syracuse University Press.

Miriam Adeney, an anthropologist, is Associate Professor of Global and Urban Ministry at Seattle Pacific University, and Research Professor of Mission at Regent College. Her publications include *How to Write: A Christian Writer's Guide* (Regent College, 1994); *God's Foreign Policy: Practical Ways to Help the World's Poor* (Eerdmans, 1984); *A Time for Risking: Priorities for Women* (Multnomah, 1987); and *Hagar's Daughters: Ministries with Muslim Women* (InterVarsity, forthcoming). A Presbyterian, she is Editor at Large for *Christianity Today*, and she has lived and worked in ten countries on four continents.

Catherine B. Allen served on the staff of Woman's Missionary Union, Auxiliary to Southern Baptist Convention, for twenty-five years, including as Associate Executive Director from 1983 to 1989. From 1990 to 1995 she was President of the Women's Department of the Baptist World Alliance, in which capacity she worked with Baptist women from over one hundred countries. Among her books are *The New Lottie Moon Story* (Broadman, 1980; WMU, 1997), *A Century to Celebrate: History of Woman's Missionary Union* (WMU, 1987), and *Laborers Together with God* (WMU, 1987). She holds an MBA from Emory University.

Angelyn Dries, O.S.F., is Associate Professor and Chair of the Religious Studies Department at Cardinal Stritch University. A past president of the American Society of Missiology, she has authored *The Missionary Movement in American*

Catholic History (Orbis Books, 1998) and *Prayer and Practice in the American Catholic Community* (Orbis Books, 2000), as well as numerous articles. Since 1992 she has been engaged in pastoral work among the Korean Catholic community in Milwaukee.

Margaret Eletta Guider, O.S.F., is Associate Professor of Religion and Society at the Weston Jesuit School of Theology. Her publications include *Daughters of Rahab: Prostitution and the Church of Liberation* (Fortress Press, 1995). She holds degrees in education from the University of Illinois and degrees in theology from the Catholic Theological Union and Harvard University. A former missionary in Brazil, she was also Associate Director of the Catholic Missions Office for the Archdiocese of Chicago.

Marsha Snulligan Haney is Associate Professor of Missiology and Religions of the World at the Interdenominational Theological Center in Atlanta, Georgia. Ordained in the Presbyterian Church, USA, in 1978, she has mission experience in Sudan and Cameroon. Her publications include *Islam and Protestant African American Churches: Responses and Challenges to Religious Pluralism* (University Press of America, 1999) and "Issues of Contextualisation: Challenges for African American Christians and Muslims," *in Studies in World Christianity* 3.2 (1997).

Melissa Lewis Heim is Lecturer in the History of Christianity at Andover Newton Theological School and is Head of the History Department at Mt. Alvernia High School in Newton, Massachusetts. A member of the Board of Managers of the American Baptist Historical Society, she holds the Ph.D. in history from Boston College.

Young Lee Hertig is Vera B. Blinn Associate Professor of World Christianity at United Theological Seminary, Dayton, Ohio. An ordained Presbyterian minister, she has served Korean immigrant churches for the last twenty years. Among her publications are *Healing the Cultural Tug of War: The Korean Immigrant Family and Church in Transition* (Abingdon, 2001) and "The Asian-American Alternative to Feminism: A *Yinist* Paradigm," *Missiology* (January 1998).

Lydia Huffman Hoyle is Associate Professor of Religious Studies at Georgetown College in Kentucky. She has published numerous articles in such journals as *International Bulletin of Missionary Research*, *Missiology*, and *Baptist History and Heritage*. A recipient of the Ph.D. from the University of North Carolina, she is a Southern Baptist.

Bonnie Sue Lewis is Assistant Professor of Mission and Native American Christianity at the University of Dubuque Theological Seminary. An elder in the Presbyterian Church, USA, she co-edited *Teaching Mission in a Global Context* (Geneva Press, 2001). Her publications include "The Contextualization of Christianity by Native American Presbyterians," in *Witness in Context*, edited by Jean S. Stoner (PCUSA, 1999). She served as a teacher in Guatemala.

Mary Joseph Maher, I.H.M., received the Ph.D. from St. Louis University. A former missionary in Brazil, during the 1970s and 1980s she coordinated and opened IHM missions throughout Africa and Latin America. She has also undertaken work in the inner city, notably among the Mexican community in Chicago. She is author of *A Compelling Vision: A History of the Overseas Missions of the Sisters, Servants of the Immaculate Heart of Mary—Monroe, Michigan* (IHM, 2000).

Dana L. Robert is Truman Collins Professor of World Mission at the Boston University School of Theology. A United Methodist, she is author of *American Women in Mission: A Social History of Their Thought and Practice* (Mercer, 1997), co-author of *Christianity: A Social and Cultural History*, 2d ed. (Prentice-Hall, 1998), and co-author of *"Occupy Until I Come": A. T. Pierson and World Evangelization* (forthcoming, Eerdmans). With M. L. Daneel, she edits the series *African Initiatives in Christian Mission*, published by the University of South Africa Press.

Silas H. L. Wu is Professor of History at Boston College where he teaches Chinese and Japanese history including the history of Christianity in China. His books include *Communication and Imperial Control in China* (Harvard University Press, 1970), *Passage to Power: K'ang-hsi and His Heir Apparent, 1661-1722* (Harvard University Press, 1979), and a recent book in Chinese on Dora Yu. A former associate of Harvard's John King Fairbanks Center for East Asian Research, he has been interested in the history of Christianity in China since his conversion to Christ in 1949.

Kevin Xiyi Yao is currently a visiting fellow at the Institute of World Religions, Chinese Academy of Social Sciences, Beijing, China. He is author of many articles on the history of Christianity in Chinese, and he has a forthcoming book in the ASM Dissertation Series, *The Fundamentalist Movement among Protestant Missionaries in China, 1920-37*. He received the Th.D. from Boston University and belongs to the Chinese Bible Church of Greater Boston.

Works Cited

MANUSCRIPT COLLECTIONS AND ARCHIVES

ABCFM (American Board of Commissioners for Foreign Missions) Archives. Houghton Library, Harvard University, Cambridge, Massachusetts.

American Madura Mission Collection. United Theological College Library, Bangalore, India.

LAM (Latin America Mission). Collection 236. Archives of the Billy Graham Center. Wheaton College, Wheaton, Illinois.

Maryknoll Mission Archives. Maryknoll (Ossining), New York.

McBeth/Crawford Collection. Idaho State Historical Society, Boise, Idaho.

McBeth, Kate C. Papers. San Francisco Theological Seminary, San Anselmo, California.

Medical Mission Sisters. Philadelphia, Pennsylvania.

Morrill, Allen and Eleanor. Papers. University of Idaho Library, Moscow, Idaho.

Olle, Mrs. Michael [Anne]. 1944. February 6. Volume 10, Scrapbook of Patna mission and mission circles. Lillian and Clara Westropp papers, 1922-1968 MC 215. Schlesinger Library, Radcliffe College, Cambridge, Massachusetts.

United Methodist Church Archives. Drew University, Madison, New Jersey.

Westropp, Lillian and Clara. Papers. 1922-68 MC 215. Schlesinger Library, Radcliffe College, Cambridge, Massachusetts.

WMU (Woman's Missionary Union), Auxiliary to the Southern Baptist Convention. Birmingham, Alabama.

PERIODICALS AND PUBLISHED LETTERS

AIC (American Indian Correspondence: The Presbyterian Historical Society Collection of Missionaries' Letters, 1833-1893). 1997. Westport, Conn.: Greenwood Press. Microfilm.

Chinese Recorder. 1914-24.

Latin America Evangelist (Evangelist). 1921-91.

LAM (The Latin America Mission). 1929. Latin America Evangelization Campaign.

The Missionary Herald. 1910-40.

Tell: Magazine for Girls. 1950-70.

Woman's Missionary Advocate. 1894-1903.

MINUTES, MANUALS, AND REPORTS

AMM (American Madura Mission). 1915-1929. *Minutes of the American Madura Mission*. Madura: American Madura Mission.

Campbell, Josephine P. 1893. *Annual Report of Woman's Foreign Missionary Society of the MEC, South*. Nashville, Tenn.

———. 1903. Report. In *Minutes of the Annual Meeting of the Korea Mission of the Methodist Episcopal Church, South.*

First Constitution of the Society of Catholic Medical Missionary Sisters. 1932. Archives of the Medical Mission Sisters. Philadelphia, Pennsylvania.

Five Deanery Mission Circle Report for 1950, Saint Francis Xavier Mission Association. 1950. Society for the Propagation of the Faith. Diocese of Cleveland, Ohio, file.

Girl's Auxiliary Leadership Guide. n.d. Birmingham: Woman's Missionary Union.

IMC (International Missionary Council). 1927. *The Place of Women in the Church on the Mission Field.* London and New York: International Missionary Council.

Jones, Lawrence. 1992. "The Black Church in America." In *Progressions: An Occasional Report.* Indianapolis: The Lilly Foundation.

Jones, Marjorie. n.d. *Intermediate Girls' Auxiliary Handbook.* Birmingham: Woman's Missionary Union.

Madura Mission Sangam. 1934. *Constitution and Rules of the Madura Mission Sangam.* Madura.

———. 1934-39. *Minutes of the Madura Mission Sangam.* Madura.

Manual for Use by Members of Intermediate Girls' Auxiliaries of Woman's Missionary Union, Southern Baptist Convention. n.d. Birmingham: Woman's Missionary Union.

"Mission to Latin America, a Progress Report." 1969. Cleveland, Ohio: Society for the Propagation of the Faith Diocesan Mission Office.

NBPC (Neah Bay Presbyterian Church). n.d. *Session Book of the Neah Bay Presbyterian Church, Neah Bay, Washington, 1922- .* Neah Bay, Washington: Neah Bay Presbyterian Church.

Shields, Joseph J. n.d. *Attitudes of American Women Religious towards the Concept of Mission.* Washington, D.C.: U.S. Catholic Mission Association.

Yui Ling-tsu [Dora Yu]. 1901. Report. In *Minutes of the Annual Meeting of the Korea Mission of the Methodist Episcopal Church, South.*

BOOKS AND JOURNAL ARTICLES

Adeney, Miriam. 1987a. "Esther across Cultures: Indigenous Leadership Roles for Women." *Missiology* 15 (July): 323-37.

———. 1987b. *A Time for Risking: Priorities for Women.* Portland, Ore.: Multnomah.

———. 2000. "Women in the World Christian Movement." *Crux* 36 (1): 31-38.

Ahmed, Huma, and Shafia Mir. 1992. "Debate: Will Islam Survive in Americas?" *The Minaret: An Islamic Magazine* (September-October): 33.

Allen, Catherine B. 1980. *The New Lottie Moon Story.* Nashville, Tenn.: Broadman Press.

———. 1987. *A Century to Celebrate: History of Woman's Missionary Union.* Birmingham, Ala.: Woman's Missionary Union.

Alves, Rubem A. 1972. *Tomorrow's Child: Imagination, Creativity, and the Rebirth of Culture.* New York: Harper & Row.

Anderson, Rufus. 1967. *To Advance the Gospel: Selections from the Writings of Rufus Anderson,* edited by R. Pierce Beaver. Grand Rapids, Mich.: Eerdmans.

Ask, Karnin, and Marit Tjornstand, eds. 1998. *Women and Islamization: Contemporary Dimensions of Discourse on Gender Relations.* New York: Berg Publishers.

Askew, Thomas A. 2000. "The New York 1900 Ecumenical Missionary Conference: A Centennial Reflection." *International Bulletin of Missionary Research* 24 (4): 146-54.

Banninga, John J. n.d. "The Woman's Hospital." Chapter 11 in *History of the Madura Mission*. Typescript. ABCFM Manuscript Histories of Missions, 1.1.

Barboza, Steven. 1994. *American Jihad: Islam after Malcolm X*. New York: Doubleday.

Barnett, H. G. 1972. *Indian Shakers: A Messianic Cult of the Pacific Northwest*. Carbondale, Ill.: Southern Illinois University Press. 1957. Reprint, Arcturus Books.

Barrett, David B. 1968. *Schism and Renewal in Africa*. Nairobi: Oxford University Press.

Barrett, David B., and Todd M. Johnson. 2001. "Annual Statistical Table on Global Mission: 2001." *International Bulletin of Missionary Research* 25 (1): 24-25.

Barthel, Diane. 1975. "The Rise of a Female Professional Elite: The Case of Senegal." *African Studies Review* 28:1-18

Bays, Daniel H. 1993. "Christian Revival in China, 1900-1937." In *Modern Christian Revivals*, edited by Edith Blumhofer and Randall Balmer. Urbana, Ill.: University of Illinois Press.

————. 1996. "The Growth of Independent Christianity in China, 1900-1937." In *Christianity in China: From the Eighteenth Century to the Present*, edited by Daniel H. Bays. Stanford, Calif.: Stanford University Press.

Beaver, R. Pierce. 1980. *American Protestant Women in World Mission: A History of the First Feminist Movement in North America*. 2d ed. Grand Rapids, Mich.: Eerdmans.

Bendroth, Margaret Lamberts. 1993. *Fundamentalism and Gender, 1875 to the Present*. New Haven, Conn.: Yale University Press.

Benhabib, Seyla. 1999. "Sexual Difference and Collective Identities: The New Global Constellation." *Signs: Journal of Women in Culture and Society* 24 (2): 335-62.

Berger, Peter L. 1969. *The Sacred Canopy*. Garden City, N.Y.: Doubleday.

Biedelman, T. O. 1982. *Colonial Evangelism*. Bloomington, Ind.: University of Indiana Press.

Birchett, Colleen, ed. 1992. *Biblical Strategies for a Community in Crisis: What African Americans Can Do*. Chicago: Urban Ministries.

Birkett, Dea. 1992. "The 'White Woman's Burden' in the 'White Man's Grave': The Introduction of British Nurses in Colonial West Africa." In *Western Women and Imperialism: Complicity and Resistance*, edited by Nupur Chaudhuri and Margaret Strobel. Bloomington, Ind.: Indiana University Press.

Bishop, J. Ivyloy. 1958. "Royal Ambassadors." In *Encyclopedia of Southern Baptists*. Nashville, Tenn.: Broadman Press.

Blackwood, Evelyn. 1995. "Senior Women, Model Mothers, and Dutiful Wives: Managing Gender Contradictions in a Minangkabau Village." In *Bewitching Women, Pious Men: Gender and Body Politics in Southeast Asia*, edited by Aihwa Ong and Michael G. Peletz. Berkeley and Los Angeles: University of California Press.

Blevins, Carolyn DeArmond. 1987. "Patterns of Ministry among Southern Baptist Women." *Baptist History and Heritage* 22 (July): 45.

Blumhofer, Edith L. 1999. "'A Little Child Shall Lead Them': Child Evangelist Uldine Utley." In *The Contentious Triangle: Church, State, and University: A Festschrift in Honor of Professor George Huntston Williams*, edited by Rodney L. Petersen and Calvin Augustine Pater. Kirksville, Mo.: Thomas Jefferson University Press.

Boff, Leonardo, and Walbert Bühlmann, eds. 1984. *Build Up My Church*. Chicago: Interprovincial Secretariat for the Missions.

Bonk, Jon. 1980. "'All Things to All Persons': The Missionary as Racist-Imperialist 1860-1918." *Missiology* 8 (July): 285-306.

Børresen, Kari Eisabeth, ed. 1995. *The Image of God: Gender Models in Judaeo-Christian Tradition*. Minneapolis, Minn.: Fortress Press.

Bosch, J. David. 1991. *Transforming Mission: Paradigm Shifts in Theology of Mission.* Maryknoll, N.Y.: Orbis Books.

Bowden, Henry Warner. 1991. "Native American Presbyterians: Assimilation, Leadership, and Future Challenges." In *The Diversity of Discipleship: The Presbyterians and Twentieth Century Christian Witness,* edited by Milton J. Coalter, John Mulder, and Louis B. Weeks. Louisville, Ky.: Westminster/John Knox Press.

Bowers, Joyce. 1984. "Roles of Married Women Missionaries." *International Bulletin of Mission Research* 8 (January): 4-7.

Bowie, Fiona, Deborah Kirkwood, and Shirley Ardener. 1993. *Women and Missions, Past and Present: Anthropological and Historical Perceptions.* Oxford: Berg Publishers.

Boyd, Lois A., and R. Douglas Brackenridge. 1983. *Presbyterian Women in America: Two Centuries of a Quest for Status.* Westport, Conn.: Greenwood Press.

Brandel-Syrier, Mia. 1984. "The Role of Women in African Independent Churches." *Missonalia* 12 (April):13-18.

Braude, Ann. 1997. "Women's History IS American Religious History." In *Retelling U.S. Religious History*, edited by Thomas A. Tweed. Berkeley and Los Angeles: University of California Press.

Brenner, Suzanna A. 1995. "Why Women Rule the Roost: Rethinking Javanese Ideologies of Gender and Self-Control." In *Bewitching Women, Pious Men: Gender and Body Politics in Southeast Asia*, edited by Aihwa Ong and Michael G. Peletz. Berkeley and Los Angeles: University of California Press.

Brewer, Betty. 1963. "GA Grown Up: Madam President." *Tell* (June 1963): 10-13.

Bronte, Charlotte. 1963. *Jane Eyre.* 1847. Reprint, New York: Airmont Books.

Brusco, Elizabeth E. 1995. *The Reformation of Machismo: Evangelical Conversion and Gender in Colombia.* Austin, Tx.: University of Texas Press.

Buchan, James. 1981. *The Expendable Mary Slessor.* New York: Seabury.

Build with Living Stones: A Program of Study on the Franciscan Missionary Charism. 1989. Pittsburgh: Franciscan Federation.

Bundy, David. 1993. "Keswick and the Experience of Evangelical Piety." In *Modern Christian Revivals*, edited by Edith L. Blumhofer and Randall Balmer. Urbana, Ill.: University of Illinois Press.

Burke, Joan. 1993. "These Catholic Sisters Are All Mammas! Celibacy and the Metaphor of Maternity." In *Women and Missions, Past and Present: Anthropological and Historical Perceptions*, edited by Fiona Bowie, Deborah Kirkwood, and Shirley Ardener. Oxford: Berg Publishers.

Burton, Antoinette. 1992. "The 'White Woman's Burden': British Feminists and 'the Indian Woman,' 1865-1915." In *Western Women and Imperialism: Complicity and Resistance*, edited by Nupur Chaudhuri and Margaret Strobel. Bloomington, Ind.: Indiana University Press.

Burton, Katherine. 1946. *According to the Pattern: The Story of Dr. Agnes McLaren and the Society of Catholic Medical Missionaries.* New York: Longmans, Green.

Calloway, Helen. 1987. *Gender, Culture, and Empire: European Women in Colonial Nigeria.* Urbana, Ill.: University of Illinois Press.

Campbell, Barbara. 1983. *United Methodist Women in the Middle of Tomorrow.* 2d ed. New York: Women's Division, Board of Global Ministries, United Methodist Church.

Campbell, Debra. 1998. "Part-Time Female Evangelists of the Thirties and Forties: The Rosary College Catholic Evidence Guild." *U.S. Catholic Historian* 5 (Summer/Fall): 371-84.

Cannon, James. 1926. *History of Southern Methodist Missions.* Nashville, Tenn.: Cokesbury Press.

Cannon, Katie Geneva. 1988. *Black Womanist Ethics.* Atlanta, Ga.: Scholars Press.

Carpenter, Joel A., and Wilbert R. Shenk, eds. 1990. *Earthen Vessels: American Evangelicals and Foreign Missions, 1880-1980.* Grand Rapids, Mich.: Eerdmans.

Chandler, John S. 1909. *Seventy-Five Years in the Madura Mission.* Madras: Lawrence Asylum Press.

Chaudhuri, Nupur, and Margaret Strobel, eds. 1992. *Western Women and Imperialism: Complicity and Resistance.* Bloomington, Ind.: Indiana University Press.

Chen Zexin, comp. 1974. *Wang Peizhen zimei jianshi* (A brief history of Sister Peace Wang). Hong Kong: Christian Publishers.

Christensen, Torben, and William Hutchison, eds. 1982. *Missionary Ideologies in the Imperialist Era: 1880-1920.* Aarhus, Denmark: Forlaget Aros.

Clark, Helen. n.d. "Chips from an Old Block." Transcribed by Veda Forrest. Unpublished manuscript. Neah Bay, Washington: Neah Bay Presbyterian Church.

Coburn, Carol K., and Martha Smith. 1999. *Spirited Lives: How Nuns Shaped Catholic Culture and American Life, 1836-1920.* Chapel Hill, N.C.: University of North Carolina Press.

Cohen, Margot. 1997. "Indonesia: Religion, Climate of Distrust." *Index on Censorship 2.*

Costello, Gerald M. 1979. *Mission to Latin America: The Successes and Failures of a Twentieth Century Crusade.* Maryknoll, N.Y.: Orbis Books.

Cothen, Grady C. 1993. *What Happened to the Southern Baptist Convention.* Macon, Ga.: Smyth and Helwys Publishing.

Crawford, Mary M. 1936. *The Nez Perces since Spalding: Experiences of Forty-one Years at Lapwai, Idaho.* Berkeley, Calif.: Professional Press.

Cummings, Mary Lou. 1991. *Surviving without Romance: African Women Tell Their Stories.* Scottdale, Pa.: Herald Press.

Cunningham, Valentine. 1992. "'God and Nature Intended You for a Missionary's Wife': Mary Hill, Jane Eyre, and Other Missionary Women in the 1840s." In *Women and Missions, Past and Present: Anthropological and Historical Perceptions,* edited by Fiona Bowie, Deborah Kirkwood, and Shirley Ardener. Oxford: Berg Publishers.

Cutrufelli, Maria Rosa. 1983. *Women of Africa.* Bath: The Pitman Press.

DeBerg, Betty A. 1990. *Ungodly Women: Gender and the First Wave of American Fundamentalism.* Minneapolis, Minn.: Fortress Press.

Dempster, Murray W., Byron D. Klaus, and Douglas Petersen, eds. 1991. *Called and Empowered: Global Mission in Pentecostal Perspective.* Peabody, Mass.: Hendrickson.

Dengel, Anna. 1927. *The Medical Missionary* 1 (October): 2.

———. 1945. *Mission for Samaritans.* Milwaukee, Wis.: Bruce Publishing Company.

———. 1949. Talks and Writings of Mother Anna Dengel. New Year's Day. Philadelphia, Pa.: Archives of the Medical Mission Sisters.

DeVault, Doris. 1970. "A Link in the Chain: A History of Girls' Auxiliary." *Tell* 18 (5): 3-8.

Dries, Angelyn. 1989. "The Americanization of Religious Life." *U.S. Catholic Historian* 10 (1, 2): 13-24.

———. 1998. *The Missionary Movement in American Catholic History.* Maryknoll, N.Y.: Orbis Books.

Drogus, Carol Ann. 1997. *Women, Religion, and Social Change in Brazil's Popular Church.* Notre Dame, Ind.: University of Notre Dame Press.

Dulin, Hilda. 1963. "Through My Life." *Tell* (May): 16.

Durant, Will. 1950. *Age of Faith.* New York: Simon and Schuster.

Eddy, G. Sherwood. 1910. "Reshaping Congregationalism: An Experiment in South India." *The Missionary Herald* (February): 67 68.

Eells, Myron. 1985. *The Indians of Puget Sound: The Notebooks of Myron Eells.* Edited by George Pierre Castile. Seattle, Wash.: University of Washington Press.

Elliot, Elizabeth. 1968. *Who Shall Ascend?: The Life of R. Kenneth Strachan of Costa Rica.* London: Hodder and Stoughton.

Ellwood, Robert S. 1997. *The Fifties Spiritual Marketplace: American Religion in a Decade of Conflict.* New Brunswick, N.J.: Rutgers University Press.

Falk, N. E. A. 1981. "Women: Status and Role in World Religions." In *Abingdon Dictionary of Living Religions.* Nashville, Tenn.: Abingdon.

Fearn, Anne Walter. 1939. *My Days of Strength: An American Woman Doctor's Forty Years in China.* New York: Harper & Brothers.

Fedders, Edward L. 1954. "Direct Apostolate by Sisters." In *Proceedings of the Lima Methods Conference of the Maryknoll Fathers,* edited by Gorden N. Fritz. Maryknoll, N.Y.: Maryknoll Fathers.

Fiedler, Klaus. 1994. *The Story of Faith Missions.* Oxford: Regnum.

Fleming, Daniel Johnson. 1916. *Devolution in Mission Administration.* New York: Fleming H. Revell Company.

Flemming, Leslie A. 1992. "A New Humanity: American Missionaries' Ideals for Women in North India, 1870-1930." In *Western Women and Imperialism: Complicity and Resistance,* edited by Nupur Chaudhuri and Margaret Strobel. Bloomington, Ind.: Indiana University Press.

Flemming, Leslie A., ed. 1989. *Women's Work for Women: Missionaries and Social Change in Asia.* Boulder, Colo.: Westview Press.

Ford, Francis X. 1953. *Stone in the King's Highway.* New York: McMullen Books.

Frey, S. Naomi. 1985. "Thens and Nows in Papua New Guinea." *COMTEC* 15.4. Oldenburg, Ind.: The Sisters of St. Francis.

Fritsch, Nina. 1998. "Mission to Women." In *Fire and Flame, the Legacy of Anna Dengel.* Philadelpia, Pa.: The Medical Mission Sisters.

Garland, Ken, and Steve Fortosis. 1991. "Historical Origins of Professional Evangelical Youth Work in the Church." *Religious Education* 86 (2): 275-84.

Garrett, Shirley. 1982. "Sisters All: Feminism and the American Women's Missionary Movement." In *Missionary Ideologies in the Imperialist Era: 1880-1920,* edited by Torben Christensen and William R. Hutchison. Aarhus, Denmark: Forlaget Aros.

Geertz, Clifford. 1973. "Religion as a Cultural System." Chapter 4 in *The Interpretation of Cultures.* New York: Basic Books.

Ginzberg, Lori D. 1990. *Women and the Work of Benevolence: Morality, Politics, and Class in the Nineteenth-Century United States.* New Haven, Conn.: Yale University Press.

Grafe, Hugald. 1990. *The History of Christianity in Tamilnadu from 1800-1975.* Bangalore, India: Church History Association of India.

Grant, Jacquelyn. 1989. *White Women's Christ and Black Women's Jesus: Feminist Christology and Womanist Response.* Atlanta, Ga.: Scholars Press.

Gross, Rita. 1995. *Buddhism after Patriarchy: A Feminist History, Analysis, and Reconstruction of Buddhism.* Albany, N.Y.: State University of New York Press.

Halberstam, David. 1993. *The Fifties.* New York: Villard Books.

Hall, Edward T. 1983. *The Dance of Life: The Other Dimension of Time*. Garden City, N.Y.: Anchor Books.

Hall, Penelope R. 2000. "When a Woman Is Not a Woman." Unpublished paper.

Haney, Marsha Snulligan. 1999. *Islam and Protestant African American Churches: Challenges and Responses to Religious Pluralism*. San Francisco: International Scholars Publications.

Hansen, Karen Tranberg. 1992a. "White Women in a Changing World: Employment, Voluntary Work, and Sex in Post-World War II Northern Rhodesia." In *Western Women and Imperialism: Complicity and Resistance*, edited by Nupur Chaudhuri and Margaret Strobel. Bloomington, Ind.: Indiana University Press.

———. 1992b. *African Encounters with Domesticity*. New Brunswick, N.J.: Rutgers University Press.

Harper, Susan Billington. 2000. *In the Shadow of the Mahatma: Bishop V. S. Azariah and the Travails of Christianity in British India*. Grand Rapids, Mich.: Eerdmans.

Hassey, Janette. 1986. *No Time for Silence: Evangelical Women in Public Ministry around the Turn of the Century*. Grand Rapids, Mich.: Academie Books.

Hastings, Adrian. 1993. "Were Women a Special Case?" In *Women and Missions, Past and Present: Anthropological and Historical Perceptions*, edited by Fiona Bowie, Deborah Kirkwood, and Shirley Ardener. Oxford: Berg Publishers.

Hayward, Victor. 1963. *African Independent Church Movements*. Edinburgh: Edinburgh House Press.

Heim, Melissa Lewis. 1994. "Making a Life in India: American Missionary Households in Nineteenth-Century Madurai." Ph.D. diss., Boston College.

Hertig, Young Lee. 1998. "The Asian-American Alternative to Feminism: A *Yinist* Paradigm." *Missiology* 26 (1): 15-22.

Hilgartner, Stephen, and Charles L. Bosk. 1988. "The Rise and Fall of Social Problems: A Public Arenas Model." *American Journal of Sociology* 94 (1): 53-78.

Hill, Patricia R. 1985. *The World Their Household: The American Woman's Foreign Mission Movement and Cultural Transformation, 1870-1920*. Ann Arbor, Mich.: The University of Michigan Press.

Hoover, Theressa. 1983. *With Unveiled Face: Centennial Reflections on Women and Men in the Community of the Church*. New York: Women's Division, Board of Global Ministries, United Methodist Church.

Hoyle, Lydia Huffman. 1999. "Teacher of Preachers: Sue McBeth and Her Mission to the Nez Perce." *Missiology* 27 (4): 475-80.

Hunter, Jane. 1984. *The Gospel of Gentility: American Women Missionaries in Turn-of-the Century China*. New Haven, Conn.: Yale University Press.

Hutchinson, Mark, and Ogbu Kalu, eds. 1998. *A Global Faith: Essays on Evangelicalism and Globalization*. Sydney: Center for the Study of Australian Christianity.

Illich, Ivan. 1970. *The Church, Development, and Change*. New York: Herder and Herder.

Ingersoll, Julie J. 1997. "The New Orthodoxy at Southern Seminary." Chapter 4 in "Engendered Conflict: Feminism and Traditionalism in Late Twentieth Century Conservative Protestantism." Ph.D. diss., University of California Santa Barbara.

Ireland, John. 1905. "Charity in the Catholic Church." In *The Church and Modern Society*. St. Paul, Minn.: The Pioneer Press.

Isichei, Elizabeth. 1993. "Does Christianity Empower Women? The Case of the Anaguta of Central Nigeria." In *Women and Missions, Past and Present: Anthropological and Historical Perceptions*, edited by Fiona Bowie, Deborah Kirkwood, and Shirley Ardener. Oxford: Berg Publishers.

Israel, Adrienne M. 1998. *Amanda Berry Smith: From Washerwoman to Evangelist.* Lanham, Md.: Scarecrow Press.

Jacobs, Sylvia. 1992. "Give a Thought to Africa: Black Women Missionaries in Southern Africa." In *Western Women and Imperialism: Complicity and Resistance,* edited by Nupur Chaudhuri and Margaret Strobel. Bloomington, Ind.: Indiana University Press.

James, Rod, ed. 1989. *The Takeover in the Southern Baptist Convention: A Brief History.* Decatur, Ga.: SBC Today.

Johnson, Carol. 1986. "Class and Gender: Yoruba Women in the Colonial Period." In *On Women and Class in Africa,* edited by Claire Robertson and Iris Berger. New York: Holmes and Meier.

Johnson, Stephen W. 1947. *The Laity and the Mission Apostolate.* Missionary Academia Series 4.5 (January).

Josephy, Alvin M. 1979. *The Nez Perce Indians and the Opening of the Northwest.* Abridged edition, New Haven, Conn.: Yale University Press, 1971. Reprint, Lincoln: University of Nebraska Press, Bison Books.

Kalven, Janet. 1999. *Women Breaking Boundaries: A Grail Journey, 1940-1995.* Albany, N.Y.: State University of New York Press.

Kang, Nam Soon. 1995. "Is the Korean Church a Community of Equals?: Korean Churchwomen's Consciousness and Their Positions in the Church." *The Journal of Korean Feminist Theology* 24: 63-88.

Kilbride, P., et al. 1990. *Changing Family Life in East Africa: Women and Children at Risk.* University Park, Pa.: Penn State University Press.

Kinnear, Angus I. 1978. *Against the Tide: The Story of Watchman Nee.* Wheaton, Ill.: Tyndale House Publishers.

Kong, Mary Braddock. 1963. *Tell* (June): 12.

Krier, Jennifer. 1995a. "Disruptive Discourses." In *Bewitching Women, Pious Men: Gender and Body Politics in Southeast Asia,* edited by Aihwa Ong and Michael G. Peletz. Berkeley and Los Angeles: University of California Press.

———. 1995b. "Narrating Herself: Power and Gender in a Minangkabau Woman's Tale of Conflict." In *Bewitching Women, Pious Men: Gender and Body Politics in Southeast Asia,* edited by Aihwa Ong and Michael G. Peletz. Berkeley and Los Angeles: University of California Press.

Krisnawati, Tati, and Artien Utrecht. 1992. "Women's Economic Mediation: The Case of Female Petty Traders in Northwest Lombok." In *Women and Mediation in Indonesia,* edited by Sita van Bemmelen, Madelon Djajadiningrat-Nieuwenhuis, Elsbeth Locher-Scholten, and Elly Touwen-Bouwsma. Leiden, Netherlands: KITLV Press.

Larsson, Birgitta. 1991. *Conversion to Greater Freedom?: Women, Church and Social Change in Northwest Tanzania under Colonial Rule.* Uppsala: Uppsala University Press.

Latourette, Kenneth Scott. 1975. *A History of Christianity.* Vol. 2, *Reformation to the Present.* San Francisco: Harper & Row.

Lee, Kwang-Soon. 1995. "An Historical Analysis on the Status and Role of Women in the Korean Church: A Retrospective and Prospective View." *Jangshin Nondan* 11: 130-53.

Lee, Witness. 1981. *Watchman Nee: A Seer of the Divine Revelation of the Present Age.* Anaheim, Calif.: Living Stream Ministry.

Lehmann, Dorothea. 1963. "Women in the African Independent Churches." In *African Independent Church Movements,* edited by Victor Hayward. Edinburgh: Edinburgh House Press.

Leonard, Juanita Evans. 1998. "Women and the Church of God (Anderson, Indiana): Mission to the Abaluyia of Western Kenya 1905-1975." Ph.D. diss., Fuller Theological Seminary.

Leung, Ka-lun. 1999. "Trichotomistic Anthropology of Watchman Nee in His *The Spiritual Man.*" *Jian Dao* 13 (December): 183-230.

Lin, Heping. 1943. *Enai Biaoben* (An example of God's grace and love). Shanghai.

Lincoln, C. Eric. 1989. "The Muslim Mission in the Context of the American Social History." In *African American Religious Studies: An Interdisciplinary Anthology,* edited by Gayraud Wilmore. Durham, N.C.: Duke University Press.

Lincoln, C. Eric, and Lawrence H. Mamiya. 1990. *The Black Church in the African American Experience.* Durham, N.C.: Duke University Press.

Longfield, Bradley J. 1991. *The Presbyterian Controversy: Fundamentalists, Modernists, and Moderates.* New York: Oxford University Press.

Lovelace, Richard F. 1979. *Dynamics of Spiritual Life: An Evangelical Theology of Renewal.* Downers Grove, Ill.: Inter-Varsity Press.

Lyall, Leslie T. 1954. *Flame for God: John Sung and Revival in the Far East.* London: Overseas Missionary Fellowship.

MacDonnell, R. W., Mrs. 1987. *Belle Harris Bennett: Her Life Work.* New York: Garland.

Magalis, Elaine. 1973. *Conduct Becoming to a Woman: Bolted Doors and Burgeoning Missions.* Prepared by Education and Cultivation Division, Board of Global Ministries, United Methodist Church.

Maher, Mary Joseph. 2000. *A Compelling Vision.* Monroe, Mich.: The Sisters, Servants of the Immaculate Heart of Mary.

Manna, Paulo. 1921. *The Conversion of the Pagan World.* Boston: Society for the Propagation of the Faith.

Marsden, George M. 1980. *Fundamentalism and American Culture: The Shaping of Twentieth-Century Evangelicalism: 1870-1925.* New York: Oxford University Press.

Marshall, Lois. 1953. "Values of Christian Education." *Tell* (June 1953): 16.

Martin, David. 1990. *Tongues of Fire: The Explosion of Protestantism in Latin America.* Oxford: B. Blackwell.

Massey, Barbara. 1990. "Training Children in Missions in Southern Baptist Churches." *Baptist History and Heritage* 25 (October): 21-28.

Mather, Juliette. 1963. "If on Life's Highway?" *Tell* (May): 3-4.

McBeth, Kate. 1993. *The Nez Perces since Lewis and Clark.* New York: Fleming Revell Co., 1908. Reprint, Moscow: University of Idaho Press.

McGee, Gary B. 1986. *This Gospel Shall Be Preached: A History and Theology of Assemblies of God Foreign Missions to 1959.* Springfield, Mo.: Gospel Publishing House.

———. 1998. "And with Fire! The Holiness Pentecostal Mission Legacy of Minnie F. Abrams of India." Unpublished paper.

Mead, George Herbert. 1934. *Mind, Self, and Society.* Chicago: University of Chicago Press.

Messer, Ellen. 1993. "Anthropology and Human Rights." *Annual Review of Anthropology.* Palo Alto, Calif.: Annual Reviews, Inc.

Monsen, Marie. 1986. *The Awakening: Revival in China, a Work of the Holy Spirit.* London: China Inland Mission.

Montgomery, Helen Barrett. 1910. *Western Women in Eastern Lands: An Outline Study of Fifty Years of Women's Work in Foreign Missions.* New York: The Macmillan Company.

Moon, Floyce. 1963. "Featuring Margaret Harris, Secretary." *Tell* (September): 15.

Mooney, James. 1991. *The Ghost-Dance Religion and the Sioux Outbreak of 1890.* Edited
    by Raymond J. DeMallie. Washington, D.C.: Government Printing Office, 1896.
    Reprint, Lincoln: University of Nebraska Press, Bison Books.

Moorhead, James H. 1994. "Presbyterians and the Mystique of Organizational Efficiency,
    1870-1936." In *Reimagining Denominationalism: Interpretive Essays,* edited by
    Robert Bruce Mullin and Russell E. Richey. New York: Oxford University Press.

Morrill, Allen Conrad, and Eleanor Dunlop Morrill. 1978. *Out of the Blanket: The Story
    of Sue and Kate McBeth, Missionaries to the Nez Perces.* Moscow, Idaho: Uni-
    versity of Idaho Press.

Mukhopadhyay, Carol and Patricia Higgins. 1988. "Anthropological Studies of Women's
    Status Revisited: 1977-1987." *Annual Review of Anthropology.* Palo Alto, Calif.:
    Annual Reviews, Inc.

Murdiati, Diati Ganis, and Dartini Sabekti Sabarish, eds. 1985. *The Women of Indonesia.*
    Revised ed. Jakarta: Department of Information of the Republic of Indonesia in
    cooperation with the Office of the Minister of State for the Role of Women.

Nasimiyu-Wasike, Anne. 1991. "Christology and an African Woman's Experience." In *Faces
    of Jesus in Africa,* edited by Robert J. Schreiter. Maryknoll, N.Y.: Orbis Books.

Neal, Marie Augusta. 1984. *Catholic Sisters in Transition.* Wilmington, Del.: Michael
    Glazier.

Newbigin, Lesslie. 1985. *Unfinished Agenda: An Autobiography.* Grand Rapids, Mich.:
    Eerdmans.

Ng, David, ed. 1996. *People on the Way: Asian North Americans Discovering Christ,
    Culture, and Community.* Valley Forge, Pa.: Judson Press.

Noll, Mark A., et al., eds. 1983. *Eerdmans' Handbook to Christianity in America.* Grand
    Rapids, Mich.: Eerdmans.

Oey, Eric. 1989. *Indonesia.* Singapore: APA Publications (HK) Ltd.

Orr, James Edwin. 1975. *The Flaming Tongue: Evangelical Awakenings 1900– .* Chicago:
    Moody Press.

Orsi, Robert. 1999. *Thank You, St. Jude: Women's Devotion to the Patron Saint of Hope-
    less Causes.* New Haven, Conn.: Yale University Press.

Otto, Anna M. 1928. "At the Madura Hospital for Women and Children." *The Missionary
    Herald* (November): 416-17.

Palmer, Bernard. 1953a. "So Far Away." *Tell* (June): 27.

———. 1953b. "So Far Away." *Tell* (September): 8.

Parker, Fred J. 1988. *Mission to the World: A History of Missions in the Church of the
    Nazarene through 1985.* Kansas City, Mo.: Nazarene Publishing House.

Pascoe, Peggy. 1990. *Relations of Rescue: The Search for Female Moral Authority in the
    American West, 1874-1939.* New York: Oxford University Press.

Paxson, Ruth. 1922. "Orthodoxy and Spirituality." *The Bulletin of the Bible Union of
    China* (July-August).

———. 1928. *Life on the Highest Plane.* 3 vols. Chicago: Moody Press.

———. 1930. *Rivers of Living Water.* Chicago: Moody Press.

———. 1936. *Called unto Holiness.* Chicago. Moody Press.

———.1939. *The Wealth, Walk, and Welfare of the Christian.* New York: Revell.

Pellow, Deborah. 1977. *Women in Accra: Options for Autonomy.* Algonac, Mich.: Refer-
    ence Publications Inc.

Penfield, Janet Harbison. 1977. "Women in the Presbyterian Church." *Journal of Presby-
    terian History:* 107-23.

Powdermaker, Hortense. 1962. *Copper Town: Changing Africa.* New York: Harper & Row.

Pretiz, Paul E., and W. Dayton Roberts. 1997. "Uncharted Waters: Evolution of a Mission (the Story of CLAME [Comunidad Latinoamericana de Ministerios Evangelicos])." Unpublished paper.

Prucha, Francis Paul. 1984. *The Great Father: The United States Government and the American Indians.* 2 vols. Lincoln, Neb.: University of Nebraska Press.

Quinn, Naomi. 1977. "Anthropological Studies on Women's Status." *Annual Review of Anthropology.* Palo Alto, Calif.: Annual Reviews, Inc.

Rankin, Jerry. 2000. Letter to the Editor, *Christianity Today* 23 (October): 13.

Relander, Click. 1986. *Drummers and Dreamers.* Seattle, Wash.: Northwest Interpretive Association and Caxton Printers.

Restrick, David. 2001. "The Church of the Nazarene and the Mozambican revolution, 1975-1982." Th.D. diss., Boston University School of Theology.

Robert, Dana L. 1993. "Revisioning the Women's Missionary Movement." In *The Good News of the Kingdom,* edited by Charles Van Engen et al., Maryknoll, N.Y.: Orbis Books.

————. 1997. *American Women in Mission: A Social History of Their Thought and Practice.* Macon, Ga.: Mercer University Press.

————. 1998. "The 'Christian Home' as a Cornerstone of Missionary Thought and Practice." Cambridge, U.K.: North American Missiology Project, Position Paper #98.

————. 2000a. "Shifting Southward: Global Christianity since 1945." *International Bulletin of Missionary Research* 24 (2): 50-58.

————. 2000b. "Holiness and the Missionary Vision of the Woman's Foreign Missionary Society of the Methodist Episcopal Church, 1869-1894." *Methodist History* 39 (1): 15-27.

Roberts, W. Dayton. 1991. "I Want to Stand beside Frank." Unpublished paper.

————. 1992. "Harry Strachan: An American Don Quixote and His Impossible Dream." Unpublished paper.

————. 1993. "Doña Susana: Susan Beamish Strachan, Missionary Trailblazer in Latin America." Unpublished paper.

Robertson, Claire, and Iris Berger, eds. 1986. *Women and Class in Africa.* New York: Holmes and Meier.

Rogers, Mary Joseph. 1922. *Discourses of Mother Mary Joseph Rogers.* 2 vols. Maryknoll, N.Y.: Maryknoll Mission Archives.

The Rule and Life of the Brothers and Sisters of the Third Order Regular of St. Francis and Commentary. 1982. Pittsburgh: Franciscan Federation.

Rupp, Leila J., and Verta Taylor. 1999. "Forging Feminist Identity in an International Movement: A Collective Identity Approach to Twentieth-Century Feminism." *Signs: Journal of Women in Culture and Society* 24 (2): 363-83.

Schreiter, Robert J. 1991. *Faces of Jesus in Africa.* Maryknoll, N.Y.: Orbis Books.

Schüssler Fiorenza, Elisabeth. 1983. *In Memory of Her: A Feminist Reconstruction of Christian Origins.* New York: Crossroad.

Scott, Anne Firor. 1991. *Natural Allies: Women's Associations in American History.* Urbana, Ill.: University of Illinois Press.

Shenk, Wilbert R. 1996. "Toward a Global Church History." *International Bulletin of Missionary Research* 20 (2): 50-57.

Shurden, Walter B., ed. 1993. *The Struggle for the Soul of the SBC.* Macon, Ga.: Mercer University Press.

Silverblatt, Irene. 1988. "Women in States." *Annual Review of Anthropology.* Palo Alto, Calif.: Annual Reviews, Inc.

Singh, Maina Chawla. 2000. *Gender, Religion, and "Heathen Lands": American Missionary Women in South Asia (1860s-1940s).* New York: Garland Publishing.

Slowick, Margaret A. 1999. *The Franciscan Third Order Regular in the United States: Origins, Early Years, and Recent Developments.* Tiffin, Ohio: Sisters of St. Francis of Tiffin.

Smock, Audrey. 1977. "The Impact of Modernization on Women's Position in the Family in Ghana." In *Sexual Stratification,* edited by Alice Schlegal. New York: Columbia University Press.

Song Shangjie (John Sung). 1991. *Wodi jianzheng* (My testimony). 10th ed. Hong Kong.

Stanley, Bob. 1990. "Committee Affirms Homemaker's Role." *The Commission* (August): 48.

Stewart, I. R. Govan. 1957. *Dynamic, Paget Wilkes of Japan.* London: Marshall, Morgan, and Scott.

Streit, Robert. 1927. *Catholic Missions in Figures and Symbols: Based on the Vatican Missionary Exhibition.* Rome: Society for the Propagation of the Faith.

Strickland, Charles E., and Andrew M. Ambrose. 1985. "The Baby Boom, Prosperity, and the Changing Worlds of Children, 1945-1963." In *American Childhood: A Research Guide and Historical Handbook,* edited by Joseph M. Hawes and N. Ray Hiner. Westport, Conn.: Greenwood Press.

Suleeman, Stephen. n.d. "Indonesian Women in the Media: A Portrait of Patriarchy." Unpublished paper.

Sullivan, Norma. 1994. *Masters and Managers: A Study of Gender Relations in Java.* St Leonards, Australia: Allen and Unwin Publishers.

Swaisland, Cecillie. 1992. "Wanted—Earnest, Self-sacrificing Women for Service in South Africa: Nineteenth-Century Recruitment of Single Women to Protestant Missions." In *Women and Missions, Past and Present: Anthropological and Historical Perceptions,* edited by Fiona Bowie, Deborah Kirkwood, and Shirley Ardener. Oxford: Berg Publishers.

Thomas, Anthony E. 1970. *PI-LU'-YE-KIN: The Life History of a Nez Perce Indian.* Ann Arbor, Mich.: University Microfilms.

Tørjesen, Karen Jo. 1993. *When Women Were Priests: Women's Leadership in the Early Church and the Scandal of Their Subordination in the Rise of Christianity.* San Francisco: HarperSanFrancisco.

Tucker, Ruth. 1988. *Guardians of the Great Commission: The Story of Women in Modern Missions.* Grand Rapids, Mich.: Academie Books.

———. 1990. "Women in Missions: Reaching Sisters in 'Heathen Darkness.'" In *Earthen Vessels,* edited by Joel Carpenter and Wilbert Shenk. Grand Rapids, Mich.: Eerdmans.

Tucker, Ruth, and Walter Liefeld. 1987. *Daughters of the Church: Women in Ministry from New Testament Times to the Present.* Grand Rapids, Mich.: Zondervan.

Van der Geest, Suaak, and Jan P. Kirby. 1992. "The Absence of the Missionary in African Ethnography, 1930-65." *African Studies Review* 35 (3): 59-103.

Verdesi, Elizabeth Howell. 1976. *In But Still Out: Women in the Church.* Philadelphia, Pa.: Westminster Press.

Walker, Deward E., Jr. 1968. *Conflict and Schism in Nez Perce Acculturation: A Study of Religion and Politics.* Pullman, Wash.: Washington State University Press.

Walls, Andrew F. 1982. "British Missions." In *Missionary Ideologies in the Imperialist Era: 1880-1920,* edited by Torben Christensen and William Hutchison. Aarhus, Denmark: Forlaget Aros.

Ware, Ann Patrick, ed. 1985. *Midwives of the Future: American Sisters Tell Their Story.* Kansas City, Mo.: Sheed and Ward, NCR Publishing Co.

Warren, Katie C., and Jo M. Bevington. 1990. "The Contributions of Children to Southern Baptists." *Baptist History and Heritage* 25 (October): 4-12.

Waugh, Earl. 1983. *The Muslim Community in North America.* Edmonton: University of Alberta Press.

Webster, John. 1998. "The Church of South India Golden Jubilee." *International Bulletin of Missionary Research* 22 (2): 50-54.

Wei Guangxi, ed. 1980. *Ni Tosheng dixiong sanci gongkai di jianzheng* (Brother Watchman Nee's public testimonies given on three occasions). Taipei: Gospel Book Room.

Welch, Sharon. 1990. *A Feminist Ethic of Risk.* Minneapolis, Minn.: Fortress Press.

Wells, Dorothy Louise. 1958. "Girls' Auxiliary." In *Encyclopedia of Southern Baptists.* Nashville, Tenn.: Broadman Press.

West, Cornel. 1988. *Prophetic Fragments.* Grand Rapids, Mich.: Eerdmans.

Whitehead, James D., and Evelyn Eaton Whitehead. 1980. *Method in Ministry: Theological Reflection and Christian Ministry.* New York: Seabury Press.

Wilder, Harriet. 1961. *A Century in the Madura Mission.* New York: Vantage Press.

Williams, Delores. 1999. "Re/membering African American Peoplehood—Resisting Its Dis/memberment." In *Dissent and Empowerment: Essays in Honor of Gayraud Wilmore,* edited by Eugene C. Turner. Louisville, Ky.: Witherspoon Press.

Women's Research and Training Centre, U.N.E.C. for Africa. 1975. "Women and National Development in African Countries: Some Profound Contradictions." *African Studies Review* 18 (3).

Wood, Robert D. 1983. *In These Mortal Hands: The Story of the Oriental Missionary Society, the First 50 Years.* Greenwood, Ind.: OMS International Inc.

Woods, Grace. 1927. *The Half Can Never Be Told.* Atlantic City, N.J.: The Worldwide Revival Prayer Movement.

———. 1936. *Revival in Romance and Realism.* New York: Fleming H. Revell Co.

Wu, Silas. 2000. *Yu Cidu: Ershi Shiji Zhongguo Jiaohui Fuxing de Xianqu* (Dora Yu: Harbinger of Christian church revival in twentieth-century China). Boston: Pishon River Publications.

Yao, Kevin Xiyi. 2000. "The Fundamentalist Movement among Protestant Missionaries in China, 1920-37." Th.D. diss., Boston University School of Theology.

Yasin, Imam Abdallah. 1996. *Islamicizing America.* Nashville, Tenn.: J. C. Winston Pub. Co.

Yates, Timothy E. 1994. *Christian Mission in the Twentieth Century.* Cambridge: Cambridge University Press.

Yu, Dora. 1916. *God's Dealings with Dora Yu: A Chinese Messenger of the Cross.* Shanghai: Mission Book Co.

———. 1927. *God's Dealings with Dora Yu: A Chinese Messenger of the Cross.* London: Morgan & Scott.

Zebiri, Kate. 1997. *Muslims and Christians Face to Face.* Rockport, Mass.: One World.

Zoba, Wendy Murray. 2000. "A Woman's Place." *Christianity Today* (August 7): 40-48.

Zwiep, Mary. 1991. *Pilgrim Path: The First Company of Women Missionaries to Hawaii.* Madison, Wis.: University of Wisconsin Press.

Index

colonialism and, 212–213; marriage in Africa, 215–217; as missionaries, 211–212; from pioneers to bureaucrats, 217–218; sin and grace for, 221. *See also* gender issues; women

stereotypes, positive, 180–181
Stewart, Milton, 77
Stock, Gertrude, 44
Stone, Mary, 77, 94, 98
Strachan, Harry, 14, 63, 64, 65, 67, 70
Strachan, Kenneth, 70–71
Strachan, Susan Beamish, 13–14, 20, 70–71; Bible Institute of Costa Rica, 68–69; early years in Argentina, 64–67; Latin America Mission, organizational structure of, 69–70; ministry beginnings, 67; missionary training in London, 64; role of, in Latin America Mission, 71

structural changes in bicultural organizations, 70–71
structural resistance of self-identity, 179–180
studies: African Instituted Churches, 216; categories of women's assignments, 123; collapse of women's mission societies, 10; decision making in Korean women, 187–188; gender issues, 23; Korean Bible women *(jeondosa)*, 189–190
Sukarnoputri, 179
Suleeman, Stephen, 178
Surviving without Romance: African Women Tell Their Stories (Cummings), 220
Swift, Eva M., 53, 58–59, 60
taboos, 2–3
Taylor, George Braxton, 103
Taylor, Horace S., 48–49
Tell magazine, 105, 106, 108
Theisen, Mary Lou, 153
theologies of evangelism: church-centric to kingdom-centric, switch from, 23–24; and women's roles in church, 21
theoretical models, 130–131
Third Order Rule, 165
Thorndike, William S., 44
Thornton, J. B., 77
Toalston, Art, 118, 120
trends, 121–122, 155, 158
Tsai, Christiana, 94, 98

twentieth century: Korean Bible women of, 186–187; missionary women in, 27–28; mission trends for Catholic women, 127–130
Utley, Uldine, 98
Vatican appeal for missionaries, 157
Vatican II, implementation of documents of, 162
Venn, Henry, 44
Vieques Chronicles, 145
Vietnam, 153
violence, 145–146, 155, 175
vision of mission, 154–155
vocations, decreasing numbers of, 23–24
Vonderhaar, Marie Rebecca, 149
Walsh, James A., 7
Walter, Anne, 88
Wang, Leland, 77, 83
Wang, Peace (Peizhen), 94, 98
Ward, Maisie, 137
Webb, Mary, 113
Western Women in Eastern Lands (Montgomery), 9
Westropp, Clara, 131–134
Wilkes, A. Paget, 75–76, 77, 78
Williams, J. E., 96
Williams, Mark, 35
Williams, Robert, 35, 37
Winfred, G. Ryappan, 48
Wisda, Anne, 153, 156
Wohlfert, Margaret, 136–137
womanist approach to mission as witness, 204, 205–207
womanist paradigm, 27
Woman's Missionary Union (WMU), 19–20, 102, 105, 113, 115; eligibility for, 103; FMB attacks on, 117–118; membership in, 125; prominent leaders of, 117; reorganization of, 119–121; sidelining of women in, 122
woman's work for woman, 15–16; development of program, 48; Maryknoll Sisters and, 138–140; in non-Christian areas, 126; research on, 21–22; as theoretical model, 130–131
women: adult education for, 214; Argentine, 68; celibate, 131; collective power of, to aid women, 131–140; consciousness in Korean, 187–189; Direct Apostolate